OECD Territorial Reviews: The Krasnoyarsk Agglomeration, Russian Federation

OECD
BETTER POLICIES FOR BETTER LIVES

Please cite this publication as:
OECD (2015), *OECD Territorial Reviews: The Krasnoyarsk Agglomeration, Russian Federation*, OECD Publishing, Paris.
http://dx.doi.org/10.1787/9789264229372-en

ISBN 978-92-64-22936-5 (print)
ISBN 978-92-64-22937-2 (PDF)

Series: OECD Territorial Reviews
ISSN 1990-0759 (print)
ISSN 1990-0767 (online)

Foreword

Place matters for policy. Public policies aimed at generating growth, jobs, equity and environmental sustainability have a greater impact when they are adapted to the economic and social realities of the places in which they are implemented. National governments are thus challenged to rethink how to harness the potential of different types of cities and regions to prepare for the future, a task that requires not only identifying the right policies but also putting in place the governance arrangements needed to support such an integrated, place-based approach. Regional and municipal governments are similarly challenged to find ways of mobilising their own specific strengths and assets, as well as to devise governance solutions adapted to their circumstances, in order to foster sustainable growth, investment and innovation.

OECD ministers endorsed this policy framework on 5-6 December 2013, during the meeting "Regions and Cities: Where Policy and People Meet" in Marseille, France. They were joined in their deliberations by ministers from a number of non-OECD partner countries, including the Russian Federation. In Marseille, they endorsed the design of a national urban policy framework to address the economic, social and environmental needs and opportunities in cities of all sizes and the need to develop new data, policy and governance tools that enable governments to better fit policies to places, thereby promoting policy action at the relevant scale. In and around large cities, this often requires efforts to overcome fragmented local governance and to improve co-ordination between cities and higher levels of government.

This *OECD Territorial Review of the Krasnoyarsk Agglomeration* has been conducted with that approach in mind. It pays particular attention to the ways in which the Agglomeration's location, population and natural endowments define its development challenges and at the ways in which policy solutions need to be adapted to those conditions. It also supports the efforts of the Krasnoyarsk Territory (*Krai*) and the municipalities that constitute the Agglomeration to devise governance solutions that allow them to address common challenges in such fields as transport, innovation and human capital formation at an Agglomeration-wide scale.

This review was undertaken in the OECD's Public Governance and Territorial Development Directorate, under the auspices of the Regional Development Policy Committee (RDPC). Created in 1999 as a unique forum for international exchange and debate, the RDPC has developed a number of activities, including a series of national Territorial Reviews. These studies follow a standard methodology and common conceptual framework, allowing countries to share their experiences and disseminate information on good practices.

Acknowledgements

The OECD Secretariat is grateful for the co-operation and support of the numerous officials, experts and businesspeople in Krasnoyarsk who contributed to the background report prepared for the study, met the OECD team preparing the review and in other ways participated in the review process. Special thanks are due to Professor Evgeniya Bukharova and Elena Dvinskikh of the Siberian Federal University, the local team co-ordinators for the review. The Secretariat is particularly grateful to the government of Krasnoyarsk Krai for its financial support and to the former Ministry of Regional Development of the Russian Federation for facilitating the project.

The OECD *Territorial Review of the Krasnoyarsk Agglomeration* was produced in the OECD's Public Governance and Territorial Development Directorate by the Regional Development Policy Division, headed by Joaquim Oliveira Martins. This report was drafted by William Tompson, David Gierten and Patrick Dubarle under the overall supervision of William Tompson, then Head of the Urban Development Programme. The analysis of market potential was undertaken by Patrick Blanchenay (OECD) and Rodrigo Paillacar (Université de Cergy Pontoise, France) under the supervision of Rudiger Ahrend, then Head of the Regional Economics and Governance Unit. Mickael Deprez provided research assistance on transport for Chapter 3. Kate Lancaster, Ulrike Chaplar, Gemma Nellies and Erin Byrne provided editorial assistance. Jennifer Allain prepared the manuscript for publication.

Table of contents

Tables

Figures

Acronyms and abbreviations

BEEPS	Business Environment and Enterprise Performance Survey (World Bank and the European Bank for Reconstruction and Development)
BRT	Bus rapid transit
CAGR	Compound annual growth rate
CBA	Cost-benefit analysis
CIS	Commonwealth of Independent States
CPI	Consumer price index
EBRD	European Bank for Reconstruction and Development
EU	European Union
FDI	Foreign direct investment
FIRE	Finance, insurance and real estate
GDP	Gross domestic product
GRP	Gross regional product
HE	Higher education
HEI	Higher education institution
IERT	Institute of Economy and Transport Development
ILO	International Labour Organization
IMF	International Monetary Fund
IT	Information technology
MME	Municipal management enterprise
NUTS	Nomenclature of territorial units for statistics
PGMs	Platinum-group metals
PIT	Personal income tax
PMR	Product-market regulation
PPP	Public-private partnership
PPP	Purchasing power parity
RDS	Regional development strategies
RIA	Regulatory impact analysis

RIS	Regional innovation system
RUB	Russian ruble
RZhD	Russian Railways
SEZ	Special economic zone
SFO	Siberian Federal District
SFU	Siberian Federal University
SME	Small and medium-sized enterprises
SNG	Sub-national government
SOE	State-owned enterprises
SWOT	Strengths, weaknesses, opportunities, trends
TOD	Transit-oriented development
VAT	Value-added tax
VET	Vocational education and training
WDI	World Development Indicators
WEF	World Economic Forum
WHO	World Health Organization
WTO	World Trade Organization
ZATO	Closed administrative-territorial formation

Executive summary

Key facts and policy issues

Key facts

- The Krasnoyarsk Agglomeration is increasingly emerging as the main economic hub of Eastern Siberia. Its relative weight in both population and economic activity continues to grow. GDP per capita is above the Russian average and recent economic performance has been somewhat stronger than overall national growth.
- Overall labour-market conditions are relatively favourable, with employment rates across the Agglomeration well above the OECD average and comparatively low unemployment. However, differences across the Agglomeration in employment, unemployment and wages suggest that the labour market is still somewhat fragmented.
- By Russian standards, the business environment appears to be relatively good, not least as regards assessments of corruption, the bureaucratic burden on business and the operation of the judicial system. However, Krasnoyarsk's location and climate represent a handicap when it comes to attracting firms and talented individuals.
- Although it is the trade and services centre of Eastern Siberia, the Agglomeration still has a relatively large share of employment and value added in manufacturing, despite some painful industrial restructuring in the early 2000s. Its strengths and weaknesses are still closely linked to the natural resource and energy sectors that are the backbone of the Siberian economy.
- The Agglomeration is also home to an important science base and a workforce with relatively high levels of human capital by both Russian and international standards. It thus has considerable innovation potential, particularly in metals and in the nuclear and space sectors. It has also recently stepped up investment in key innovation infrastructures, such as business incubators.

Key policy challenges

- While the Agglomeration's economy is likely to remain heavily dependent on the primary sector for the foreseeable future, a degree of economic diversification could create new opportunities for high-productivity employment and also reduce vulnerability to commodity price cycles.
- Fostering diversification will, in turn, require the creation of a better climate for entrepreneurship in the Agglomeration. Given its location, climate and small market size, Krasnoyarsk must do more than its peers to stimulate

entrepreneurship and to retain firms and talent. This is one reason the small and medium enterprise (SME) sector seems to be under-developed in Krasnoyarsk.

- The Agglomeration appears to be far short of realising its innovation potential. Both indicators such as patent data and enterprise surveys suggest that its innovation system is not performing as well as those of many other Russian regions, including Tomsk, its near neighbour in the Siberian Federal District.
- The position of the "closed cities" of Zheleznogorsk and Zelenogorsk is an important constraint on developing the Agglomeration's innovation capacities. There has long been a vision of Zheleznogorsk as a city of high-tech production and a centre for the design and development of innovative new technologies, but the regulatory regime governing the city remains very restrictive.
- Weak co-ordination of land-use and transport planning at the level of the Agglomeration reduces efficiency and contributes to labour-market fragmentation. It also impedes the development of the housing market.
- External connectivity also remains a challenge, owing to the Agglomeration's location and transport bottlenecks that affect the Russian Federation as a whole.

Key recommendations

- There is a need for an **Agglomeration-wide labour-market strategy**, including education and training, as well as active labour-market initiatives. Particular attention should be paid to vocational education and training systems, which face changing demand patterns, increasing competition from higher education and rising demand from employers to reduce the gap between the content of education and training and the requirements of firms.
- **Support for small and medium enterprises** should be streamlined and strengthened. Current SME support programmes are substantial but also fragmented, resulting in dispersion and duplication of effort, complications for entrepreneurs and low levels of support overall. Entrepreneurship training should also be incorporated in many more curricula at specialised secondary and tertiary levels of education.
- The main focus of **innovation support** should shift from investment in infrastructures to "softer instruments", including: horizontal approaches like the recently launched technology platforms, more support to innovative start-ups and small firms, deeper inter-regional co-operation and new modalities for linking the "closed cities" to the Agglomeration.
- An **Agglomeration-wide approach to spatial planning** is needed, one that integrates transport, land-use and economic development planning. This would help curb sprawl, reduce transport bottlenecks and redevelop centrally located brownfield sites.
- Transport policies need to aim at improving internal and external connectivity, in particular by exploring bus rapid transit and other new modes of **public transport provision** and by overcoming the regulatory barriers to realising the **potential of Emelyanovo to develop as an international transport hub**.

Assessment and recommendations

The Krasnoyarsk Agglomeration is increasingly emerging as the main economic hub of Eastern Siberia

With a population of 1.175 million in 2011, the urban agglomeration constituted by the city of Krasnoyarsk and six adjacent municipalities is the economic and administrative centre of Krasnoyarsk Krai, the Russian Federation's second-largest region by territory but also one of its most sparsely populated. The Krasnoyarsk Agglomeration is also the most important concentration of population and economic activity in Eastern Siberia. Its importance to the larger region is growing, moreover, as it is one of the few places in Siberia to experience population growth in recent years, against the backdrop of demographic decline at the level of both the Siberian Federal District and the Russian Federation as a whole.

The Agglomeration's economy rests on natural resources – particularly metals and energy, the sectors that constitute the basis of the Krai's considerable wealth. Industry accounts for around 44% of value added and 21% of employment in the Agglomeration; services account for just about 41%. Even so, the Agglomeration concentrates the urban activities of the Krai, a territory covering more than 2.3 million km^2 (13.7% of the Russian Federation's territory) with a population of just over 2.8 million in 2011. Thus, the Agglomeration, despite the large share of industry in total value added, is home to almost 80% of trade, transport, tourism and communications in the Krai, as well as almost one-third of financial services and real estate activities. Moreover, the concentration of services in Krasnoyarsk is increasing.

The vision and strategy of the Agglomeration have evolved over time

The Krasnoyarsk Agglomeration was first conceived as an inter-municipal investment project involving the Krai, the city of Krasnoyarsk and the adjoining municipalities – the Berezovsk, Emelyanovo, Mana and Sukhobuzim Districts, as well as the smaller cities of Divnogorsk and Sosnovoborsk. Since then, the vision for the Agglomeration has evolved, albeit with some starts and stops along the way, towards a growing awareness of the entire area as a single functional economy. However, since there is no legislative basis in the Russian Federation for the concept of "urban agglomeration" (what would be called "metropolitan areas" elsewhere), progress towards institutionalising the Agglomeration has been very slow and the leadership of the Krai government has been critical.

This is consistent with the experience of many metropolitan areas in the OECD: even relatively modest-sized urban agglomerations are often quite fragmented and the obstacles to collective action are frequently substantial. Leadership from higher levels of government is often required to bring about cross-jurisdictional co-operation among municipalities. Even if all the municipalities in a large urban area or region stand to gain from co-operation, it is possible that none of them have the capacity and incentives to take on the costs of gathering the necessary information, mobilising others, etc. Some external support is often needed to overcome collective-action problems.

The Agglomeration is relatively wealthy and productive by Russian standards but still has considerable catch-up potential

In 2011, the Agglomeration's gross domestic product (GDP) per capita was about 5% above the Russian average and slightly higher than that of St. Petersburg, the country's second major city. The Krai as a whole ranked 9th among Russia's 83 regions in terms of GDP per capita. Yet there is clearly room for catch-up growth here: measured in 2008 USD PPP, the Agglomeration's per capita GDP was only just over half that of Antofagasta, the mining region in northern Chile, which, in turn, was slightly above the OECD average.

The Agglomeration's productivity performance is unusual for such a resource-dependent region, inasmuch as over half of total employment – and more than 70% of private-sector employment – is in sectors with above-average productivity. This contrasts favourably with the situation in many resource-based economies, where a small proportion of workers are concentrated in very high-productivity activities but most others are in low-productivity sectors. This positive situation reflects the continuing strength of manufacturing in the Agglomeration even after more than a decade of painful economic restructuring. That said, there are weak spots: in particular, productivity in financial services and real estate activities is surprisingly low. This points to an area where considerable work may be needed, in view of entrepreneurs' complaints about access to finance.

Although the population is growing, the Agglomeration faces demographic challenges

Although birth and death rates have been improving in recent years and compare favourably with Russian-wide averages, population growth in the Agglomeration is largely a result of its increasing attraction to migrants: less than a decade ago, only about one-third of new arrivals in the Agglomeration came from outside the Krai, but this share has been rising steadily and was above 40% in 2011. Nevertheless, the demographic situation still presents social and economic challenges for Krasnoyarsk. First, mortality rates remain elevated by OECD standards and are especially high in some parts of the Agglomeration – three of its constituent municipalities still have death rates that exceed birth rates. Moreover, the Agglomeration has an unusually (for the Russian Federation) large share of population in the 20-34 age group, but the share of those 35 and up has been falling. It appears that many people – particularly the highly skilled – are leaving in their prime; having come to the city to study and start their careers, they seem to move on in their 30s.

Labour market conditions are relatively favourable, though there is considerable variation from place to place

The Agglomeration is characterised by relatively high levels of employment by OECD standards: labour-force participation rates in 2010 ranged from around 73.5% in Emelyanovo, an area hit hard by industrial restructuring, to 82.9% in Mana – all above an OECD average in 2012 of just under 71% – and total unemployment is also comparatively low. However, the concentration of unemployment in specific parts of the Agglomeration has been increasing. As population has become increasingly concentrated in the city of Krasnoyarsk, so has unemployment – a development consistent with low-skilled and surplus workers being pushed out of places on the periphery of the Agglomeration by industrial restructuring and seeking employment in the city itself.

Inter-sectoral wage differentiation is typical for the Russian Federation. Budget-sector wages have risen rapidly relative to the Krai average, reflecting an all-Russian trend, as strengthening public finances made it easier to address public-sector wages in the good years prior to the crisis. Since 2008, public-sector wages have been above the averages for the Russian Federation, the Siberian Federal District and the Krai. Geographic wage disparities, mirroring productivity differentials, are sharp – in Krasnoyarsk wages are on average 1.5-2.0 times higher than on the periphery of the Agglomeration. They are lowest in the Sukhobuzim and Mana Districts and the city of Sosnovoborsk.

The Agglomeration's major economic assets challenges are largely defined by its geography

The Agglomeration's major economic strengths and weaknesses are closely linked to its location, natural resources and climate. First, as noted above, the enormous natural resource wealth of Krasnoyarsk Krai constitutes the foundation of the city's economy. Altogether, the Krai accounts for around 80% of the country's nickel production and is the largest producer of nickel in the world. It also holds 75% of the Russian Federation's cobalt, 70% of its copper, 16% of its coal and 10% of its gold extraction. More than 95% of Russia's known resources of platinum-group metals (PGMs) are located within the Krai, which also produces 20% of the country's timber. The Krai's global importance as a PGM producer is difficult to exaggerate: it is the world's leading producer of palladium (above 40% of global supply in 2010) and ranks second to South Africa in the production of platinum and other PGMs. Such endowments have served as the basis for the relatively good growth that both the Krai and the Agglomeration have enjoyed in recent years.

The benefits of this natural wealth are tempered, however, by the relative geographic isolation of the Agglomeration, which has limited the expansion and diversification of the local economy, as well as by the comparatively harsh climatic conditions that prevail. Winters are both long and severe, with average temperatures in January of –18°C even in the relatively warm southern parts of the Krai (–36°C in the north). Such cold affects the cost of production of many goods and services, as well as the well-being and cost of living of the population. Remote location and a difficult climate are by no means insuperable obstacles to success – the prosperity of such diverse places as Alaska, New Zealand and parts of Canada testifies to the contrary – but they do imply specific problems for both public and private sectors to resolve. Local markets tend to be thin and characterised by relatively weak competition, while transport costs to larger markets are high, particularly given Krasnoyarsk's reliance on relatively expensive (overland and air) transport. The scope for realising economies of scale or benefiting from agglomeration economies is limited.

Policy makers and firms in Krasnoyarsk are all too familiar with these problems. They point to the very fundamental reality that an export-oriented economy located far from the major centres of demand faces an exceptional competitiveness challenge, particularly in manufacturing. Tradables producers outside the primary sector thus require an edge in terms of efficiency to offset the handicap of distance – they need to be that much better than their rivals; being just as good may not be enough. They also need other sources of competitive advantage to offset the limited ability to exploit scale or agglomeration economies, e.g. by focusing on unique qualities of products, where scarcity can add value.

A degree of economic diversification would create new opportunities for the population

The economy of the Agglomeration, and the Krai as a whole, is very likely to remain heavily dependent on its existing strengths in natural resources. These are considerable and there is no reason why they should not provide a basis for reasonably good growth over the long run. Yet the diversification of economic activity remains a priority. The case for working towards further diversification is two-fold.

- It will reduce somewhat the vulnerability of the economy to commodity-price cycles.
- It will create new opportunities for high-productivity employment. Perhaps the chief difficulty with heavy reliance on extractive industries is that they are very capital intensive but do not employ much labour.

The risk is that a mining or oil-producing region has a small number of extremely high-productivity jobs in the core sector and the high-value business services linked to it, and a much larger number of jobs in relatively low-productivity proximity services. Given Krasnoyarsk's population and human capital, such an outcome would represent a waste of economic and human potential. The point of a diversification strategy, therefore, is not so much to bring about a fundamental shift in the sectoral structure of the economy as to create new opportunities for people with skills and talent to employ them productively in and around Krasnoyarsk. This will entail a focus on entrepreneurship, human capital formation and innovation.

The Agglomeration's business environment is relatively good by Russian standards

Krasnoyarsk offers at least some advantages to entrepreneurs. In particular, recent enterprise surveys suggest that the Agglomeration's business climate is better than that of most places in Russia. While such issues are difficult to assess with precision, managerial responses to surveys like the World Bank-EBRD "Business Environment and Enterprise Performance Survey (BEEPS)" suggest that firms in the Agglomeration suffer less from corruption and have fewer difficulties with issues like licences, permits and inspections than most other firms in the Russian Federation. They also have fewer concerns about the operation of the judicial system. Their biggest headaches concern access to land and access to finance.

A recent comparison of 100 major Russian cities highlights some other strong points that should not be overlooked. Krasnoyarsk ranks in the top 20% among major Russian cities in terms of household purchasing power and in the top 10% in terms of the quality of its built environment. Despite its remote location, it ranks near the top in terms of measures of external connectivity, as well.

Nevertheless, given its location and climate, the Agglomeration is handicapped in the competition with other Russian cities to retain firms and talented individuals. It must therefore do more than its more favourably located rivals to stimulate entrepreneurship and innovation and to retain firms and talent. Being as good – or even a bit better – is not enough. Yet there is considerable potential for the constituent units of the Agglomeration to pursue this end by working together to create a more competitive, attractive urban area and, in particular, to create the best possible conditions for entrepreneurs and innovators.

Support for small and medium enterprises could be streamlined and strengthened

Despite the quality of the business environment, the small and medium-sized enterprise (SME) sector is under-performing. It accounts for just 17% of employment, and service-based and mining-related small companies are few in number. Moreover, the evidence suggests that most SMEs have rather weak absorption capacities and their innovation potential cannot be fully tapped. While there are some outstanding exceptions to this generalisation – such as the Divnogorsk-based SKAD Light Alloy Wheels – the broader picture is troubling, especially since SMEs are increasingly considered as the driving force behind new products and processes.

The authorities in and around Krasnoyarsk are aware of this and SME support programmes are substantial. The problem is that they are also fragmented. A proliferation of programmes results in dispersion of effort, complications for entrepreneurs and very small levels of support. Given the limited sums available for such support, streamlining and consolidation would seem to be essential. In addition, most SME policies target the purely financial dimension of SME activities. While access to finance is a key constraint on SME development and needs to be addressed, policy can also influence SME behaviour by, for example, emphasising inter-firm co-operation or helping to upgrade social capital and inter-firm networks. There is also more that could be done in terms of human capital formation, particularly entrepreneurship education. The Agglomeration would benefit from a more comprehensive plan to guide SME promotion, worked out by the authorities in concert with the expert and business communities.

The multi-dimensional *Región Fértil* Initiative in Antofagasta, a relatively remote mining city in Chile, could provide important lessons for such an experiment in Krasnoyarsk. Bringing together local enterprises, public organisations academic institutions and media under the sponsorship of the regional government, *Región Fértil* seeks to "join all forces" in order to build an entrepreneurial ecosystem capable of strengthening the impact of public and private initiatives and help raise the innovation and entrepreneurship performance of the region.

Training for entrepreneurship is crucial at secondary and even more at tertiary levels of education. It would be useful to review the entrepreneurship-related curricula in the different institutions in Krasnoyarsk and to consider the ways to upgrade and amplify them. The experience of the Brandenburg Institute for Entrepreneurship and SMEs (BIEM) in Germany might be considered as a useful basis for drawing some lessons.

BIEM is the entrepreneurship institute of the regional development agency and nine public higher education institutions, including universities and universities of applied sciences. BIEM activities include entrepreneurship education, start-up support, entrepreneurship research and networking with business support organisations and other universities.

Education and training policies could usefully be consolidated at the scale of the Agglomeration

Increasingly, the municipalities of the Agglomeration are being drawn together into a single functional urban economy, with increased commuting, new infrastructure and industrial relocation altering the shape of labour market flows in quite important ways. In this context, there is a need for an Agglomeration-wide approach to labour market strategy, including education and training, as well as active labour market initiatives. Policy interventions, which are currently somewhat fragmented, should target the appropriate scale: the functional labour market of the Agglomeration. This will need to pay particular attention to vocational education and training (VET) systems, which face changing demand patterns, increasing competition from higher education and rising demand from employers to reduce the gap between the content of education and professional training and the actual requirements of local industries. In 2012, it was estimated that 35% of tertiary graduates and 40% of graduates of secondary vocational institutions were unprepared for employment on completion of their studies.

The Krai authorities are working actively on the issue. The Krai Ministry of Education and Science has taken steps to restructure the secondary VET system with a view to producing graduates with skills more relevant to the local labour markets. International experience suggests that interactions between vocational institutions and industry are crucial to ensuring up-to-date training content, equipment and facilities as well as providing career guidance and introducing new programmes. The Agglomeration needs to prioritise partnerships between business and the public sector and to strengthen the incentives for universities to expand their continuous training programmes.

The Krasnoyarsk Agglomeration's innovation system is under-performing relative to its potential

For historical reasons, Krasnoyarsk contains significant innovation assets, particularly associated with metals and the nuclear and space sectors, including a substantial science base and high overall levels of human capital, by both Russian and international standards. However, a wide range of indicators suggest that Krasnoyarsk's innovation system does not perform particularly well compared to many other places in Russia, including Tomsk, its near neighbour in the Siberian Federal District. This holds true for such indicators as patents, new products or services brought to market, the share of innovative goods and services in total sales, new production methods or organisational-managerial innovations.

That said, the potential of the Agglomeration to generate innovations remains considerable, and there are some positive trends observed. First, Krasnoyarsk's major higher education institutions have been climbing up the SCImago institutions rankings in recent years as the emphasis on research and engagement with the business sector increases. In addition, the innovation system does appear to be relatively efficient, in the sense that the relationship between the input side (spending on research and development, R&D staff, etc.) and the measured outputs in terms of patents, compares favourably to many other places in Russia. In addition, Krasnoyarsk's innovation system clearly reflects the structure of the economy as a whole, with activity focused on those sectors: it is thus much more oriented towards engineering, production processing, automated monitoring, information technology (IT) for production and integrated management, in contrast to the more research-driven approach that prevails in places like neighbouring Novosibirsk.

The position of the "closed cities" is a constraint on innovation

Some of the greatest innovation potential in Krasnoyarsk is to be found in two so-called "closed administrative-territorial formations" (ZATOs): Zheleznogorsk, which lies near the heart of the Agglomeration, and Zelenogorsk, which is not far from it. These two towns were originally created as closed military research-industrial complexes and they remain under strict federal access regimes today, owing to the sensitive nature of their nuclear and space research. Indeed, Zelenogorsk still does not appear on most public maps. The authorities are well aware of the scientific and commercial potential of these two ZATOs, and Zheleznogorsk is especially important to the future of the Agglomeration. For some time past, there has been a long-term vision of Zheleznogorsk as a city of high-tech production, acting as a centre for the design and development of innovative new technologies. An incubator has been operating since 2004 and an industrial park will be completed over the 2013-17 period. However, ZATO status does not facilitate the interactions with external actors. The cities' competitiveness is hampered by restrictive regulations with regard to import of technologies and co-operative exchanges with non-ZATO communities and firms.

The authorities have been stepping up innovation-promotion efforts

Much relevant policy is vested at the level of the Krai rather than with the municipalities that constitute the Agglomeration, but these initiatives are focused in and around the city of Krasnoyarsk, because that is where the Krai's innovation assets are concentrated. The Krai Ministry of Investments and Innovation designs the regional innovation policy with the help of the Governor's Council for Innovative Development and the Innovation Council of Krasnoyarsk. It has recourse to a relatively large spectrum of instruments, including pecuniary incentives (e.g. public procurement, subsidies for commercialisation of research and purchase of equipment, partial funding of training expenses and so on), as well as indirect support through assistance for international co-operation and the organisation of public events (fairs, exhibitions, conferences).

So far the policy has emphasised the development of innovation infrastructure and improved public-private co-operation. The region is now developing a Technopark, the Krasnoyarsk Regional Innovative Technology Business Incubator (KRITBI) opened its doors in 2011; there is also a city incubator. In addition, the ministry has sought to encourage co-ordination between business, higher education and the public sector is encouraged within the framework of 13 regional technology platforms. There is also federal support channelled through such programmes as the Russian Foundation for Basic Research and the Foundation for Assistance to Small Innovative Enterprise (FASIE).

Numerous KRITBI projects have also benefited from federal support for young researchers.

Policy can do more to stimulate innovative activity

In terms of the future, there are four priorities for policy to explore, in addition to continuing to develop the initiatives now under way:

- *Deepening horizontal approaches.* The technology platforms represent an excellent start, in that they focus on technologies rather than sectors and thus bring together actors and firms that might not otherwise collaborate. This is promising and should be taken further, keeping policy fairly neutral as to sectors, but perhaps reducing the number of platforms (13 may be more than the local economy requires or can sustain fruitfully). With this in mind, the authorities should be wary of cluster initiatives, which in Russia are often sectorally focused and can confuse clusters with old Soviet-era territorial production complexes. Broad networks relying on light instruments look more promising than cluster policies.
- *Supporting innovative small firms.* As noted above, start-ups and SMEs are critical elements of a successful innovation system. Start-up support for small innovative firms has recently been augmented substantially; this support should be maintained and extended.
- *Better linking the "closed cities" to the Agglomeration.* The challenge is to better use the innovation assets of these cities while respecting the federal authorities' legitimate security concerns. For both cities, it is critical to facilitate horizontal linkages between high-tech SMEs in the ZATOs and the universities and firms outside of them. The experience of the United States in managing the Oak Ridge National Laboratory (ORNL), which was the cradle of the US atomic bomb project during World War II and is still the largest laboratory of the US Department of Energy. Legislation adopted in the United States in the 1980s enables collaborative R&D, patent licence agreements and technical outreach, while preserving the security of the ORNL's sensitive activities.
- *Strengthening inter-regional co-operation for innovation.* Inter-regional and intercity co-operation in Siberia has remained underdeveloped. Some (limited) steps have nevertheless been taken. For example, the information satellite platform involves not only the Siberian Federal University (SFU) and the Siberian State Aerospace University but also the Siberian branch of the Russian Academy of Sciences, the Tomsk Polytechnic University and Tomsk State University. However, such examples are few and the potential for development is enormous. EU initiatives such as the Interreg programme could serve as models for strengthening co-operation among the regions and cities of Siberia.

The Agglomeration would benefit from better co-ordination of land-use and transport planning across the constituent municipalities

Among the strategic priorities for the Agglomeration is the "economically efficient and environmentally sustainable use of land". If this goal is to be achieved, the authorities will need to co-ordinate changes in housing provision, the relocation of industries in the Agglomeration and transport planning at an Agglomeration-wide scale. The choice of new industrial locations should be co-ordinated with Agglomeration-wide transport planning in order to minimise the need for new infrastructure and to optimise commuting flows related to new industrial locations, while former industrial sites in central areas will need mixed-use, transport-oriented redevelopment. In accordance with current legislation, spatial planning, zoning and civil construction are dealt with in each municipal entity separately. The Krai Ministry of Economics and Regional Development has defined its own guidelines for inter-municipal co-ordination, but it does not provide an explicit framework for co-ordinating transport or land-use planning across municipalities. However, federal law does allow municipalities to conclude voluntary contractual agreements. Better integration of land-use and transport planning might necessitate the creation on a contractual basis of a separate inter-municipal advisory body.

In any case, where the plan of one municipality affects the interests of another municipality or a regional planning document, the Urban Planning Code specifies the rules, criteria and procedures for inter-municipal approval of plans. Yet this regulatory framework for reconciling spatial plans among municipalities does not provide guidance or a framework for *pro-active* inter-municipal planning – hence the desirability of an Agglomeration-wide advisory body. Such a body would need to be open to representatives of the Krai and the Federation but could act upon relevant inter-municipal planning issues in the Krasnoyarsk Agglomeration. Experiences with inter-municipal planning organisations in cities like Vancouver and Chicago could offer useful models and lessons.

Better co-ordination of spatial planning could also help strengthen the housing market and curtail the trend towards sprawl

Most residential development in the Agglomeration is currently implemented in greenfields, as low-rise housing in peripheral areas. Such development patterns negatively affect the economic and environmental efficiency of territorial development, not least by raising the cost of infrastructure and service provision and increasing resource consumption, notably due to higher energy consumption in buildings and longer commutes. Freeing up centrally located industrial land for other uses could benefit the Agglomeration economically and environmentally. Centrally located former industrial land plots not only have the advantage of being connected to urban infrastructures and services, but are also attractive for developers due to their size, which offers opportunities for centrally located residential, commercial or mixed-use development at efficient scales. This would also reduce the cost of addressing the Agglomeration's housing needs. Better planning also needs to be accompanied by a reduction in the distortions that shape land markets, so that agents can reallocate land uses in urban territories in economically more efficient ways.

Such an approach could also contribute to the formation of a dynamic rental market. Currently low rental rates in Russia are discouraging developers from investing in multi-family buildings for rental housing. Furthermore, terms for private developers in land-use agreements with public authorities using "model rent agreements" are often not attractive enough to encourage investments. The underdeveloped rental market makes the Agglomeration's labour market more rigid, affecting firms in finding their needed human capital, particularly small and medium-sized companies. Some of the public land to be redeveloped in urban areas could, for example, be dedicated to constructing affordable rental housing; or developers may be given incentives to include a minimum share of rental space in new buildings.

Coherent approaches to transport and infrastructure are central to the Agglomeration's future

Upgrading the Agglomeration's transport networks and improving internal connectivity are high on the agenda of policy makers in Krasnoyarsk. Better co-ordination of all aspects of internal connectivity is critical to the Agglomeration's future as a functional urban economy. This is a multi-dimensional challenge and it will need to be tackled in a co-ordinated fashion: addressing individual constraints in isolation, in a reactive fashion, could make things worse in the long run. Thus it is important that attempts to de-bottleneck the road network via the construction of new roads and bridges be accompanied by steps to improve public transport, which is not currently an attractive alternative to the private car for most users.

Dormant potential might lie in Krasnoyarsk's unfinished metro system but this is likely to be a prohibitively costly option, especially for reaching places outside the centre of the city itself. Bus rapid transit (BRT) could offer a better alternative. Any plan to complete the metro should be compared to alternative solutions such as BRT, which is likely to be cheaper and more flexible. BRT would create less spatial and infrastructure path dependence. BRT could better be adapted to changes in commuting patterns and land use arising from, for example, the relocation of industries currently situated in the centre of Krasnoyarsk and the development of new residential settlements. Furthermore, synergies could be achieved between extending and improving road infrastructure for both BRT and car use.

Much can be done to enhance the external connectivity of the Agglomeration

The other critical dimension of the Agglomeration's transport challenges concerns external rather than internal connectivity. Given its location and assets, it has the potential to develop as a reasonably serious Eurasian transport and logistics hub, and the authorities in Krasnoyarsk have considerable ambitions in this direction. Many of the obstacles to realising this ambition fall in the domain of federal regulatory and infrastructure policies, which constrain the development of rail and air cargo traffic. However, the Krai and the local authorities can take action – this is particularly true of air cargo, since rail and road networks to the rest of the world are not within the competence of policy makers in Krasnoyarsk.

The international airport in Emelyanovo is the central element of the Agglomeration's potential to develop into an international transport hub. Emelyanovo serves both international and domestic air travel and cargo in the Krasnoyarsk Agglomeration, and it ranks third in terms of domestic air passengers and third for the number of regional airports it serves (22). Emelyanovo has significant potential to serve international air cargo stopovers. At present, though, most such stopovers occur in neighbouring countries, despite Krasnoyarsk's convenient location. Lufthansa Cargo estimates that it can optimise its routing and shorten flying times to the Far East by using Krasnoyarsk as a stopover instead of Astana in Kazakhstan, but technical landing charges at the airport are very high, even by Russian standards, and Russian international airports overall are characterised by inefficient customs procedures, high kerosene prices and expensive air navigation fees for air cargo.

Taken together, these factors curb the attractiveness of Emelyanovo for international air cargo companies. The authorities are trying to correct this. With respect to airport customs procedures, Emelyanovo is engaged in one of two Russian pilot projects implementing the International Air Transport Association's e-Freight handling standards. This allows paperless and cheaper cargo handling and increases efficiency of service delivery, reliability and transparency. However, more effort is needed to tackle the different challenges currently holding back Krasnoyarsk's potential to develop an international air transport hub.

Krasnoyarsk should also proceed with plans to develop an intermodal transport logistics centre. The volume of container cargo transit between Asia and Europe is expected to increase over the next years, and the Russian Federation's share of international containers could be much higher. Whether or not this will be achieved depends on the competitiveness of container transport via international sea routes versus the competitiveness of Russian rail container transport. The sea route from the People's Republic of China to European Union countries is almost four times longer than the Russian rail track and costs are over USD 250 more per container. Russian container transport needs to become more reliable and more flexible. Given Krasnoyarsk's position at the cross-roads of important road and rail links, as well as astride the Yenisei, a logistics centre with storage facilities and inter-modal connection and transhipment facilities could develop as a key asset for the Agglomeration.

To sum up

Krasnoyarsk's importance to both the Krai and the whole of Eastern Siberia continues to grow. The region and the city are among the more prosperous places in the Russian Federation and the foundations for further growth are strong. Nevertheless, much remains to be done if the Krasnoyarsk Agglomeration is to realise its full potential in terms of economic growth, innovation and quality of life. An integrated approach to territorial development will be needed. This will entail both careful co-ordination of sectoral policies, especially in the fields of transport, land use and labour markets, as well as stronger, more institutionalised co-operation among the municipalities that constitute the Agglomeration under the leadership of the Krai.

Figure 0.1. **Krasnoyarsk Krai and the Krasnoyarsk Agglomeration**

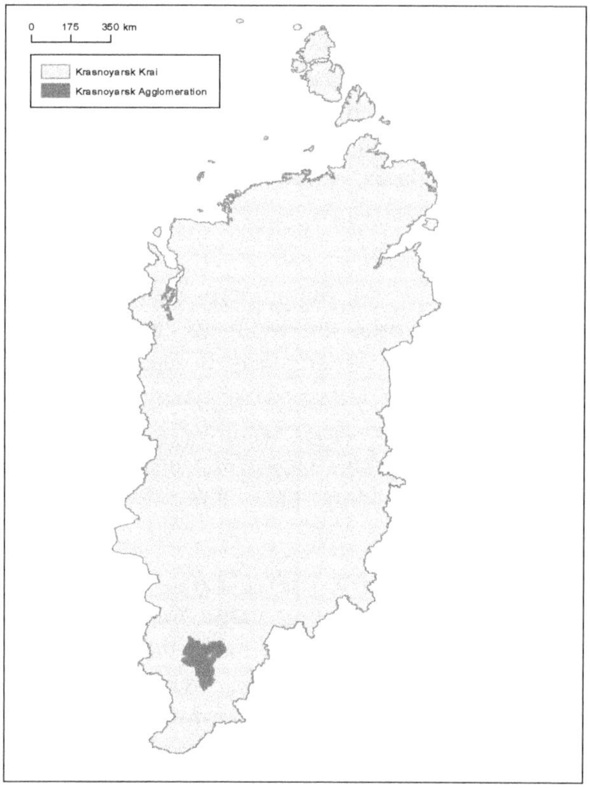

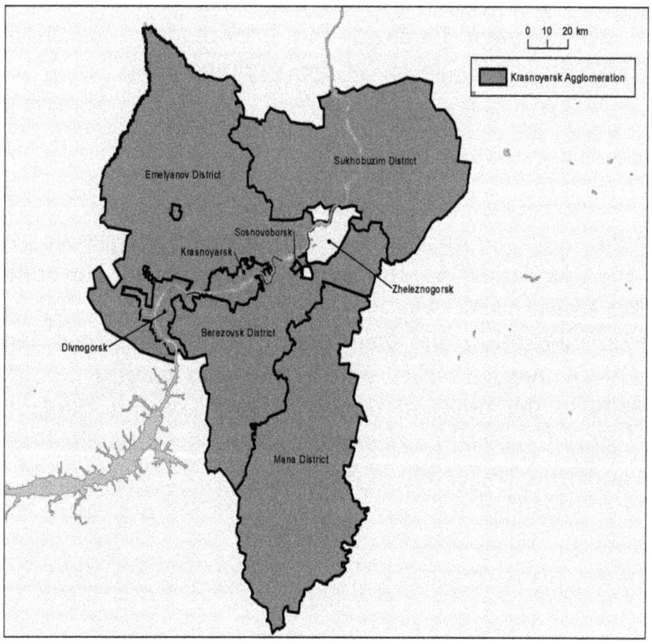

Chapter 1

Understanding the Krasnoyarsk Agglomeration*

This chapter situates the Krasnoyarsk Agglomeration in the context of Krasnoyarsk Krai and the Russian Federation and assesses the major economic, urban and social challenges facing the Agglomeration. It examines demographic and economic trends, highlighting the Agglomeration's strengths in terms of resource wealth, human capital and science assets. It also defines the development challenges created by its geography, including a severe climate, long distances to major markets and a relatively sparse settlement pattern. Finally, it looks at the need and potential for further diversification of economic activity in the Agglomeration.

* The statistical data for Israel are supplied by and under the responsibility of the relevant Israeli authorities. The use of such data by the OECD is without prejudice to the status of the Golan Heights, East Jerusalem and Israeli settlements in the West Bank under the terms of international law.

Introduction

This chapter presents an overview of the demographic, social and economic trends and challenges facing the Krasnoyarsk Agglomeration, which constitutes the main urban hub of Krasnoyarsk Krai and the largest urban area in Eastern Siberia. The Agglomeration is centred on the city of Krasnoyarsk, which is the administrative capital of the Krai, and it also encompasses the Berezovsk, Emelyanovo, Mana and Sukhobuzim Districts, as well as the smaller cities of Divnogorsk and Sosnovoborsk. Together they form a functional urban area that represents the most important concentration of economic activity in Eastern Siberia. The economy of the Agglomeration is largely dominated by natural-resource extraction activities in the surrounding areas and in the rest of the Krai, which have influenced in many ways the dynamics and structure of the city of Krasnoyarsk and its hinterland. The benefits of this natural wealth are tempered, however, by the relative geographic and economic isolation of the Agglomeration, which has limited the expansion and diversification of the local economy, as well as by the comparatively severe climatic conditions that prevail.

The goal of this chapter is to understand how these opportunities and constraints have shaped the Krasnoyarsk Agglomeration and to outline some of the policy issues that face the Krai and the constituent municipalities of the Agglomeration as they seek to generate growth and enhance the quality of life for the area's inhabitants. The discussion begins with a look at Krasnoyarsk Krai as a whole, in the context of the Russian economy, since economic realities in the Agglomeration are in no small measure determined by the activities that take place elsewhere on the territory of the Krai. It then zeroes in on trends in the Agglomeration itself before stepping back, as it were, to consider the fundamental nature of some of the policy issues confronting both the Krai and the Agglomeration – above all, those concerned with four key dimensions of geography: natural resources, climate, location and density of settlement. On the basis of this analysis, the chapter, finally, sketches the major challenges to be addressed in the chapters that follow.

Krasnoyarsk Krai in the context of the Russian Federation

The Russian Federation has struggled to regain the economic momentum lost during the contraction of 2008-09

The performance of Krasnoyarsk Krai can only be understood in the context of Russian economic performance overall. In recent years, this has been better than that of many OECD countries but still relatively disappointing. During the period from 1999 until 2008, the Russian Federation (hereafter "Russia") experienced a period of extremely strong growth following the transition recession of the 1990s. Between 1999 and 2008, real gross domestic product (GDP) grew at an average annual rate of just under 7%, buoyed by rising terms of trade, which supported a boom in domestic consumption. GDP per capita nearly doubled in real terms. As argued in OECD (2006, 2009), this run of strong growth was based on a number of factors, which were clearly transitory.

- The gains in competitiveness that Russian producers enjoyed after the 1998 financial crisis largely disappeared by the mid-2000s, thanks to the steady appreciation of the rouble and rising unit labour costs.
- There was less and less scope for Russian industry to go on raising output by increasing capacity utilisation without substantially greater investment.

- The terms of trade could not go on rising indefinitely, and it was always clear that the impact on growth of commodity price increases would inevitably attenuate even if oil prices remained high, as the economy adjusted to the new terms of trade.

The model of growth that prevailed in the early 2000s thus left Russia vulnerable when the global financial crisis erupted in late 2008. Real GDP fell by almost 8% in 2009 and was only marginally above 2008 levels in 2011. An initially quick recovery from the crisis (about half of the 11% peak-to-trough decline in output was recovered in the second half of 2009) soon lost momentum. As energy prices stabilised and then fell, and labour and capital utilisation rates recovered, growth slowed in 2012 and 2013 before stalling in 2014. Investment growth more or less came to a halt, mining output declined and private consumption growth was increasingly sustained by increasing household debt. Though still outperforming the OECD average, the Russian Federation's performance was unimpressive alongside that of the other BRICS countries (Brazil, Russian Federation, India, China and South Africa) (Figure 1.1).

Figure 1.1. **Real GDP growth, BRIICS countries and OECD**

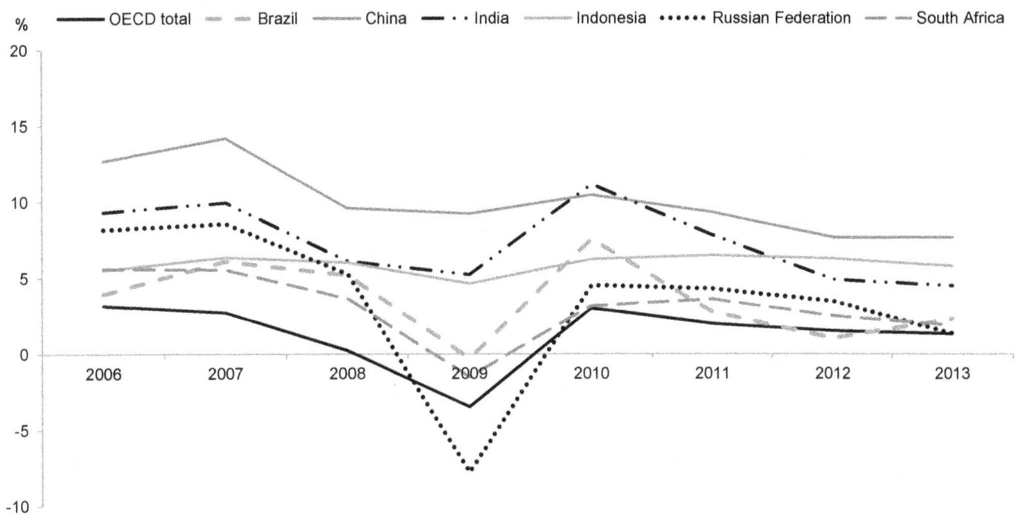

Source: OECD (2014a), *OECD Economic Outlook: Statistics and Projections* (database), http://dx.doi.org/10.1787/eo-data-en.

Transmission of the global crisis to Russia followed two major channels. First, with a ratio of external assets to GDP of 500% in 2010, Russia is more financially integrated than many other emerging economies; this exposed it to the financial downturn in high-income countries, although some argue that the deleveraging partially mitigated these effects in Russia and Turkey. Secondly, with natural-resource sectors accounting for a large part of Russian growth (Ahrend, 2006), the country was hit by fluctuations in commodity prices in the years 2008-09 and by their stabilisation in the more recent past (Figure 1.2).

Figure 1.2. **Commodity price index**

January 2005 = 100

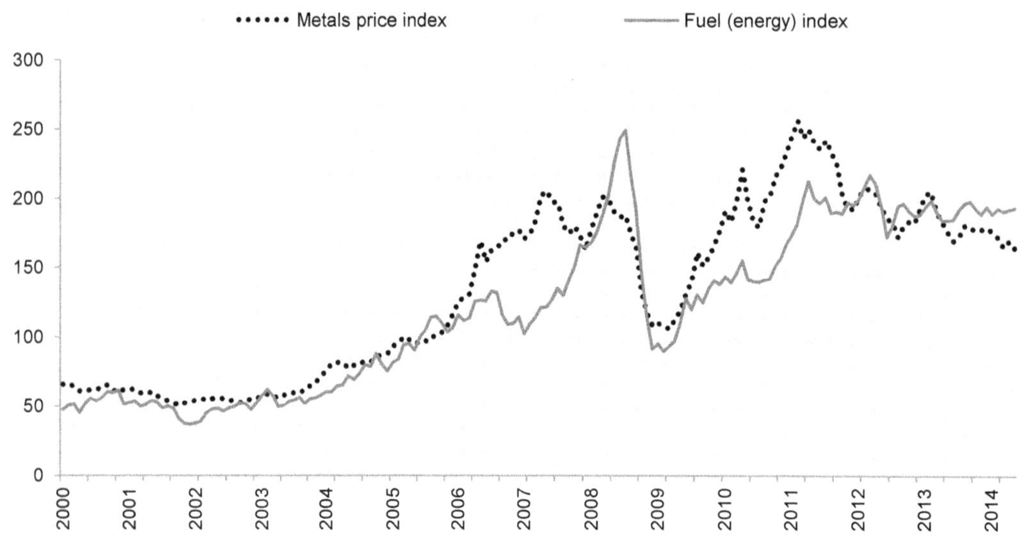

Note: The metals index includes copper, aluminium, iron ore, tin, nickel, zinc, lead and uranium prices. The fuel index includes crude oil, natural gas and coal prices.

Source: IMF (n.d.), Primary Commodity Prices http://www.imf.org/external/np/res/commod/index.aspx (accessed June 2014).

Figure 1.3. **Relative income and productivity levels, 2012**

As percentage points above/below US levels

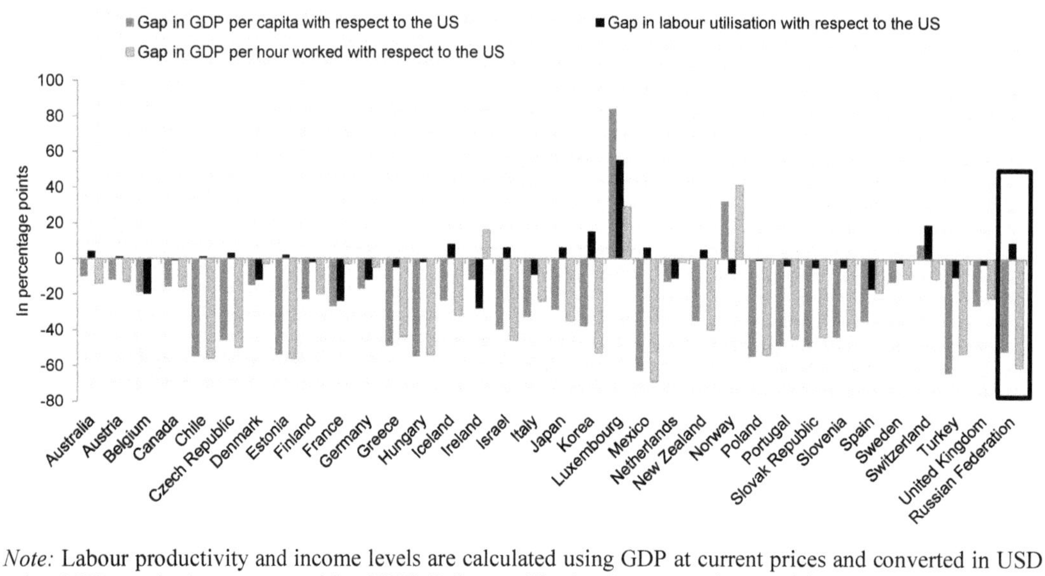

Note: Labour productivity and income levels are calculated using GDP at current prices and converted in USD using 2009 purchasing power parities (PPP). Labour utilisation is measured as total hours worked per capita. Labour productivity and labour utilisation levels estimates for Israel, the Russian Federation and Slovenia are based on hours worked for the year 2008. Euro area includes Austria, Belgium, Finland, France, Germany, Greece, Ireland, Italy, Luxembourg, the Netherlands, Portugal, the Slovak Republic, Slovenia, and Spain. France includes overseas departments.

Source: OECD (2014b), *OECD Productivity* (database), http://www.oecd.org/std/productivity-stats/.

The Russian Federation's productivity challenge is intimately linked to the problem of resource dependence. There are two issues here. The first is that the productivity performance of the resource sector itself proved somewhat lacklustre even in the good years leading up to the global crisis, as was that of the large non-market sector (Table 1.1). Given the continuing importance of the primary sector in the economy, this has to be a concern for policy makers. The second problem is that the minerals and hydrocarbons sectors are highly capital-intensive but employ few people: in the official data, resource extraction accounted for around 11% of GDP in 2012 (without taking account of the knock-on effects of mining and hydrocarbon production on other sectors), but it employed under 2% of the workforce. Oil production in 2012 reached a post-Soviet high of 10.3m barrels/day, making Russia the world's largest oil producer. However, Russia cannot be a simple petro-economy: its output in per capita terms was a fraction of that recorded in oil-producing countries with small populations, like Kuwait, Norway and Saudi Arabia. The country's resource sectors alone will never be able to provide an acceptable standard of living for the great mass of the population, even if one makes very aggressive assumptions about both future mineral and hydrocarbon prices and about its ability to increase resource extraction (Sutela, 2005). Given Russia's population and its considerable human capital endowments, a flourishing non-resource urban sector is likely to be critical to long-term prosperity, as well as social and political stability.

Table 1.1. **GDP decomposition, 1995-2008**

	Value added share (current prices)		Annual real growth rates (%)			
	1995	2008	Value added	Labour input	Capital input	Multi-factor productivity
Total economy	100.0	100.0	4.61	1.30	3.22	2.27
Market economy	86.1	84.0	4.82	1.27	2.89	2.56
Goods	25.6	18.3	2.92	-1.01	0.51	3.23
High skill-intensive	3.6	3.6	3.92	-2.54	-0.18	5.57
Low skill-intensive	22.0	14.8	2.72	-0.71	0.64	2.78
Services	40.4	41.0	5.82	1.72	3.92	3.14
High skill-intensive	5.1	11.2	10.70	1.20	2.78	8.97
Low skill-intensive	35.3	29.8	4.60	1.85	4.20	1.69
Extended mining	20.1	24.7	4.87	2.67	3.35	**0.84**
Non-market economy	13.9	16.0	3.41	1.52	5.12	0.60

Source: OECD (2014c), *OECD Economic Surveys: Russian Federation 2013*, OECD Publishing, Paris, http://dx.doi.org/10.1787/eco_surveys-rus-2013-en based on M. Timmer and I. Voskoboynikov (2013), "Is mining fuelling long-run growth in Russia? Industry productivity growth trends since 1995", GGDC Research Memorandum.

In short, Russia needs to create a large number of productive jobs in competitive activities outside the primary sector. This is but one of a number of reasons for Russian policy makers to focus on the diversification of economic activity and, in particular, on fostering the emergence of competitive, tradable producers outside the resource-extraction sector. Other motivations include the heightened vulnerability to external shocks that resource dependence entails and the institutional pathologies often associated with heavy reliance on natural resource sectors (OECD, 2006; Ahrend, 2006). In principle, there are policy options that might address these latter concerns and enable the Russian Federation to continue to enjoy strong growth with limited diversification (World Bank, 2014). However, when it comes to employment, there is little option, and this constitutes perhaps the most compelling motivation for seeking to diversify economic activity: without it, Russia cannot make the most of its population's talents or allow the great mass of its citizens to pursue productive, rewarding careers.

Resource wealth may make economic diversification more difficult

In at least two important respects, Russia's resource wealth complicates the business of diversification. As is well known, the presence of a large and highly profitable resource sector can complicate life for producers of non-resource tradables. Rising commodity prices attract labour and capital into the primary sector, which – thanks to resource rents – can offer higher wages and rates of return than other sectors (a process sometimes referred to as factor drainage). The change in relative prices squeezes the competitiveness of the non-resource tradable sector (Corden and Neary, 1982), a phenomenon often referred to as "Dutch disease".[1] In addition, a commodity boom can fuel domestic demand, putting upward pressure on prices, especially in non-tradable sectors. This further hurts the competiveness of non-resource tradables producers. The strengthening of the exchange rate is often the most visible symptom of this phenomenon, but it can unfold even in the absence of nominal appreciation.[2] Such pressures can be very hard, even on established producers of manufactures and other non-resource tradables; they are even tougher to overcome for nascent firms and sectors trying to establish themselves in highly competitive global markets, so diversification can be particularly difficult for an economy with a booming primary sector.

Such "Dutch disease" pressures constitute only one part of the macroeconomic challenge. The other concerns the impact of growth volatility on diversification. González, Iacovone and Subhash (2013) find that the volatility of Russia's growth, which is in part a product of its specialisation in primary resource sectors, may itself be bad for diversification. Commodity-exporting countries are often particularly vulnerable to growth volatility, owing to swings in commodity prices, which can be rather large even over very short periods. At issue is the way in which boom-and-bust cycles affect the selection of firms for exit. In a perfectly functioning market, more productive firms survive and less productive firms are forced to exit. In reality, there is also an incumbency advantage: other things being equal, older firms are more likely to survive than new ones. Lenders and suppliers, for example, may be less likely to support new entrants under stress than they are to back older firms, with which they have longer relationships. In Russia, older firms frequently enjoy an additional advantage in terms of their relationships with the public authorities (so-called "administrative resource"). As González, Iacovone and Subhash (2013) show, the problem is that the relative importance of incumbency, as opposed to productivity, appears to be greater in downturns. Sharp cycles are thus more likely to weed out productive new firms, as opposed to less productive older ones.

Diversification will require sound macroeconomic management and structural reform

As the foregoing implies, any attempt to sustain growth over the long term and to foster the emergence of new tradable activities and sectors will require extremely prudent macroeconomic management. The authorities must use their fiscal powers, in particular, to buffer the economy to some extent from commodity price fluctuations and thereby to ensure that sudden shifts in the terms of trade do not result in significant imbalances between domestic supply and demand (OECD, 2006; Ahrend, 2006). Russia has already done much to mitigate such risks, via the creation of fiscal mechanisms for saving a large share of the country's commodity windfalls, in an effort to avoid boom-and-bust cycles.

A fiscal rule introduced in December 2012 limits the budgetary use of oil revenues to that calculated at a benchmark five-year average of past oil prices (to be gradually increased to a ten-year average by 2018). Oil revenues above the benchmark prices are directed to the Reserve Fund until it reaches a level of 7% of GDP. Above that level, at least half are directed to the National Welfare Fund while the rest can be spent on infrastructure investment. Such an arrangement not only helps to reduce fluctuations in aggregate domestic demand, it can reduce upward pressure on the exchange rate, thus mitigating the "Dutch disease" problems of non-resource tradable sectors (OECD, 2006).

This is an important positive step, building on the fiscal framework the Russian Federation established in the mid-2000s, prior to the global crisis – a framework that arguably helped the country weather the crisis better than it could have otherwise. However, OECD (2014c) observes that the rule does not control for the use of oil and extra-budgetary funds, for the transfer of spending responsibilities to the regions without providing sufficient additional resources[3] or for the use of guarantees. It also recommends that the authorities further strengthen the medium-term fiscal framework by better clarifying the capital and current transactions underlying the fiscal rule. Moreover, as OECD (2006: 98) showed in the pre-crisis period, the framework focuses on hydrocarbon revenues and does a rather poorer job of sterilising windfalls from other resource sectors, which can be very important indeed. The result was a strong, if unintended, pro-cyclical fiscal stance in the years prior to the global contraction of 2008-09.

In addition, raising Russia's productivity performance – and shifting to a growth model less reliant on the primary sector and the external conjuncture – will require a range of reforms to establish a more favourable business climate, particularly when it comes to reducing corruption, strengthening the rule of law and reducing red tape. The Russian authorities have been increasingly active on these fronts in recent years, although it is too early to judge the impact of recent measures on economic performance. Surveys of both entrepreneurs and citizens suggest a high level of scepticism about anti-corruption efforts, but there is some evidence that the drive to reduce the bureaucratic burden on firms and to improve the functioning of the commercial courts is bearing fruit (OECD, 2014; Granville, 2013). Also critical will be steps to strengthen competition, which remains weak in many markets, often thanks to the continuing dominance of the economy by large, often state-owned, enterprises. To an exceptional degree, the Russian Federation's industrial "ecosystem" is dominated by a few very large players: prior to the crisis, just 100 enterprises accounted for close to 60% of Russia's GDP (OECD, 2011).

At the same time, Russia's firm ecology includes a growing population of small and medium-sized enterprises (SMEs). Nevertheless, these still account for only about 25% of employment, compared to a level of about 50% on average in OECD countries. This underdevelopment reflects in part the dominance of the big players, but it is also a product of regulatory barriers, poor access to finance and the generally poor business climate. The evidence suggests that weak institutional environments are far more damaging to newer and smaller firms than to established incumbents. Large capital-intensive firms (i.e. the major players in the resource sector) are generally better able to protect their interests, as well as to bear the costs of corruption when they incur them. For new firms and sectors, which are often on the brink of viability during the early learning-by-doing phase of their development, the cost of informal payments to officials or the inability to enforce contracts efficiently can be the difference between survival and exit. Since the factors that favour large firms (and impede the emergence of strong SMEs) effectively reduce the pressure on large firms to become more efficient, the relative dearth of SMEs is likely to be directly related to productivity performance.[4]

Russia's non-resource tradable sector faces one other important problem that is of particular relevance to places like Krasnoyarsk: transport bottlenecks (Figure 1.5). The world's largest country by surface area, Russia has greater transport needs than most. Unfortunately, its transport networks are in need of significant improvement. The World Economic Forum's Global Competitiveness Index (WEF, 2013), based on both official statistics and surveys of business executives in 148 countries, recently ranked the Russian Federation's roads 136th in the world, its ports 88th and its air transport 102nd. The road network is a particular problem: it is roughly as extensive as that of France, a country one-twentieth the size of Russia, and is in many places of very poor quality.[5] Russian rail transport ranked 31st globally, but, as will be seen, the railways are not without problems of their own, and these are highly relevant to producers located far from both foreign markets and the two major metropolitan areas, Moscow and St. Petersburg. One recent appraisal concludes that maintenance activities on Russia's transport networks are not sufficient to prevent the degradation of the infrastructure (Institute of Economy and Transport Development, 2012).

Figure 1.4. **Competitiveness and quality of transport infrastructure**

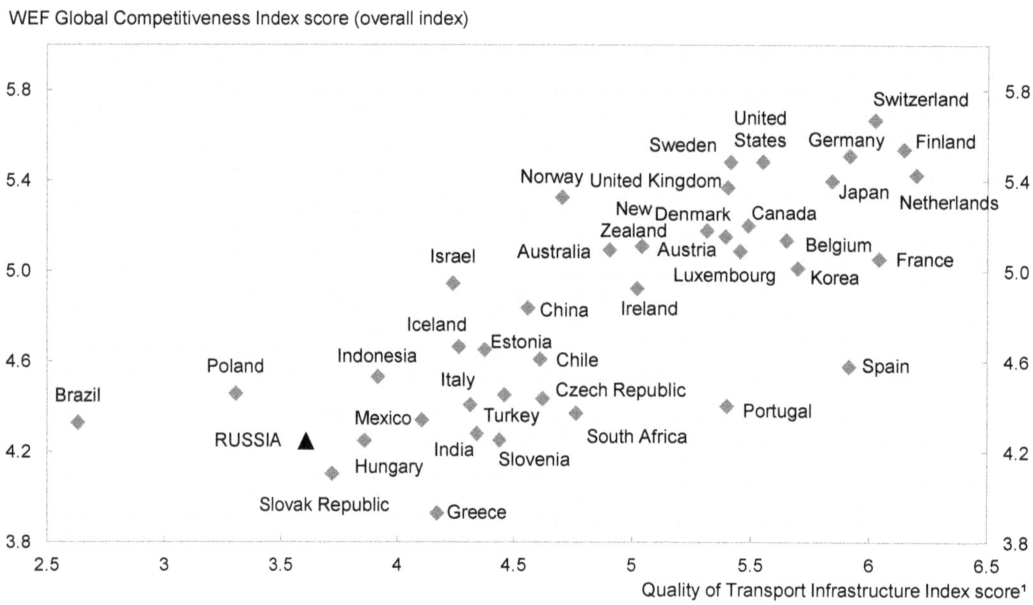

Notes: Simple average of four quality indicators (roads, railroad infrastructure, port infrastructure, air transport infrastructure). The responses are to the questions "How would you assess roads in your country?"; "How would you assess the railroad system in your country?"; "How would you assess port facilities in your country?", for landlocked countries, the question is as follows: "How accessible are port facilities?"; "How would you assess passenger air transport infrastructure in your country?" (1 = extremely underdeveloped; 7= well developed and efficient by international standards).

Source: World Economic Forum (2013), *The Global Competitiveness Report 2013-2014*, World Economic Forum Geneva, available at: http://www10.iadb.org/intal/intalcdi/PE/2013/12834.pdf.

While the Russian Federation's railway network is the third-longest in the world and is in many respects far superior to its road network, the monopoly position of Russian Railways (RZhD) is a problem. The RZhD owns the infrastructure and is also the only company allowed to operate locomotives – it has effectively blocked all attempts by other players to enter this market, although some 200 licences had been issued by mid-2013. Against this backdrop, tariffs have risen rapidly in recent years and the RZhD has come under increasing criticism for alleged anti-competitive practices; it has frequently been fined by the Federal Anti-Monopoly Service for abuse of its market power.[6] SMEs, in particular, suffer from problems with the rail network, finding it very difficult and costly to ship goods by rail – a factor which is of particular relevance in the context of any discussion of economic diversification. As will be seen, this is an issue of particular relevance for Krasnoyarsk.

OECD (2014c) also draws attention to barriers to competition in air transport, which is important given the size of the country and the problems with roads and rail infrastructure. Although the air carriage market is generally very competitive, ground services (fuelling, technical services, etc.) are highly monopolised, resulting in poor quality and high prices. This is because the legislative framework governing the relationship between carriers and airports is not yet fully developed and, in some regions, airport and air carriage businesses have not been separated. Prices for aircraft fuel are approximately 30% higher than in other countries, and other airport services are twice as expensive (Fridland, 2013). That is why a significant share of in-bound air cargo is delivered to airports in neighbouring countries and then shipped on its final leg by road. High technical landing and air-navigation fees also limit the growth potential of international cargo transit, an area where, as will be seen, Krasnoyarsk has some ambitions. OECD (2014c) argues that, to address these shortcomings, Russia needs to finalise separation between airports and airlines, improve the regulation of local monopolies and strengthen competition policy enforcement. Low-cost carriers also face legal obstacles, as according to the Russian Federation Aviation Code, carriers are obliged to provide the full range of passenger services (on-board meals, baggage handling, etc.) without exception. Relaxing such requirements would encourage a low-price segment for passenger air transport.

Krasnoyarsk Krai is one of the Russian Federation's largest but most thinly populated regions

Covering an area of 2 339 700 km^2 in the centre of the Eurasian landmass, Krasnoyarsk Krai is the Russian Federation's second-largest federal subject by territory (the Krai occupies 13.7% of Russia's territory). Somewhat more than 3.5 times the size of France, the Krai stretches around 3 000 kilometres from the Taymyr Peninsula on the Arctic Ocean in the north to the Sayan Mountains in Southern Siberia, close to the Mongolian border. However, with only 2% of Russia's population, the Krai ranks 77th among the Russian Federation's 83 federal subjects in terms of population density, with roughly 1.2 inhabitants per square kilometre – well below the Russian average of 8.4 or even that of the Siberian Federal District (3.7). It is rich in natural resources, which are the mainstay of the Krai's economy and which have enabled the Krai to reach higher levels of per capita income than most of Russia's regions. The economic challenges facing Krasnoyarsk Krai are in many respects those that confront Russia as a whole, though in some cases they are more acute. Above all, there is the task of building a competitive non-resource economy in a difficult climatic and geographic context. As will be seen, Krasnoyarsk faces much more serious accessibility and transport issues than most of the Russian Federation, being one of the most remote places on earth when location is assessed in terms of proximity to the world's economic centres of gravity. This is by no means an insuperable obstacle to success – the prosperity of such diverse places as Alaska, New Zealand and parts of Canada testifies to the contrary – but it does imply specific problems for both public and private sectors to resolve.

The Krai's population has begun to recover after a period of decline

The declining population trend that affects Russia as a whole is evident in Krasnoyarsk Krai. The population fell from 3.01 million inhabitants in 2000 to a low of 2.71 million in 2008; the trend has recently started to reverse, however, with a modest resurgence in population during 2008-11. In 2011, the population reached 2.83 million. Both the contraction and recovery of population in the Krai have been far sharper than the corresponding trends for the country as a whole (Figure 1.5). Fluctuations in the Krai's population are driven primarily by fertility and mortality. Net migration oscillates between inflows and outflows from year to year, but the variation remains in the narrow range of -0.24% to +0.36% of the population.

Figure 1.5. **Population trends in Krasnoyarsk Krai and the Russian Federation**

Population in 2000 = 100

Source: Federal Service for State Statistics.

Geographically, the population of the Krai is concentrated in two agglomerations that together comprise almost half of its population. In 2010, Norilsk, in the far north of the Krai, accounted for 6.2% of the population, while the Krasnoyarsk Agglomeration represented 41%. This reflects an on-going process of concentration of population in the major cities: the Agglomeration's share of the Krai total was up five percentage points on 2000. In this respect, too, the Krai is typical of trends across Russia and many other countries, where, against the backdrop of weak overall demographic dynamics, people – particularly those of working-age – are increasingly concentrating in cities, particularly big cities. This concentration process, moreover, has a fractal quality: one can observe such concentration at different geographic scales, from the globalised mega-cities of the world to the concentration of population in the major towns of largely rural counties (OECD, 2012c).

Resource endowments have helped make the Krai one of Russia's wealthiest regions

Krasnoyarsk Krai is one of the Russian Federation's most important regions in terms of natural resource wealth. Altogether, it accounts for around 80% of the country's nickel production and is the largest producer of nickel in the world (16.7% of global supply in 2010). It also holds 75% of Russia's cobalt, 70% of its copper, 16% of its coal and 10% of its gold extraction. More than 95% of the country's known resources of platinum-group metals (PGMs) are located within the Krai, which also produces 20% of the country's timber. The Krai's global importance as a PGM producer is difficult to exaggerate: it is the world's leading producer of palladium (above 40% of global supply in 2010) and ranks second to South Africa in the production of platinum and other PGMs.[7] The major rivers that flow through the Krai to the Arctic Ocean – above all, the Yenisei and its tributaries (the Kan, the Angara, the Podkamennaya Tunguska and the Nizhnyaya Tunguska) have given the Krai tremendous potential for hydroelectric power generation, the development of which has been critical to the region's important aluminium sector. In recent years, oil production has also begun to develop in the Krai.

With a GDP of RUB 1.19 trillion (Russian rubles) in 2011 (USD 34.4bn), Krasnoyarsk Krai ranked eighth among Russia's federal subjects in terms of aggregate GDP and ninth in per capita terms (Figure 1.6). Over the years, though, the difference between the Krai's per capita GDP and the national average has been growing – though both have been rising. In 2005, GDP per capita in the Krai was just over 20% above the national average; in 2011, it was roughly 32% higher than the national average (Figure 1.7). The economic activity of the Krai is dominated by the abundance of natural resources and cheap energy (notably through the Krasnoyarsk Dam on the Yenisei), which enables it to export both unrefined minerals and energy-intensive commodities. The Krai has been able to benefit from the surge in the world prices of commodities since the beginning of the millennium. It is worth noting, however, that the geographic distribution of value added creation in the Russian Federation is highly concentrated in Moscow, and in 2011 the GDP of the Krasnoyarsk Krai only represented 12% of that of Moscow. Even so, the Krai remained the largest economy in the Siberian Federal District in aggregate and by far the most productive in per capita terms.

During the decade to 2008, the Krai grew at an average annual rate of around 5.1%. Though strong by OECD standards, this was not exceptional for the Russian Federation at the time. Indeed, the Krai underperformed both the national average and the two capitals, although it fared much better in per capita terms, as rising output coincided with a sharp decline in population up to 2008. As Figure 1.7 shows, the Krai, Moscow and St. Petersburg followed similar trends up to 2007. Krasnoyarsk weathered the global downturn surprisingly well, despite its commodity orientation – suggesting perhaps that tax and other institutional arrangements governing Russia's resource sector insulate the Krai itself against swings in commodity prices to some extent. Following a contraction that was relatively modest compared to the Russian Federation as a whole in 2009 (-1.5 percentage points), Krasnoyarsk recorded growth rates of 5.7-5.8% in 2010-11, well above the rates prevailing for the country as a whole. It is also noteworthy that the Krai ranked sixth among Russian federal subjects in the growth of fixed capital formation over 2008-12. Almost half of Russian regions still had lower levels of investment in 2012 than before the crisis, while Krasnoyarsk was up almost 60% – a large part of this increase was linked to the development of new oil fields in the Krai. As will be in seen in subsequent chapters, the business climate in Krasnoyarsk is generally better than for the average Russian region, and this may also contribute to investment growth.

Figure 1.6. **Top 20 federal subjects by gross regional product**

Current prices, 2011

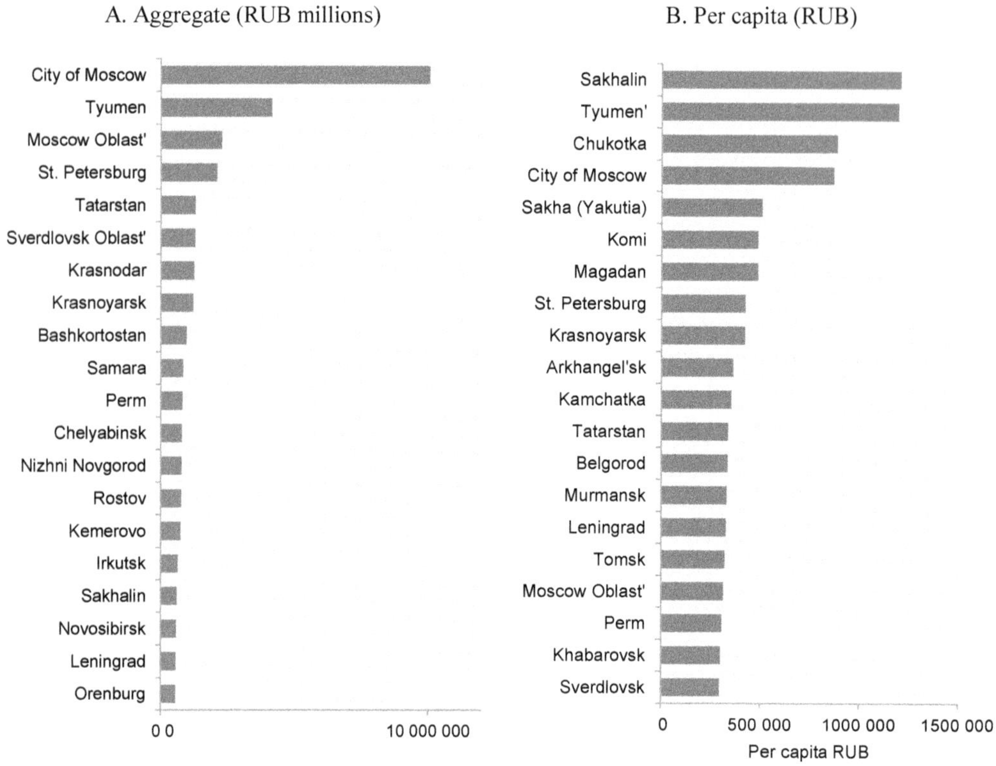

Source: Federal Service for State Statistics.

Figure 1.7. **GDP growth: Russian Federation and selected Russian regions**

1998 = 100

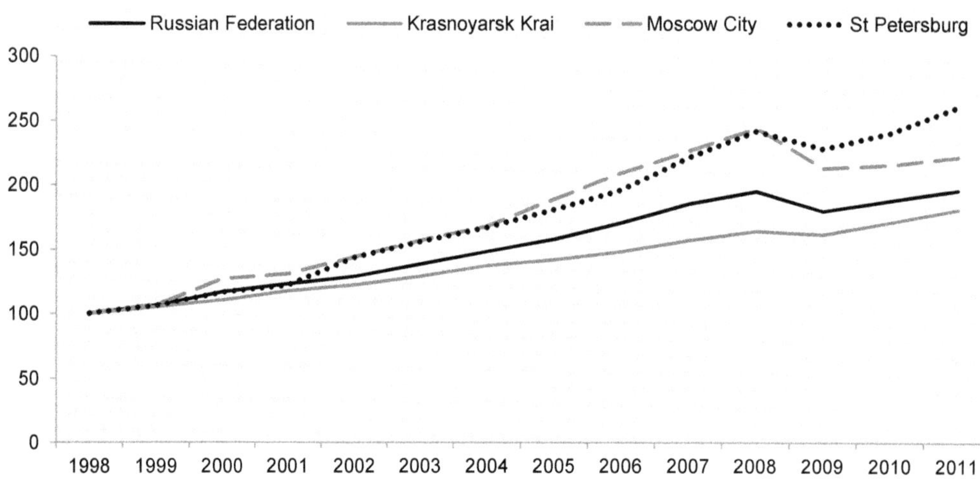

Source: Federal Service for State Statistics.

Activities involving such resources account for an important share economic activity and employment. In 2011, mining, manufacturing, gas, electricity and water supply accounted for almost 56% of the Krai's gross regional product (Figure 1.8). This makes the Krai far more industrial, in terms of output, than is Russia as a whole: these sectors accounted for about 30% of Russian GDP in 2011. For the Russian Federation as whole, construction and services – including public services – accounted for close to 60%, as compared with 40% in Krasnoyarsk Krai. Being highly productive, capital-intensive activities, however, mining and manufacturing account for a far smaller share of employment: in 2011, resource extraction accounted for only 2.2% of employment in the Krai, as against more than 18% of GDP, while the corresponding figures for manufacturing were 13.8% and 33.8%. Thus, 16% of the Krai's workforce generates over half of gross regional product. Employment in industry fell sharply in the first half of the 2000s – as a number of important industrial concerns failed – but then it stabilised in the latter half of the decade and declined only slightly in the context of the crisis. If production and distribution of energy, gas and water are added to the manufacturing and mining shares, then just under 20% of employment in the Krai is in industry.

Figure 1.8. **Krasnoyarsk Krai sectoral structure of activity, 2011**

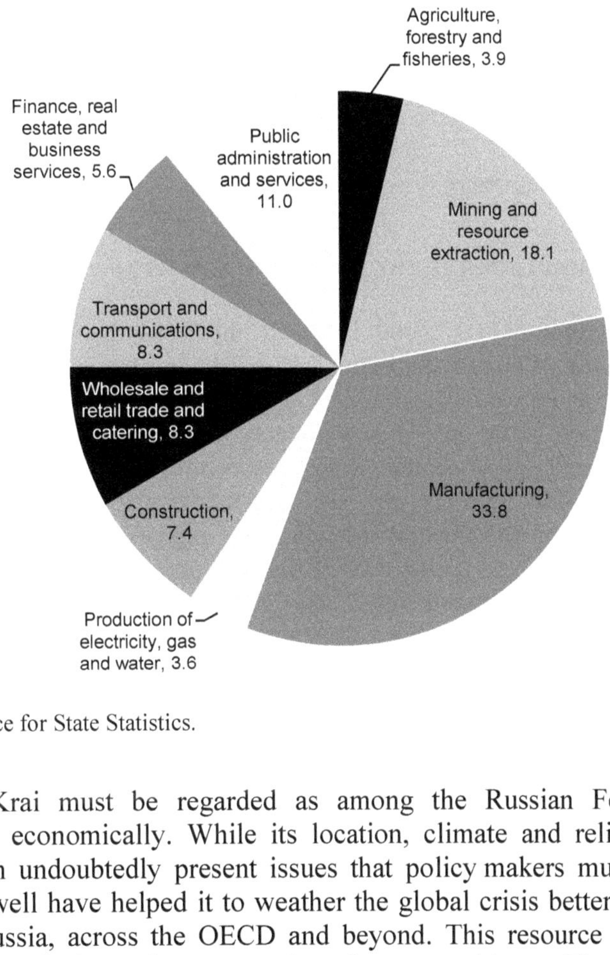

Source: Federal Service for State Statistics.

Overall, the Krai must be regarded as among the Russian Federation's more successful regions economically. While its location, climate and reliance on primary resource extraction undoubtedly present issues that policy makers must address, those very factors may well have helped it to weather the global crisis better than many other regions, within Russia, across the OECD and beyond. This resource strength will not disappear but it does limit employment options for many citizens. The primary focus of economic policy should thus be to build on this strength to create more – and more productive – employment opportunities for the great mass of the Krai's inhabitants. This will involve diversifying the production structure of the Krai. There is little doubt that, if the Krai is to develop competitive new activities, these will to a great extent be concentrated in its primary urban centre: the Krasnoyarsk Agglomeration.

Figure 1.9. **Structure of employment in Krasnoyarsk Krai, 2011**

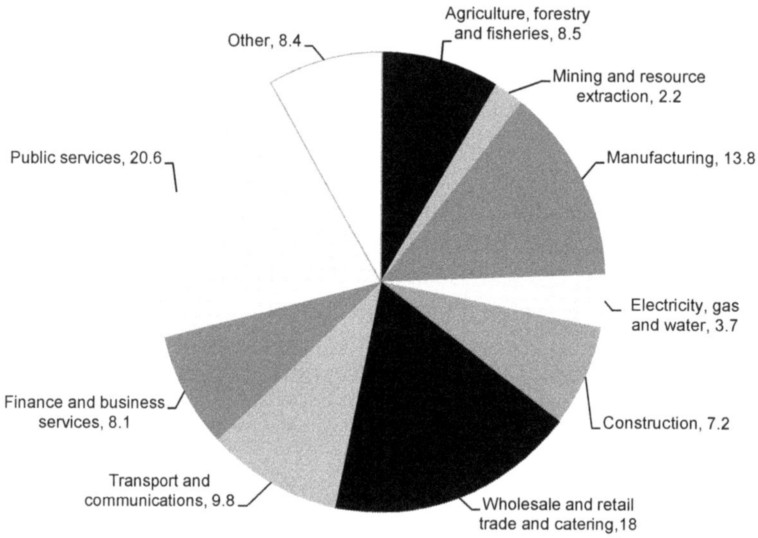

Source: Federal Service for State Statistics.

The Krasnoyarsk Agglomeration in the context of the Krai

With a population of 1 175 000 in 2011, the Krasnoyarsk Agglomeration is the biggest concentration of population in the Krai and is home to over 41% of its population. Its aggregate GDP is comparable to that of neighbouring Zabaikal'skii Krai. At the heart of the Agglomeration is the city of Krasnoyarsk, home to 84% of the Agglomeration's population. It accounts for an estimated 86.5% of employment in the Agglomeration and 94.2% of its total GDP. The six other components of the Agglomeration are together home to the remaining 185 000 inhabitants.[8] The city of Krasnoyarsk is not only the largest but by far the densest component of the Agglomeration, with a population density of over 2 600 inhabitants/km^2 in 2011, followed by Sosnovoborsk (2 257 inhabitants/km^2). Divnogorsk, though a city, has a relatively low density of settlement (just under 65 inhabitants/km^2) and the other components of the Agglomeration are largely rural, with population densities below 10 persons/km^2.

The Agglomeration's relative weight in the Krai, and in Eastern Siberia as a whole, is increasing

The population of the Agglomeration rose 7.4% between 2000 and 2011. Over the same period, the Russian Federation lost approximately 2% of its population, while Krasnoyarsk Krai lost 6% (Figure 1.10). This is not wholly atypical for Russia, inasmuch as many parts of the country have experienced a growing concentration of population in the major cities against the backdrop of declining population for the surrounding regions and for the country as a whole. As noted above, the Agglomeration's share of the Krai population was up around five percentage points over the period from 2000 to 2011. The appeal of the Agglomeration to migrants is seen in Figure 1.11, which shows net inward migration to the Agglomeration every year since 2000, despite significant outflows.

Importantly, this tendency has been increasing over the years: every year, net migration inflows represent an increasing proportion of the population of the Agglomeration.[9] In 2010, the Agglomeration gained more than 14 000 residents through migration, an increase representing 1.23% of its population. The same year, the rest of the Krai lost 0.73% of its population due to net outflows of migrants.

Figure 1.10. **Population dynamics**

Year 2000 = 100

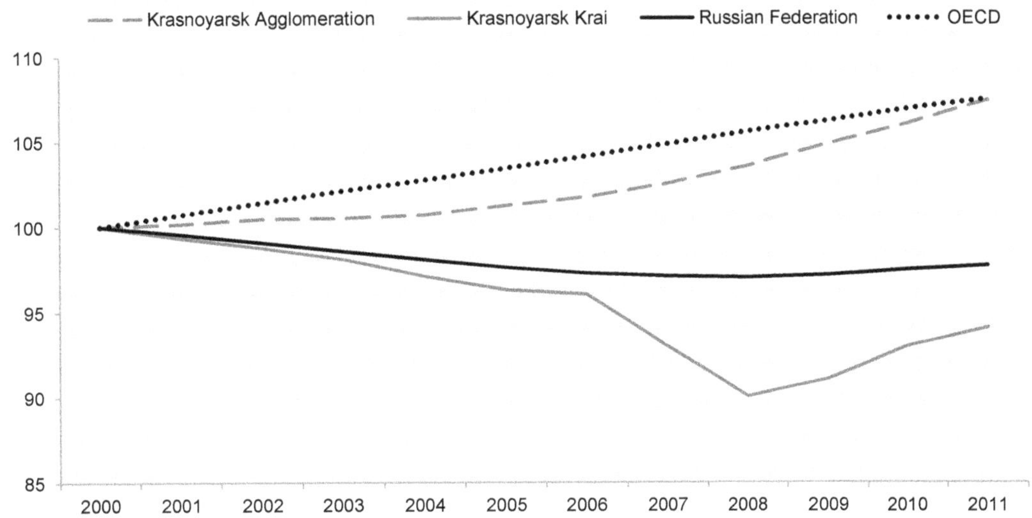

Source: Federal Service for State Statistics, SFU (2012), "Background report for the OECD Territorial Review of Krasnoyarsk", Siberian Federal University, Krasnoyarsk, Russian Federation.

Figure 1.11. **Net migration flows as a share of total population**

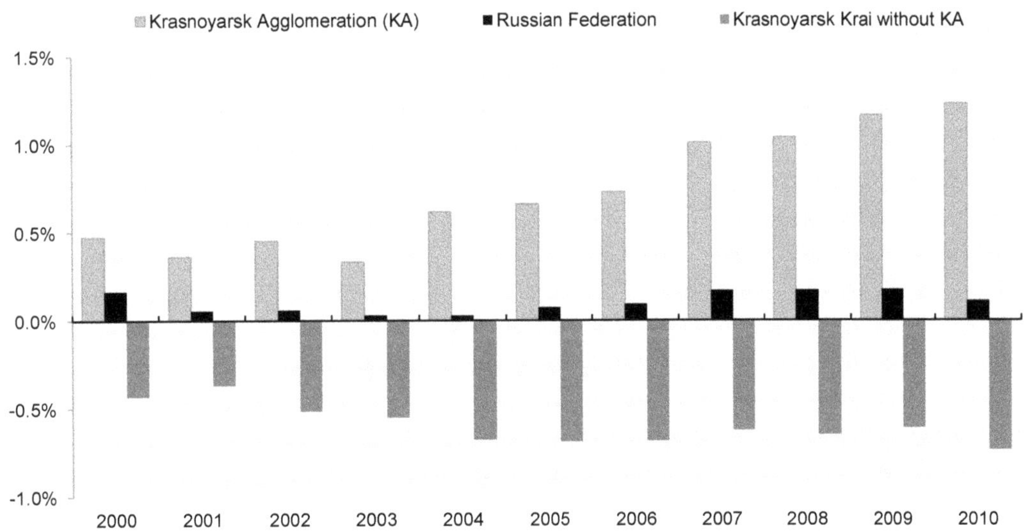

Source: Federal Service for State Statistics; SFU (2012), "Background report for the OECD Territorial Review of Krasnoyarsk", Siberian Federal University, Krasnoyarsk, Russian Federation.

The increasing attractiveness of the Agglomeration can also be seen in the origin of the migrants. Until around 2006, only around one-third of new arrivals in the Agglomeration came from other subjects of the Russian Federation, but since then that share has jumped to somewhat above 40%. Most of this migration centres on the city of Krasnoyarsk. In 2000, it accounted for 77.1% of inflows into and 74.2% of outflows from the Agglomeration, but by 2011, these figures had reached 83.2% and 73.2% respectively. The increasing trend shows that the Agglomeration (and, above all, the city) has been able to attract migrants from greater and greater distances over time. Largely as a result of such trends – migrants tend to be relatively young, on average – the Agglomeration enjoys a population that is younger than the national average. In particular, the population aged 15-39 years old is relatively large as a share of the total, when compared to the rest of the country. Some 30% of the Agglomeration's population is aged 20-34, an age category that only represents 25% of the national population. This suggests that the Agglomeration is particularly attractive for students and younger workers, who can acquire skills and begin their careers there. However, there is evidence that a disproportionately large share of young adults leave the Agglomeration later in life. Thus, while the share of 20-34 year-olds in the total population rose from 23% to 29% over 1999-2011, the share of those aged 35-39 fell from 23.9% to 20.5%. While older cohorts are still under-represented relative to the national average, the differential is far smaller than for young adults. The Agglomeration thus risks being perceived as a place to study and/or start a career rather than to settle.

Both younger and older cohorts are both under-represented in the Agglomeration, compared to the all-Russian average (Figure 1.12), though it is important to note that only the under-15 year old age group is under-represented when compared to the Krai as a whole. The Agglomeration seems to be characterised by lower fertility rates, particularly in the cities of Krasnoyarsk, Divnogorsk and Sosnovoborsk, but the share of those in the 50-65 age group is larger than for the Krai as a whole. This latter phenomenon may reflect differences in death rates affecting this group and/or migration from the Krai to the Agglomeration as retirement approaches.

Figure 1.12. **Age structure of the population: Krasnoyarsk Agglomeration and the Russian Federation, 2010**

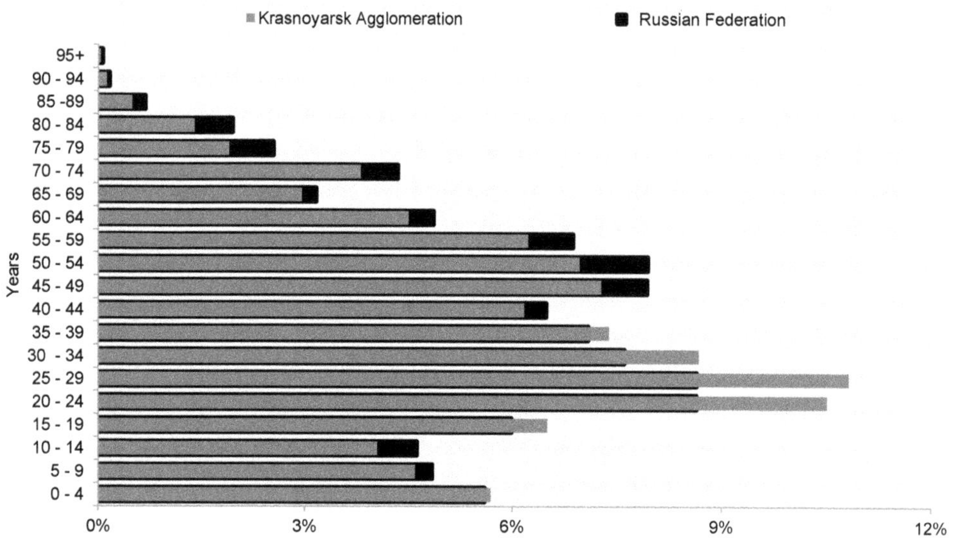

Source: Federal Service for State Statistics; SFU (2012), "Background report for the OECD Territorial Review of Krasnoyarsk", Siberian Federal University, Krasnoyarsk, Russian Federation.

Mortality rates remain high

The Russian Federation as a whole has long faced a demographic problem in the form of unusually high mortality rates for most age cohorts, particularly among men. This tendency was worsening until the middle of the last decade, before improving after 2004-05 (Figure 1.13). As a result, the country has displayed strong and persistent differentials between male and female life expectancy at virtually all ages. Krasnoyarsk Krai has experienced a similar evolution over time, albeit with lower average mortality rates, due to female mortality being consistently lower than in the rest of the country. After a small increase from 13.63 (per 1 000 population) to 14.3 between 1999 and 2003, mortality started to decline in the Agglomeration, to reach a level of 11.53 in 2010, thus following the general trend of the country. It is still high, however. This is the real demographic problem facing Krasnoyarsk and Russia as a whole: excess mortality is far more of an issue than declining fertility. The latter phenomenon is part of a global trend and is typical of countries with rising incomes per capita. The Russian Federation's mortality rates, by contrast, tend to be closer to those of countries with far lower levels of income.

Figure 1.13. **Mortality rates: The Russian Federation and Krasnoyarsk Krai**

Source: Federal Service for State Statistics; SFU (2012), "Background report for the OECD Territorial Review of Krasnoyarsk", Siberian Federal University, Krasnoyarsk, Russian Federation.

The average mortality rates in the Agglomeration remain below the Russian national average but are much higher than in OECD countries (Figure 1.14). The overall reduction in mortality rates across all the Agglomeration in recent years has not erased very large local disparities. In 2000, the mortality rate in the Mana District was almost twice as high as that of Sosnovoborsk, and recent improvements have hardly reduced the difference. Unfortunately, the data are not detailed enough to allow the calculation of age-adjusted mortality rates, but at least part of the difference does indeed appear to reflect differences in age structure – the three areas in the Agglomeration with the highest mortality rates are also those with the highest shares of population over the age of 50. This difference in age structure is also reflected in the balance of births and deaths in the various constituent communities of the Agglomeration (Figure 1.15). Since birth rates are similar across all parts of the Agglomeration, the differences in mortality rates are the main source of variation in demographic dynamics. Demographic indicators have improved in all parts of the Agglomeration in recent years, but this has been sufficient to generate a positive dynamic only in the city of Krasnoyarsk, Sosnovoborsk, Divnogorsk and Berezovsk. The causes of this improvement are difficult to pinpoint on the basis of the available data: cohort effects (i.e. changes in the age structure of the population) may play a role, as well as inflows of younger migrants to the Agglomeration and increased expenditure on healthcare provision.

Figure 1.14. **Mortality rates within the Krasnoyarsk Agglomeration and OECD average**

Deaths per 1 000 population

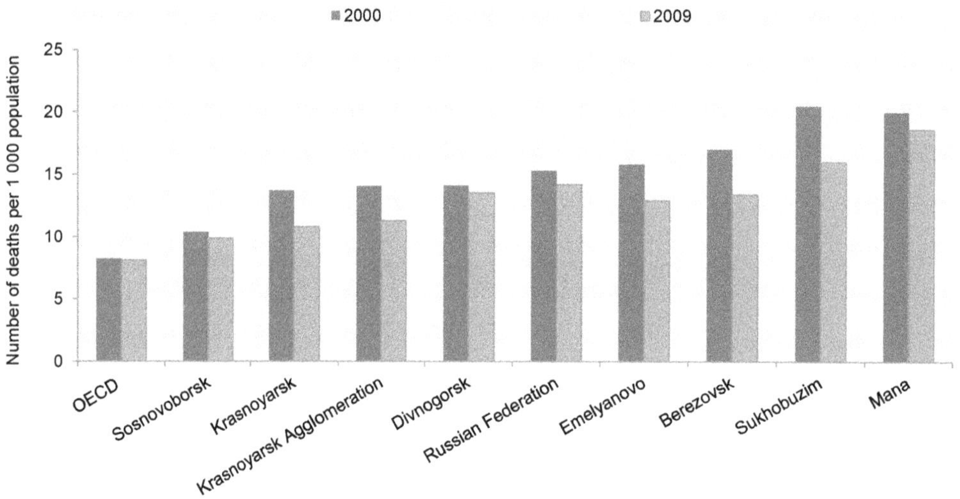

Source: SFU (2012), "Background report for the OECD Territorial Review of Krasnoyarsk", Siberian Federal University, Krasnoyarsk, Russian Federation.

Figure 1.15. **Birth rates minus death rates**

Per 1 000 population

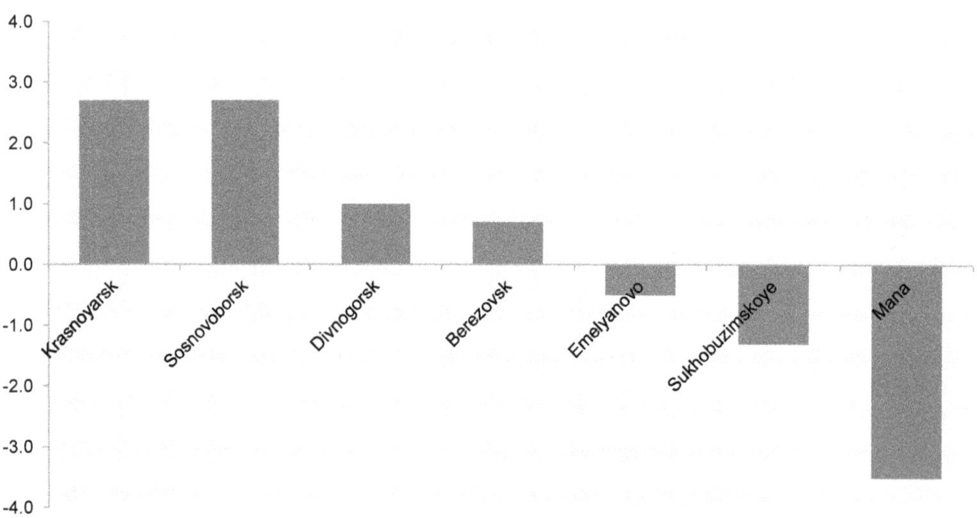

Source: SFU (2012), "Background report for the OECD Territorial Review of Krasnoyarsk", Siberian Federal University, Krasnoyarsk, Russian Federation.

The settlement pattern of the Agglomeration is increasingly concentrated

The city of Krasnoyarsk is increasingly concentrating the population of the Agglomeration. Its share of the Agglomeration's total population has risen slowly but steadily, from 82.5% in 2000 to just over 84.1% in 2011. This is yet another dimension of the trend towards increasing concentration alluded to above and mirrors the growing share of the Agglomeration in the Krai's population. As Figure 1.16 suggests, there has been a trend over the years for denser areas to grow and less dense areas to experience population decline.

Figure 1.16. **Population change as a function of initial density**

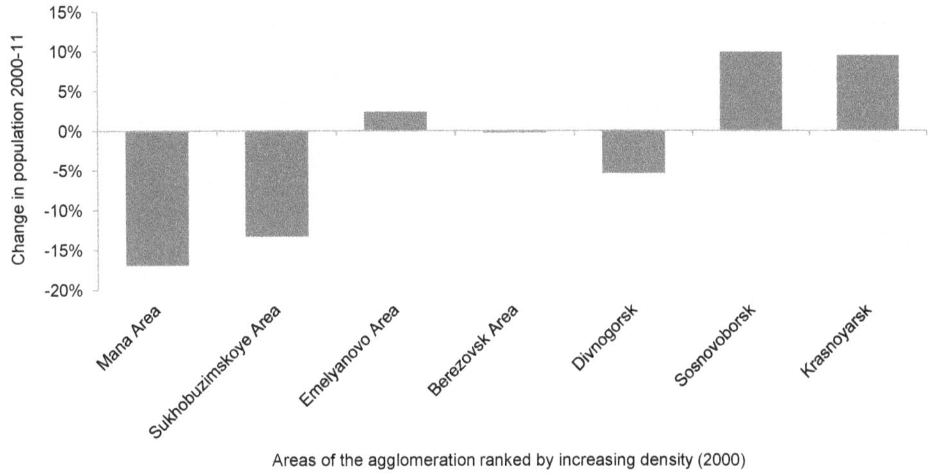

Note: Areas of the Agglomeration are ranked by increasing density for the year 2000.

Source: SFU (2012), "Background report for the OECD Territorial Review of Krasnoyarsk", Siberian Federal University, Krasnoyarsk, Russian Federation.

The Krasnoyarsk Agglomeration enjoys a GDP per capita on a par with the national average

In 2010, the Agglomeration's GDP per capita was RUB 255 350, comparable to that of St. Petersburg (the national average was RUB 262 130). It remains, however, well below the OECD average. In particular, it is well below the GDP per capita enjoyed by other cities that also rely on natural resources (Figure 1.17). Calgary is the economic hub for the oil industry in the province of Alberta in Canada. Antofagasta (Chile) has heavily specialised in mining. Of course, differences in output per head do not translate directly into income differentials. In resource-rich regions, the presence of natural-resource rents, which are often taxed away or otherwise transferred out of the region, means that income levels do not "map" onto productivity levels as neatly as they might elsewhere. In Antofagasta, for example, household disposable income in 2011 was around 35% above the national average, while GDP per capita was about 3 times as high as the national figure (OECD, 2013b).

As is clear from Figure 1.18, the city of Krasnoyarsk is characterised by far higher levels of productivity than its hinterland: GDP per capita in the city was almost seven times that reported for Sukhobuzim District. This partly reflects commuting patterns. In 2012, around 46% of employed people in the surrounding cities and districts of the Agglomeration commuted to Krasnoyarsk (up 9 percentage points on 2000), including almost 80% of the employed inhabitants of Berezovsk District and around 60% of the working population of Sosnovoborsk. The value added that these commuters generate is thus "credited" to Krasnoyarsk city rather than to the places where they live. Demographic factors are also at work. Sukhobuzim, Mana and Emelyanovo have, on average, somewhat older populations than the Agglomeration as a whole, while Krasnoyarsk's population is somewhat younger. Strikingly, though, labour-force participation rates are, by OECD standards, rather high across the Agglomeration: in 2010, they ranged from around 73.5% of the working-age (15-64) population in Emelyanovo, an area hit hard by industrial restructuring, to 82.9% in Mana – all above an OECD average in 2012 of just under 71%. In short, the communities with a relatively larger share of older workers do not exhibit much lower labour-force participation, suggesting that early withdrawal from economic activity is not much of an issue.[10]

Figure 1.17. **GDP per capita**

2008 PPP USD

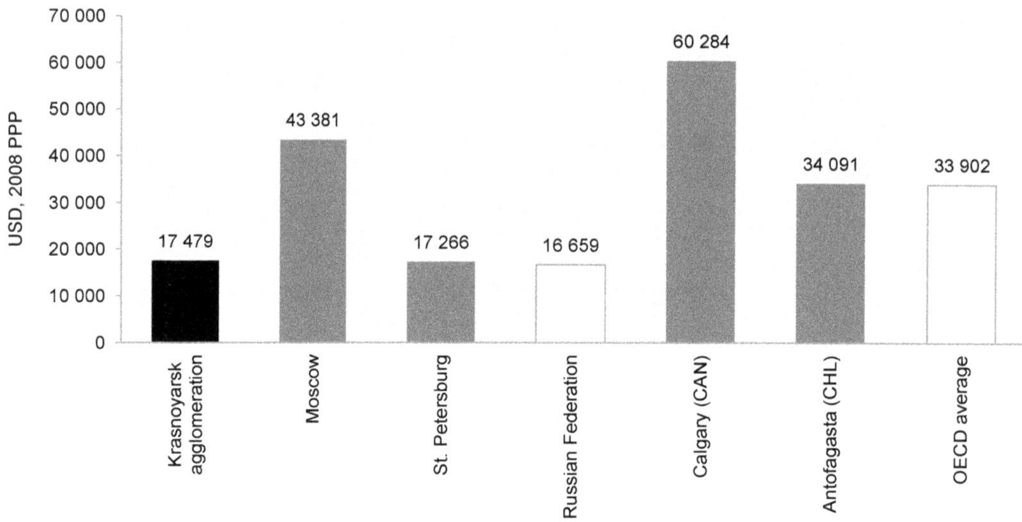

Sources: SFU (2012), "Background report for the OECD Territorial Review of Krasnoyarsk", Siberian Federal University, Krasnoyarsk, Russian Federation; Federal Service for State Statistics; OECD (2014d), *OECD Regional Statistics* (database), http://dx.doi.org/10.1787/region-data-en.

In any event, commuting flows probably play a larger role than demography in accounting for these differentials: the influence of commuting is apparent in the data on household incomes shown in the left-hand panel of Figure 1.18: the household income differentials are dramatically smaller than those for output (whether per worker or per capita). The more interesting measure is, in any case, relative productivity. This, too, is far higher in the city, so it does not appear that labour market and demographic factors account for all of the differences in GDP per capita. When GDP per worker is measured, the gaps between the city and its neighbours remain very large, confirming that the most productive enterprises are concentrated in the city. Even so, the productivity differences are far smaller than the GDP per capita differentials, except in the cases of Emelyanovo and particularly Sukhobuzim, which doubtless reflects the impact of commuting and demographic factors.

Figure 1.18. **Productivity and income in the Krasnoyarsk Agglomeration, 2010**

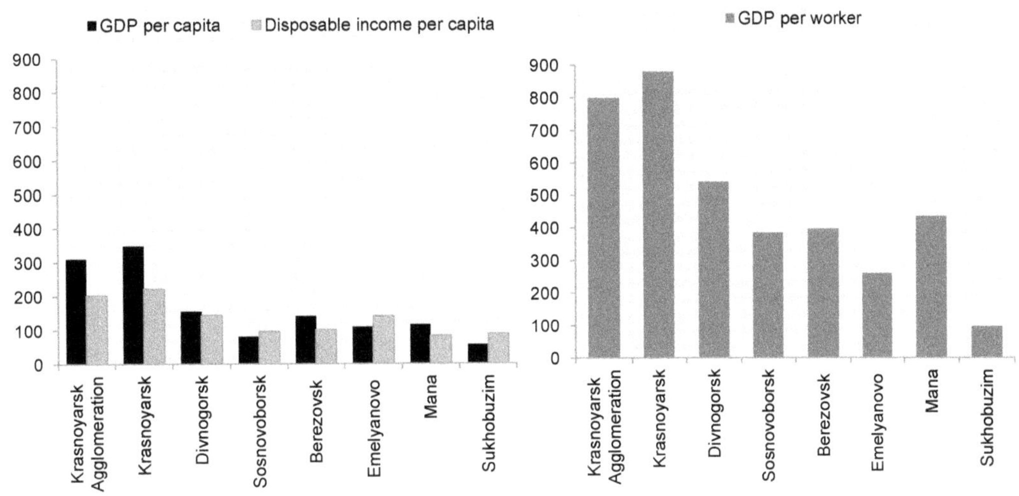

Note: Data for disposable income are for 2009.

Source: SFU (2012), "Background report for the OECD Territorial Review of Krasnoyarsk", Siberian Federal University, Krasnoyarsk, Russian Federation.

In sectoral terms, resources and energy constitute the backbone of the economy

The Krai's abundance of natural resources shapes the pattern of activity in the Agglomeration, which acts as the economic hub of the Krai's hinterland. In 2011, mining, manufacturing, and the production and distribution of electricity, gas and water constituted the biggest sector in the Agglomeration, generating almost 44% of GDP. In 2011, metallurgy accounted for over half of industrial production (55.8%), with the food industry (11.8%) and the production of machinery and equipment (10%) following far behind it in second and third places. The Agglomeration is also home to important trade and services activities: these account for another 47% of its value added, compared to only 22% at the level of the Krai as a whole (Figure 1.19). Market services (sectors 4 and 5 in the figure) account for only 11% of the economic activity taking place in the Krai outside the Agglomeration. The Agglomeration thus generates 78% of the Krai's value added in trade, transport, tourism and storage, activities that are less capital intensive but instead rely on the labour and human capital found in the Agglomeration.

As is clear from Figure 1.20, it is in these typically urban sectors that the Agglomeration represents a disproportionately large share of the Krai's activity – in all other major sectors, it is "underweight" relative to its share of the Krai's overall population or GDP. That said, it must be noted that these activities in many cases are located in Krasnoyarsk precisely because of links to the resource sector; realistically, there would not be a large urban centre in Krasnoyarsk absent the resource sector. Additionally, because Krasnoyarsk is relatively remote from other large cities, it is likely to concentrate more functions than a city of its size might be expected to have in an urban hierarchy.

Figure 1.19. **Share of value added by activity, 2011**

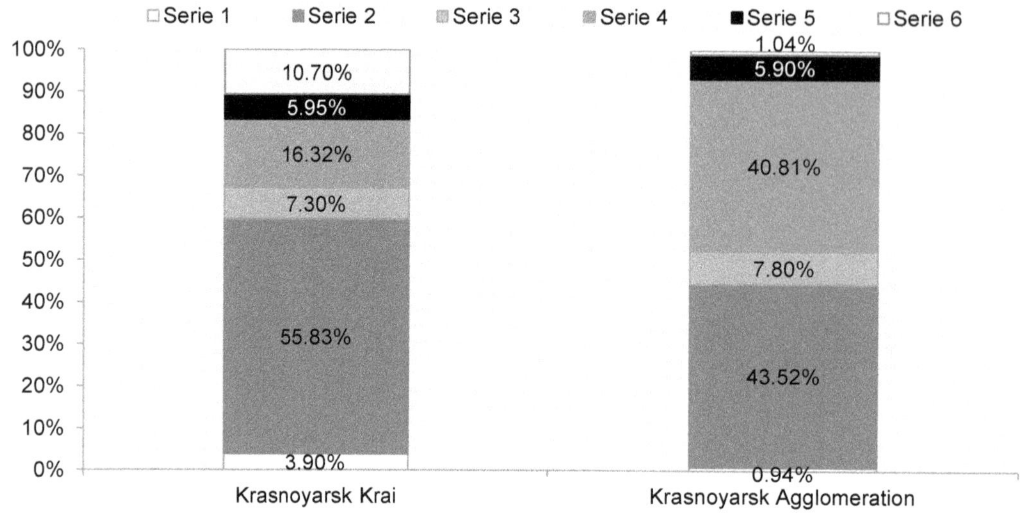

Notes: Sectors are defined as follows:

1 Agriculture, hunting, forestry, fishing and fisheries
2 Mining; manufacturing; gas, electricity and water supply
3 Construction
4 Wholesale and retail trade; repairs of motor vehicles, motorcycles, household appliances and personal items; hotels and restaurants; transport, storage facilities, communications
5 Financial activities, real estate transactions, lease, and service provision
6 Public administration and military security, mandatory social security, education, healthcare and social services; provision of other utilities, social and personal services; private households' activities involving hired workers

Source*: Federal Service for State Statistics;* SFU (2012), "Background report for the OECD Territorial Review of Krasnoyarsk", Siberian Federal University, Krasnoyarsk, Russian Federation.

Figure 1.20. **Relative weight of the Krasnoyarsk Agglomeration in various sectors in the Krai, 2011**

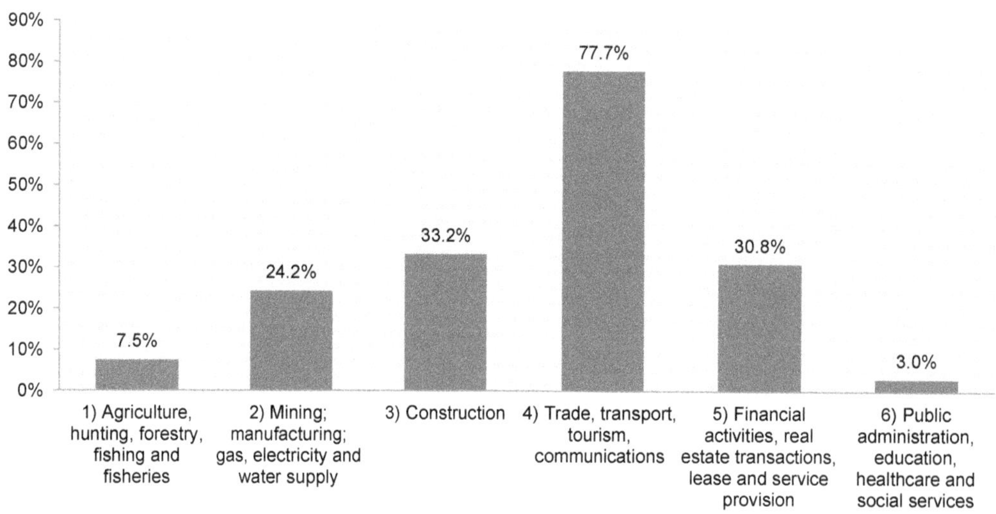

Source: SFU (2012), "Background report for the OECD Territorial Review of Krasnoyarsk", Siberian Federal University, Krasnoyarsk, Russian Federation.

The share of market services has stayed relatively constant in the Agglomeration's value added. This reflects the consistent importance of services in the city of Krasnoyarsk (Figure 1.21). In the rest of the Agglomeration, the share of services has fallen sharply in recent years, from 55% of value added in 2007 to 26% in 2011. In other words, the share of services has halved in the Agglomeration periphery during those five years, which suggests that the crisis and its aftermath may have accelerated the concentration of service activities within the Agglomeration itself. At the same time, the share of value added generated by industry in the communities around the city rose from 40% to 66%. This increase has been driven by rising natural resource exports, which have led to a big increase in the share of the extractive industries (sector 2).

Figure 1.21. **Evolution of the share of market services in GDP**

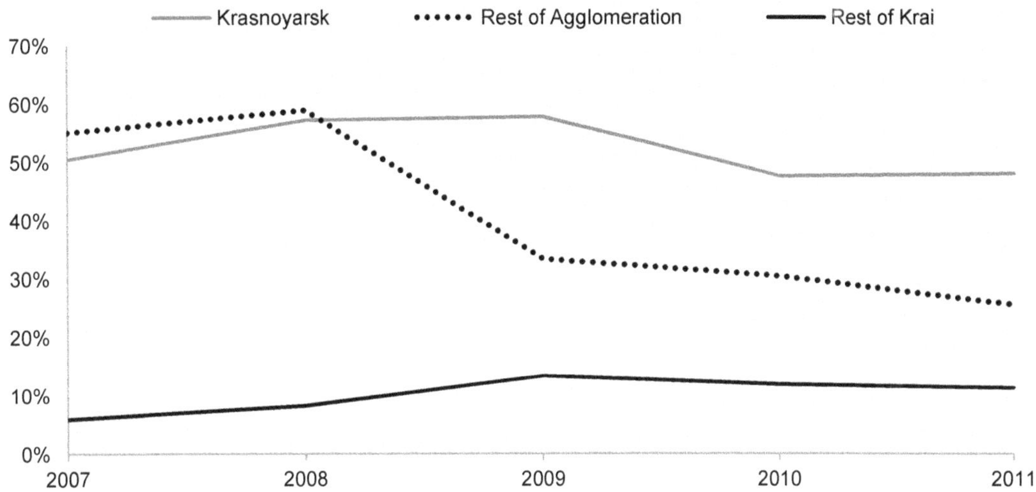

Source: Federal Service for State Statistics, SFU (2012), "Background report for the OECD Territorial Review of Krasnoyarsk", Siberian Federal University, Krasnoyarsk, Russian Federation.

The extractive industries were hit hard by the sudden fall in the price of commodities of 2008, although the Agglomeration was less severely affected than the rest of the Krai (Figure 1.22), largely due to its more diversified pattern of economic activity. Even so, the Agglomeration remains highly dependent on export prices, especially minerals and metal prices. Like the Krai – and, indeed, the Russian Federation as a whole – it is therefore extremely vulnerable to fluctuations in commodity prices. While Russian performance is indeed linked more strongly to hydrocarbons than to other commodities, metals prices, which are more important to the economy of Krasnoyarsk, tend to move with oil prices – and thus, with growth.

Overall labour-market conditions are favourable but there is considerable spatial variation

As noted above, the Agglomeration and its constituent cities and districts show comparatively high levels of employment and labour-force participation. Total unemployment is also comparatively low. The economic expansion that started at the beginning of last decade brought about a significant drop in unemployment in the Agglomeration, despite an influx of migrants and a relatively young population. Apart from a sharp spike in unemployment in 2009, there has been fairly steady progress, and unemployment is now below both Russian and OECD averages (Figure 1.23). Unemployment rates in all of the constituent units of the Agglomeration have also fallen over in the last dozen years and, at least until 2008, they tended to converge, with the greatest improvements occurring in the places with initially higher unemployment (Figure 1.24). That trend seems to have broken with the crisis: although there has been no return to the huge differentials seen in 2000, unemployment rates in the Mana District, which have been consistently high over the years, were still four times higher in 2012 than those recorded in Divnogorsk.

Figure 1.22. **Trends in GDP and metals prices**

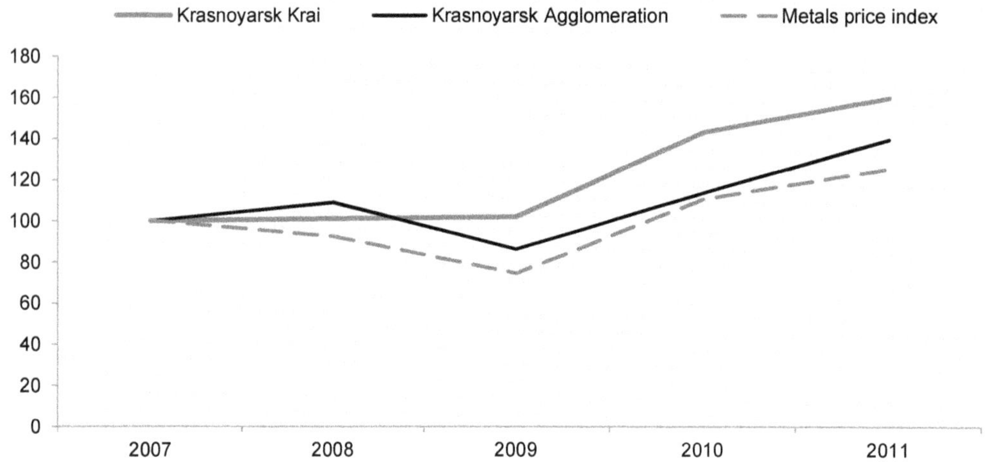

Note: The metals price index includes copper, aluminium, iron ore, tin, nickel, zinc, lead and uranium price indices.

Source: SFU (2012), "Background report for the OECD Territorial Review of Krasnoyarsk", Siberian Federal University, Krasnoyarsk, Russian Federation, Datastream.

Figure 1.23. **Unemployment rates, 1999-2012**

ILO method

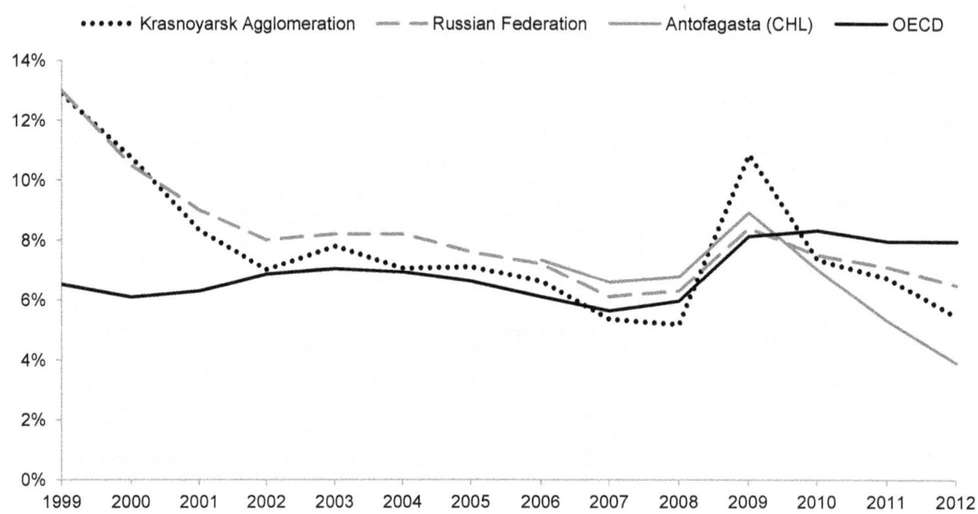

Sources: OECD (2014a), *OECD Economic Outlook: Statistics and Projections* (database), http://dx.doi.org/10.1787/eo-data-en; Federal Service for State Statistics; SFU (2012), "Background report for the OECD Territorial Review of Krasnoyarsk", Siberian Federal University, Krasnoyarsk, Russian Federation.

Figure 1.24. **Variation in unemployment in the Krasnoyarsk Agglomeration**

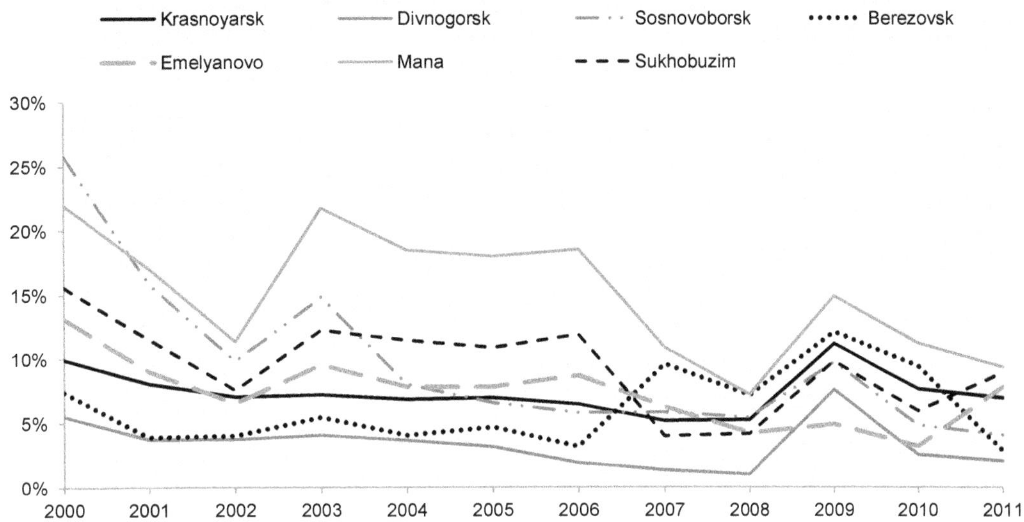

Source: SFU (2012), "Background report for the OECD Territorial Review of Krasnoyarsk", Siberian Federal University, Krasnoyarsk, Russian Federation.

Figure 1.25 shows the evolution of the population-weighted Gini coefficient for the different parts of the Agglomeration (see Box 1.1). If all constituent units had the same rate of unemployment, the coefficient would be 0. If, on the other hand, all the unemployment of the Agglomeration was concentrated in one of its areas, the coefficient would be 1. Clearly, the distribution of unemployment across the Agglomeration has become more and more uneven over time. While unemployment has fallen significantly in the periphery of the Agglomeration, it has not done so in the city itself, which represents the bulk of the Agglomeration's active population. As population has become increasingly concentrated in this city, so has unemployment – a development consistent with low-skilled and surplus workers being pushed out of rural places by mechanisation and industrial restructuring. Redeploying such workers is a particular challenge in an urban economy that lacks an internal dynamic (its primary source of growth is exogenous – the primary sector).

Box 1.1. **Using the Gini coefficient as a measure of concentration or dispersion**

The Gini coefficient is an index taking values between 0 and 1 that measures the distribution of a certain variable in a sample population. It was initially devised as a way to measure the inequality of income distribution in a population. In the extreme, if all individuals in the population have the same income, the Gini coefficient will be 0. If, on the other hand, all the income is concentrated in the hands of one individual, the coefficient will be 1. The more the distribution is skewed towards a few individuals in the sample, the higher the coefficient will be. This measure can be readily applied to the distribution of any economic variable in a sample.

Inter-sectoral wage differentiation is typical for the Russian Federation. Budget-sector wages are improving, having risen from 55% of the Krai average as recently as 2005 to about 80% in 2011. This reflects a general Russian trend, as strengthening public finances made it easier to address public sector wages in the good years prior to the crisis (budget-sector wages in the Krai and the Agglomeration jumped dramatically from 2007 to 2008, roughly doubling in the Agglomeration), but this tendency has been especially pronounced in the Agglomeration. In 2005, average wages for budget-sector workers in the Krasnoyarsk Agglomeration were about 75% of the national average (and 62-63% of the Krai average). Since 2008, they have been above the averages for the Russian Federation, the Siberian Federal District and the Krai. Geographic wage disparities, mirroring the productivity differentials described above, are sharp – in Krasnoyarsk wages are on average 1.5-2.0 times higher than on the periphery of the Agglomeration. They are lowest in Sukhobuzim and Mana Districts and the city of Sosnovoborsk.

Figure 1.25. **Population-weighted Gini coefficient of unemployment rates in the Krasnoyarsk Agglomeration**

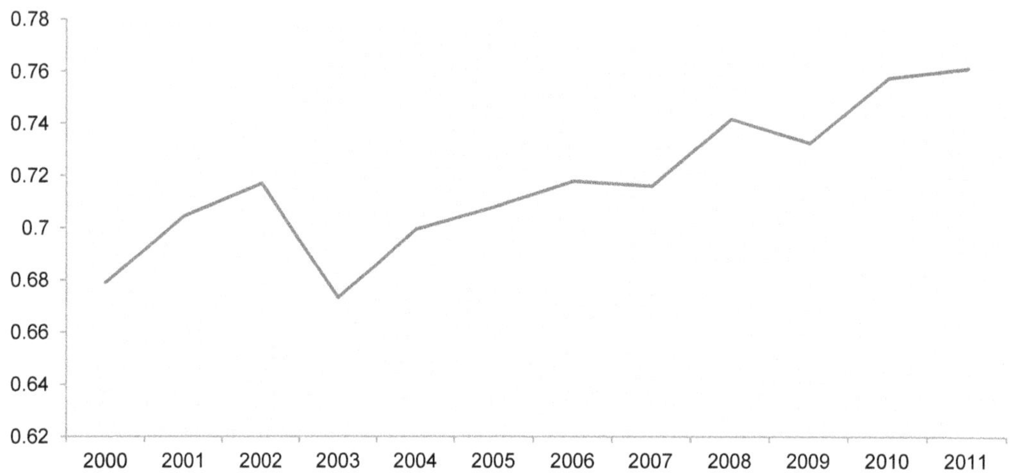

Source: SFU (2012), "Background report for the OECD Territorial Review of Krasnoyarsk", Siberian Federal University, Krasnoyarsk, Russian Federation.

The importance of resources is reflected in the structure of employment and human capital

The importance of the resource sector for the Agglomeration is also reflected in the sectoral distribution of employment (Figure 1.26). In 2011, industry (including mining, manufacturing, and the production and supply of water, electricity and gas) represented 21% of employment in the Agglomeration. This was, not surprisingly, a far larger share than found in Moscow but comparable to other resource-rich regions, as well as St. Petersburg. The share of market services (combining sectors 4 and 5) was significantly lower than in comparator regions, except Alberta, and the employment share of sector 6 – the public sector – rather larger.

The variations in productivity across sectors in the Agglomeration are striking (Figure 1.27). In particular, sector 2 (mining, manufacturing and energy) stands out, as does sector 4 (trade, tourism, transport, communications). The former result is entirely predictable, given the value of resource rents; the latter may well reflect the predominance of smaller firms in the sector, as SMEs typically face greater pressure to be productive. Perhaps the major negative surprise concerns the productivity of high-value market services (finance, insurance and real estate or FIRE), which appears to be precisely in line with the Agglomeration average. Given the increasing concentration of such activities in the Agglomeration, this is bad news. The data are, of course, skewed by sector 6, since more than a third of the working population is employed in the provision of public services (education, healthcare, military, etc.) but these are not properly reflected in the estimates of value added by sector for the Agglomeration.[11] To correct for this problem, Figure 1.28 presents the estimates for the private sector only. The productivity advantage of the industrial sector largely disappears and that of non-FIRE market services is much reduced. FIRE still emerges as having below-average productivity. The importance of physical capital in manufacturing, extractive industry and energy provision generates high labour productivity in those activities, although there is likely to be considerable variation among them.

Figure 1.26. **Distribution of employment by sector**

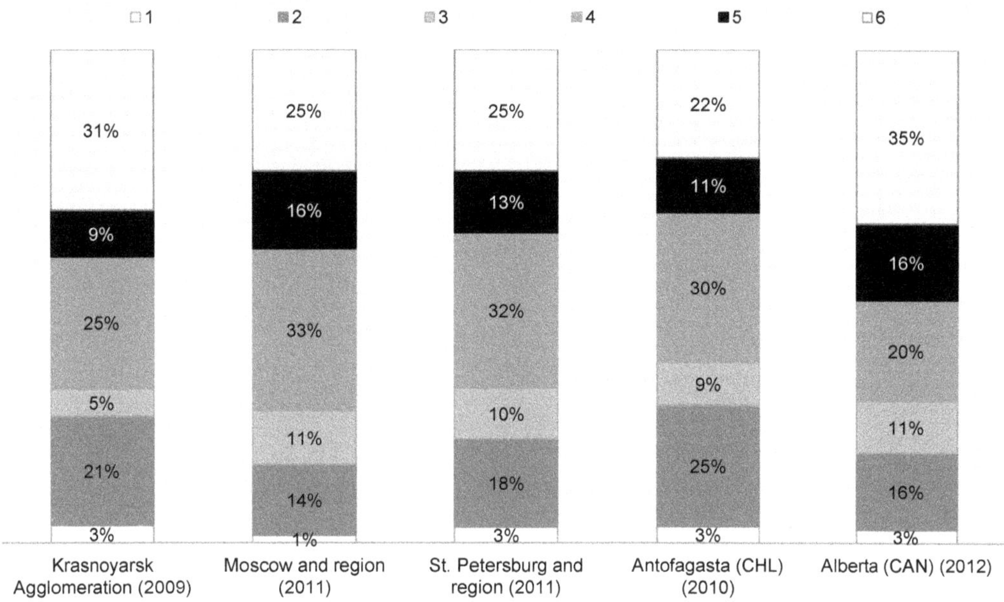

Notes: Sectors are defined as follows:

1 Agriculture, hunting, forestry, fishing and fisheries
2 Mining; manufacturing; gas, electricity and water supply
3 Construction
4 Wholesale and retail trade; repairs of motor vehicles, motorcycles, household appliances and personal items; hotels and restaurants; transport, storage facilities, communications
5 Financial activities, real estate transactions, lease, and service provision
6 Public administration and military security, mandatory social security, education, healthcare and social services; provision of other utilities, social and personal services; private households' activities involving hired workers

Sources: OECD (2014d), *OECD Regional Statistics* (database), http://dx.doi.org/10.1787/region-data-en; Federal Service for State Statistics; SFU (2012), "Background report for the OECD Territorial Review of Krasnoyarsk", Siberian Federal University, Krasnoyarsk, Russian Federation.

The data for the Agglomeration do not permit consideration of separate sub-sectors, but national-level data suggest that productivity in mining and resource extraction is perhaps five times the levels found in the rest of the industrial sector. However, the contrast between sector 4 (trade, transport, communication) and sector 5 (FIRE) is more puzzling, and suggests that sector 4 in the Agglomeration consists of more capital-intensive activities whereas sector 5 would be more labour-intensive. Although sector 5 contributes less than 10% to the GDP of the Agglomeration, it is a sector that could greatly benefit from enhanced skills in the labour market.

Figure 1.27. **Comparison of sectoral structures of value added and employment**

Krasnoyarsk Agglomeration, 2009

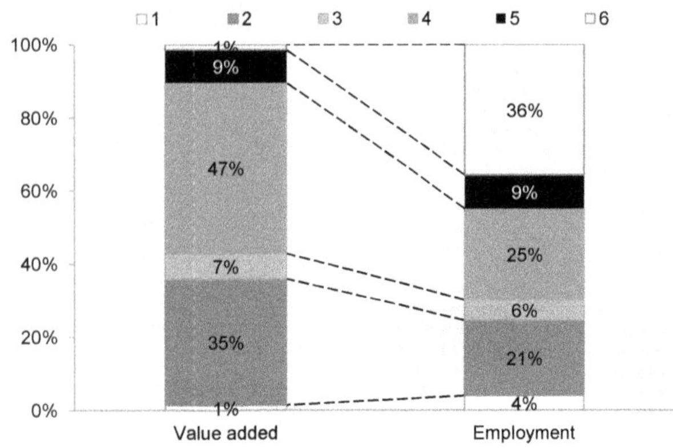

Figure 1.28. **Value added and employment, private sector only**

Krasnoyarsk Agglomeration, 2009

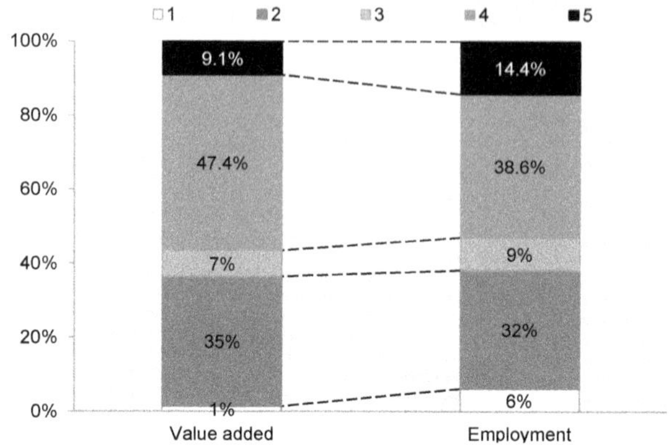

Notes: Sectors are defined as follows:

1 Agriculture, hunting, forestry, fishing and fisheries

2 Mining; manufacturing; gas, electricity and water supply

3 Construction

4 Wholesale and retail trade; repairs of motor vehicles, motorcycles, household appliances and personal items; hotels and restaurants; transport, storage facilities, communications

5 Financial activities, real estate transactions, lease, and service provision

6 Public administration and military security, mandatory social security, education, healthcare and social services; provision of other utilities, social and personal services; private households' activities involving hired workers

Source: SFU (2012), "Background report for the OECD Territorial Review of Krasnoyarsk", Siberian Federal University, Krasnoyarsk, Russian Federation.

A comparison of employment and number of firms (Figure 1.29) highlights the concentration of industrial employment in larger firms, which is no surprise given the role of large primary-sector enterprises in the Krasnoyarsk economy. The capital intensity of these activities implies greater scope for economies of scale and even creates significant barriers to entry, as high fixed costs bar small firms from competing in the market. Sectors 4 and 5 are, on the other hand, populated by more atomised firms. Although 25% of private sector employment occurs in sector 4, it accounts for 45% of the Agglomeration's firms operating in the private sector.

The Agglomeration's population is relatively well educated on the whole

The Krai benefits from a generally well-educated population by international standards, although its levels of education attainment are similar but marginally below the average for the country (Figure 1.30). The share of the population with lower levels of education tend to be slightly over-represented at the level of the Krai compared to the rest of the country, and vice versa for higher levels of education, but differences remain small and the population compares well with those of many OECD countries. Although data on educational attainment for the Agglomeration are not available for the recent past, it is

Figure 1.29. **Comparison of sectoral structures of private sector employment and firm population**

Krasnoyarsk Agglomeration, 2009

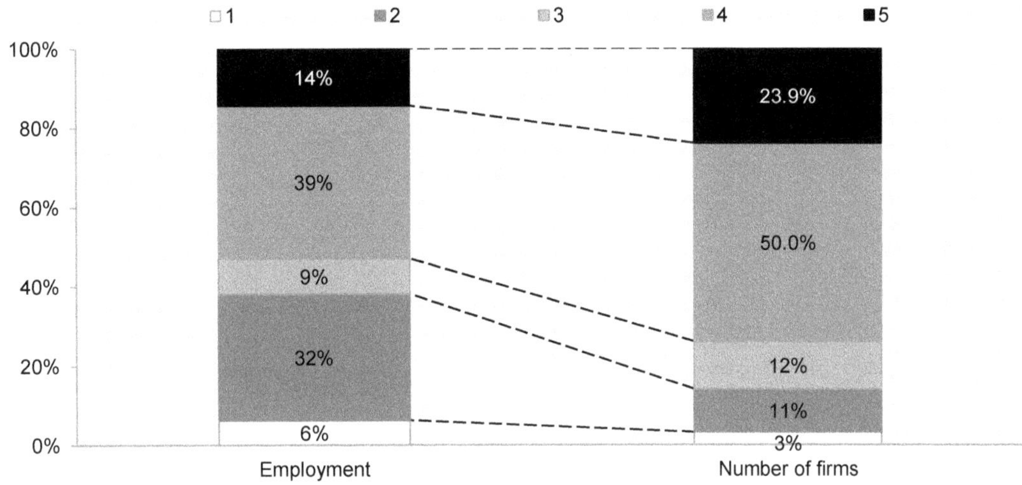

Notes: Sectors are defined as follows:

1 Agriculture, hunting, forestry, fishing and fisheries

2 Mining; manufacturing; gas, electricity and water supply

3 Construction

4 Wholesale and retail trade; repairs of motor vehicles, motorcycles, household appliances and personal items; hotels and restaurants; transport, storage facilities, communications

5 Financial activities, real estate transactions, lease, and service provision

Source: SFU (2012), "Background report for the OECD Territorial Review of Krasnoyarsk", Siberian Federal University, Krasnoyarsk, Russian Federation.

likely that the city and its immediate hinterland have higher levels of human capital than the Krai as a whole. For instance, in 2002 the share of the population above 15 that had only completed primary education was 11.9% in the city, compared to 15% at the level of the Krai, while the share with higher or post-graduate education was 22.6% in the city versus only 14.4% in the Krai. This is due to the fact that the city is home to most of the Krai's higher education institutions; in 2010, it accounted for 87.4% of the Krai's enrolment in higher education. With 25 600 students enrolled in secondary education, the Agglomeration also represented 53% of the enrolment in non-vocational secondary education in the Krai. Education spending in 2011 accounted for roughly one-third of the spending of public budgets of the Agglomeration's constituent units, up from just under 23% in 2000. This increase has helped the Agglomeration maintain its attractiveness as an important educational hub for the Krai as well as for other parts of Siberia.

Student performance on the Unified State Examination, a nationally standardised examination that takes place at the end of secondary education across the whole of the Russian Federation, tends to reinforce this impression. In 2012, school-leavers in the Agglomeration achieved an average score across all subjects of 59.8 (out of 100), higher than the corresponding scores of 57.2 for Russia as a whole and 54.5 for the Krai. Since the great majority of examinees in the Krai are within the Agglomeration, the gap between Agglomeration and Krai averages implies that students elsewhere in the Krai are performing far less well on average.

Figure 1.30. **Educational attainments of the adult population (ages 15+), 2010**

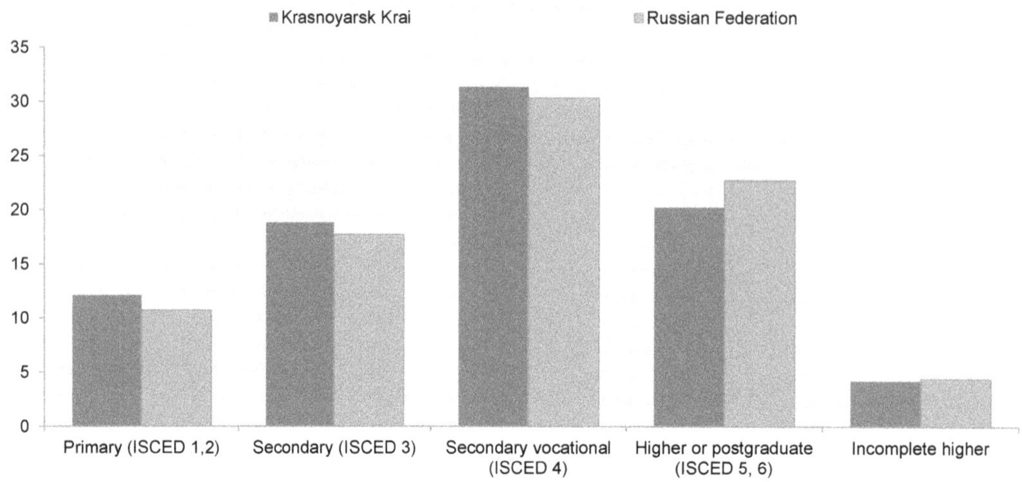

Source: Federal Service for State Statistics.

The importance of extractive industries in the life of the Krai and the Agglomeration is reflected in the pattern of higher degrees and research pursued in the Agglomeration. In 2011, 37% of the "Candidate of Sciences" (PhD-equivalent) degrees awarded in the Agglomeration were related to geosciences and engineering (Figure 1.31). Medicine and other sciences also constitute an important segment, with 29%. The educational system is oriented towards science and engineering to a significant degree, reflecting the needs of the local economy (notably in geoscience and medicine).

Figure 1.31. **Candidate of Sciences degrees awarded by subject in the Agglomeration and in the Russian Federation as a whole**

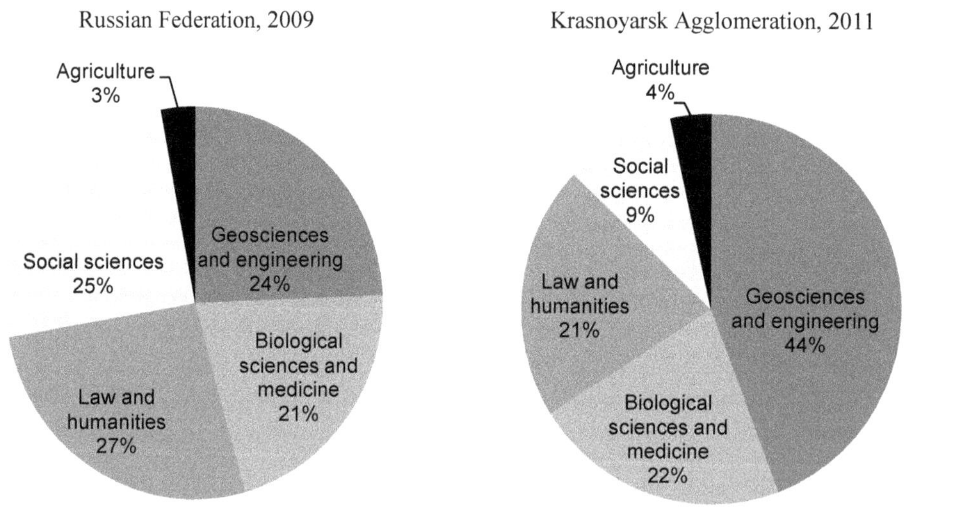

Source: SFU (2012), "Background report for the OECD Territorial Review of Krasnoyarsk", Siberian Federal University, Krasnoyarsk, Russian Federation.

The Agglomeration's innovation system also reflects its specialisation

As will be seen in Chapter 2, invigorating the Agglomeration's innovation system is a major priority for the Krai and the city authorities. Krasnoyarsk is home to an important science base, including enterprises and research institutes in the nuclear and space sectors, as well as metallurgy and related fields. The evidence suggests that, in innovation terms, Krasnoyarsk has not been performing up to its potential, however, and the authorities have been increasingly active in recent years in investing in innovation infrastructures and programmes designed to realise that potential. One factor working for the Agglomeration is that a large part of the local educational and research establishment corresponds to the structure of the economy; this may seem a banal observation but it is not always the case. In many OECD and non-OECD regions, major research strengths are not associated with local productive capacities; they still bring real benefits to the region but their work is primarily linked to production elsewhere.[12]

Geography and economic development

Questions of economic geography loom large in this review. This partly reflects the natural wealth of Krasnoyarsk, but three other factors discussed above are also critical: distance to markets, climate and, above all, density of settlement. The geography of a place is effectively defined by a combination of physical ("first-nature") and human ("second-nature") geographies. The more people inhabit a place, the more its character will be defined by second-nature geography – by human beings and their activities. Where settlement is sparse, first-nature geography inevitably looms larger – less human settlement and activity necessarily implies a larger role for natural factors. Yet distance matters, too. After all, there are two major pockets of dense settlement in Krasnoyarsk Krai, of which the Agglomeration is by far the larger, and there are other major cities in Siberia.

The economic benefits of agglomeration are not entirely unrelated to questions of location. It is one thing to be a city of 1 million people in Eastern Siberia and quite another to be a city of 1 million or so in, for example, the densely urbanised triangle defined by Berlin, London and Milan. The cities of Siberia still face many of the challenges and opportunities typical of rural places. However, they are also likely to benefit from their remoteness in some respects, as it is common for remote cities to have higher-order functions than their size would suggest, simply because the distance to bigger places is great (and a poor transport network reinforces this effect). Moreover, the Siberian cities are where they are primarily on account of the natural resources to be found there – bringing the element of resource wealth back into the picture. With these considerations in mind, this final section of Chapter 1 reflects on recent research in economic geography and what it implies for the development of the Krasnoyarsk Agglomeration and the surrounding Krai.

Even in a technologically advanced, globalising world, geography still matters

There are a number of ways in which geography can influence economic development. The first is that proximity may have a favourable impact on productivity, through various channels operating via product and labour markets. Proximity strengthens competition – consumers of intermediate inputs and final goods have more choice of potential suppliers. Secondly, proximity can offer firms new opportunities to enhance productivity by allowing them to benefit from so-called "agglomeration economies" (see below). These two factors are mutually supportive, insofar as the large market size makes it possible to realise economies of scale without undermining competition. They imply that long distances to major markets, as well as low density of settlement, represent economic challenges. Recent OECD work exploring the extent to which cross-country dispersion in economic performance can be accounted for by economic geography points to a number of findings that are relevant for many Russian regions, including Krasnoyarsk, and also for the Krasnoyarsk Agglomeration itself (Box 1.2).

Box 1.2. The contribution of economic geography to GDP per capita

Employing an augmented Solow model as a benchmark and using data on 21 OECD countries over the period 1970-2004, Boulhol, de Serres and Molnar (2008) look at: *i)* a variety of indicators of proximity to major markets; *ii)* the specific impacts of telecommunications and transport costs; and *iii)* the significance of natural resource endowments. Their major conclusions may be summarised as follows:

- While the impact of proximity/distance depends to some extent on the measure used, all of the indicators of distance are found to have a statistically significant effect on GDP per capita, with the exception of population density. For countries such as Australia and New Zealand, lower access to markets compared to the OECD average could lower GDP per capita by up to 10%. Countries like Belgium and the Netherlands, conversely, are found to benefit greatly from their location at the heart of Europe.
- With respect to transport and telecommunications costs, they find no evidence that the importance of distance in the transportation of goods has diminished since 1970, despite the fact that transport costs have fallen relative to the value of transported goods. Transport costs continue to have a negative and significant impact on GDP per capita, depressing it in remote countries like Australia and New Zealand and raising it in, for example, Canada and the United States, albeit by a smaller margin: the effect appears to be asymmetrical, hurting peripheral countries more than it helps centrally located ones. (The smaller effects found here are consistent with the idea that transport costs are only one aspect of costs related to distance.)
- The cost of international telecommunications, by contrast, has fallen to the point where it is not significant for any OECD country.
- Despite the widespread discussion in the economic literature of "Dutch disease" and a possible "resource curse", the results suggest that resource-rich countries do, other things being equal, have higher levels of GDP per capita. Countries, like Australia, Canada and Norway, at least, have managed to escape the resource curse, such as it may be.

In one extension of the model, the authors explore the possibility that the returns to investment in research and development are negatively affected by geographic remoteness. They find that the effectiveness of private R&D intensity is significantly influenced by the degree of urban concentration but not by distance to major markets, a result with potentially important (and encouraging) implications for Krasnoyarsk.

Perhaps the most important policy implication of this analysis is that policy makers should ensure that transport costs are not inflated by regulations that reduce efficiency and impede competition. Transport sectors have traditionally been heavily regulated and are often largely exempt from the provisions of standard competition legislation. While many OECD countries have liberalised domestic transport sectors in recent decades, international transport is still subject to extensive regulation, much of which undermines competition, particularly in road, rail, maritime and air freight. Cartels and lack of cabotage rights are common (Clark, Dollar and Micco, 2004).

Source: Boulhol, H., A. de Serres and M. Molnar (2008), "The contribution of economic geography to GDP per capita", *OECD Economics Department Working Papers*, No. 602, OECD Publishing, Paris, http://dx.doi.org/10.1787/242216186836; Clark, X., D. Dollar and A. Micco (2004), "Port efficiency, maritime transport costs and bilateral trade", *NBER Working Papers*, No. 10 353, March.

Siberia's climate affects both living costs and firm competitiveness

In one very important sense, Krasnoyarsk benefits tremendously from its geography. As noted above, its resource wealth forms the backbone of the economy, which is, by Russian standards, comparatively successful. Nevertheless, geography also presents major drawbacks for the development of the Krai's economy. First, the continental climate is severe: even in the warmer reaches of the southern part of the Krai, the average temperature in January is -18°C (in the north, -36°C), and winters are long. This has implications for the cost of production of many goods and services as well as the well-being and cost of living of the population. Mikhailova (2004) links the cold to higher infant mortality rates and lower productivity in sectors such as construction. She finds the most significant impact of cold to be on energy consumption, concluding on the basis of cross-sectional analysis that consumption of various kinds of energy by manufacturing firms increases by 2.5-4% when the average January temperature drops by 1°C. Similar results were obtained for residential energy consumption. Like Gaddy and Hill (2003), Mikhailova links the cost of the cold in the Russian Federation to past policies, noting that Soviet planners' determination to settle the far north and east of the country resulted in larger populations in relatively cold climates than would otherwise have been observed – at a time, moreover, when populations in all other northerly countries were increasingly concentrated in relatively warmer places. Falling populations across much of Siberia and the Russian Far East in 1991 thus represent a partial unwinding of this policy.

The good news here is that there is much that can be done to cut energy costs. Despite substantial progress since the start of the transition, the Russian Federation remains one of the most energy-intensive economies in the world (Figure 1.32). This contributes to local air pollution as well as greenhouse gas emissions; the rate of premature mortality attributable to low air quality is among the highest in the world (OECD, 2014c). If Russia achieved the same energy efficiency as its OECD peers, it could save 30% of consumed energy (IEA, 2011). The Russian government's official goal is to reduce the energy intensity of GDP by 40% by 2020. Federal and regional programmes adopted in pursuit of this goal have included tax credits, state subsidies and loan guarantees for efficiency improvement projects. However, implementation of these initiatives has been uneven and often delayed and effective mechanisms to monitor the achievement of programme objectives are often absent, partly because target indicators were often not well-specified (OECD, 2014c).

Fuel production and consumption subsidies in the Russian Federation are still estimated at more than 2% of GDP (IEA, 2012; OECD, 2013a). OECD (2011a) identifies a disparity between domestic energy prices and marginal social cost of energy consumption as the most important challenge for improving energy efficiency, and this remains a missing element of the existing policy framework. Since then, slower growth has led to backtracking on plans to reduce the cross-subsidisation reflected in the gap between low domestic and higher export gas prices. Indeed, domestic prices of utilities are to be either frozen or increased more slowly than inflation in the next three years. Nevertheless, the government foresees an increase in prices above newly introduced consumption norms for households and progress continues on other lines of policy. While energy consumption meters are legally required, only 40% of residential houses and 20-25% of apartments have them installed so far. Non-metered consumption is to be subject to higher tariffs starting in 2015.

Figure 1.32. **Energy intensity and emissions**

A. Energy consumption per unit of GDP, 2011
Tonnes of oil equivalent (toe) per 2005 USD 1 000 of GDP calculated using PPPs

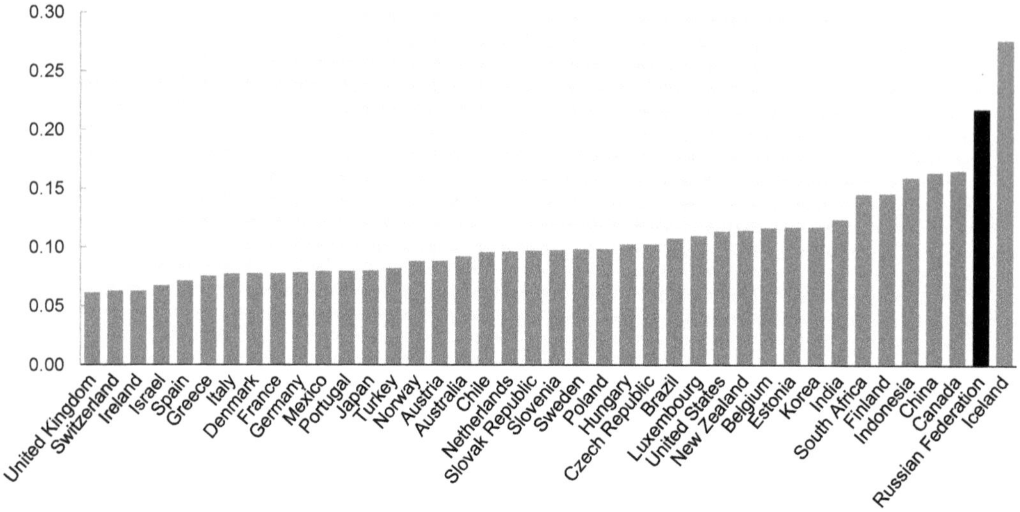

B. Total greenhouse gas emissions per unit of GDP, 2011
kg of CO_2 equivalent/2005 USD PPP

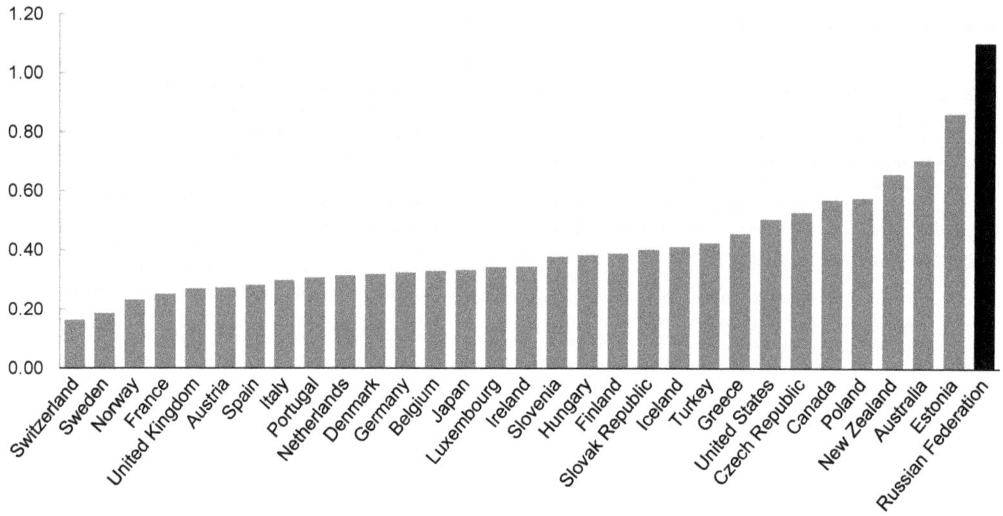

Note: Data for greenhouse gas emissions are excluding emissions/removals from LULUCF (land use, land-use change and forestry).

Sources: OECD (2014c), *OECD Economic Surveys: Russian Federation 2013*, OECD Publishing, Paris, http://dx.doi.org/10.1787/eco_surveys-rus-2013-en, based on United Nations Framework Convention on Climate Change (UNFCC), "Greenhouse Gas Inventory Data"; World Bank, *WDI database*; IEA (2012), "World energy indicators and world energy balances".

For an economy like Krasnoyarsk's, with a specialisation in energy-intensive industrial sectors, the potential pay-offs to enhanced energy efficiency are enormous. While many of the key parameters of policy are set by the federal authorities, Chapters 2 and 3 will explore the potential for action at the level of the Krai and the Agglomeration to improve efficiency in transport, housing and industry.

Krasnoyarsk, like much of the Russian Federation, also faces problems associated with climate change. On some recent estimates, average temperatures in Siberia had already risen by as much as 1.6°C between the middle of the last century and 2009. Global climate models also suggest that temperatures in Eastern Siberia could rise by 2.1-2.4°C by 2050, and that the intensity and variability of precipitation will both increase. Higher precipitation is expected year-round but especially in winter, when precipitation is projected to rise by around 17% (World Bank, 2009a). Perhaps the most serious – and unpredictable – challenge stems from the impact of climate change on permafrost zones. The permafrost line is receding and this is already affecting biodiversity and leading to coastal erosion and the collapse of exposed buildings and infrastructure. Transport and energy infrastructures are particularly vulnerable, but so are many urban dwellings. Moreover, permafrost is estimated to hold about twice the amount of carbon in the atmosphere. While some of the carbon released as permafrost thaws will be captured by the encroachment of trees in the tundra, the carbon emissions arising from microbial decomposition of organic carbon in thawing permafrost could amount to about half those generated by global land-use change during this century (Schuur et al. 2008).

That said, it is worth noting that climate change, for all its costs and hazards, will also offer some new opportunities to Krasnoyarsk. World Bank (2009a) points to new opportunities for offshore oil exploration in the Arctic and increased crop potential in Siberia and the Russian Far East. Warmer weather will also lead to lower energy consumption for much of the year, an undoubted benefit to such an energy-intensive economy. Moreover, the Yenisei is largely navigable outside its upper reaches, which rise in Mongolia. This means that, as Arctic maritime transport becomes feasible for longer and longer periods of the year, Krasnoyarsk – the city, as well as the Krai – will gain a potentially important new outlet to the sea. A new freight route through the Arctic could reduce the shipping time from China to Rotterdam by as much as 15 days when compared with the current route via the Suez Canal (Financial Times, 2013).

Low density of settlement has important implications for productivity

Economic activity is not naturally dispersed; rather it tends to concentrate in certain geographic spaces rather than others, mainly owing to the benefits associated with economies of agglomeration. People want to live where firms – and therefore job opportunities – are concentrated, and firms want to locate where demand – and therefore population – is large. Agglomeration economies occur when firms enjoy increasing returns to scale (IRS) in a particular place. This could be because of the presence of natural advantages (i.e. natural resources, location, etc.), monopolistic protection, political factors (e.g. the decision to create a capital city or administrative centre) or some other reason. The presence of IRS also induces other firms to locate there, as people come in search of higher wages, a wider range of job opportunities and better/more varied amenities and consumption opportunities. Part of the advantage of large cities thus stems from their attractions for high-productivity firms and for individuals with high levels of human capital; in other words, a selection effect is at work. However, there is clear evidence that this selection process is magnified by agglomeration dynamics: other things being equal, individuals and firms become more productive in denser places. This reflects the opportunities that cities afford for sharing assets, improving matches on the labour market and knowledge diffusion (Box 1.3). The result of these combined selection effects and agglomeration dynamics is that cities tend to be more productive, on average, than non-urban places (the major exceptions tend to be resource-rich rural regions).

Box 1.3. Agglomeration economies

Three main mechanisms work to produce agglomeration economies:

1. Mechanisms that deal with sharing of:
   - Indivisible facilities such as local public goods or facilities that serve several individuals or firms. Some examples, other than public goods, are facilities such as laboratories, universities and other large goods that do not belong to a particular agent but where some exclusion is implicit in providing them.
   - The gains from the wider variety of input suppliers that can be sustained by a larger final goods industry. In other words, the presence of increasing returns to scale along with forward and backward linkages allow firms to purchase intermediate inputs at lower costs.
   - The gains from the narrower specialisation that can be sustained with higher production levels. Several firms specialise in producing complementary products, reducing overall production costs.
   - Risks. This refers to the idea that an industry gains from having a constant market for skills. If there are market shocks, firms can adjust to changes in demand if they have access to a deep and broad labour market that allows them to expand or contract their demand for labour.
2. Matching mechanisms by which:
   - Agglomeration improves the expected quality of matches between firms and workers, so both are better able to find a good match for their needs.
   - An increase in the number of agents trying to match in the labour market also improves the probability of matching.
   - Delays are alleviated. There is a possibility that contractual problems arising from renegotiation among buyers and suppliers will result in one of the parties losing out to the other party in a renegotiation. However, if the Agglomeration is extensive enough, agents can find an alternative partner.
3. Learning mechanisms based on the generation, diffusion and accumulation of knowledge. This refers not only to the learning of technologies, but also the acquisition of skills.

OECD metropolitan regions benefit from agglomeration effects and thus tend to display higher levels of productivity, higher rates of employment and higher levels of GDP per capita than other regions. These benefits, however, are limited by congestion costs, diseconomies of scale and oversupply of labour, among other potential negative elements, and many metropolitan regions have in recent decades tended to underperform national economies.

Sources: Duranton, G. and D. Puga (2004), "Micro-foundations of urban agglomeration economies", *Handbook of Regional and Urban Economics*, in: J.V. Henderson and J.F. Thisse (ed.), *Handbook of Regional and Urban Economics*, edition 1, Vol. 4, Chapter 48, pp. 2 063-2 117 Elsevier; OECD (2009), "OECD Economic Outlook interim report", OECD, Paris, April.

Recent OECD research suggests that agglomeration benefits increase with city size: the bigger the city, the greater the agglomeration dynamic. For a given city size (in terms of population), agglomeration benefits appear to increase with labour density – that is, with the spatial concentration of economic activity within the city. They also appear, other things being equal, to increase with the share of services in total value added and with overall levels of human capital. This last point is particularly significant: highly skilled individuals become even more productive when interacting with other highly skilled individuals. With respect to Krasnoyarsk Krai, this suggests that the increasing concentration of the Krai's population in and around the Krasnoyarsk Agglomeration is good news. First, it involves a relocation of population towards the south of the Krai. Secondly, it represents a strengthening of potential agglomeration economies in Krasnoyarsk, which could be good for both productivity and innovation. Moreover, these findings underscore the importance of investment in education and skills. Even if, as noted above, a large number of skilled workers tend to leave the Agglomeration and the Krai for other parts of the Russian Federation, the evidence strongly suggests that the benefits of greater investment in human capital are substantial – "brain drains" may reduce the local returns to such investment but they remain significant and positive nonetheless.

Agglomeration economies are not the automatic consequence of population density: large urban areas can miss many of their potential benefits if infrastructure bottlenecks or other impediments prevent the formation of deeper labour, product and factor markets (OECD, 2012a). As will be seen in the chapters that follow, there is much that Krasnoyarsk city and its neighbours can do to deepen these agglomeration processes. Better transport networks across the entire Agglomeration, co-ordinated approaches to skills development and labour-market policies, along with other steps to strengthen policy co-ordination across the Agglomeration's constituent units could help increase the density and intensity of economic interactions taking place in and around the city. Policies to strengthen competition and create more favourable conditions for entrepreneurship are also important. One of the main tasks for the authorities in the Krai and in the Agglomeration is thus to forge this large urban area into a truly integrated and well-functioning urban economy.

Krasnoyarsk is also disadvantaged by its relatively remote location

Economic remoteness, or peripherality, is always a relative term – it is about being connected or unconnected to somewhere. However, it is possible to assess the global position of a place *vis-à-vis* the main centres of demand using a market potential indicator such as that described in Box 1.4. The indicator presented here rests on population, GDP and physical distance (albeit distinguishing between overland and maritime distances). Adjustments are made to take into account shared borders, common languages and colonial ties but not to reflect such factors as trade agreements, export baskets or industrial structures. This is because these latter factors are endogenous to economic and policy processes. As can be seen from Table 1.2, Krasnoyarsk Krai ranks among the bottom 10 Russian regions of the 79 federal subjects for which sufficient data are available. Among all the regions included in the study, it ranks 363rd out of 409.[13] Its level of remoteness is comparable to that of Queensland in Australia. While Krasnoyarsk is certainly a remote area by the standards of the large majority of OECD countries, most Australian and all New Zealand regions are more remote, as are a majority of regions in Brazil, Chile or South Africa, and – more generally – most countries in South America and Sub-Saharan Africa. Moreover, the prosperity of places like New Zealand, Australia and Alaska is a reminder that remoteness may be an economic handicap but it is not a necessary bar to economic success.

Table 1.2. **Regional market potential of selected Russian regions**

Top 10 Russian regions by market potential (international ranking in brackets)	Bottom 10 Russian regions by market potential (international ranking in brackets)
1. Federal City of Moscow (5)	70. Irkutsk Oblast (361)
2. Federal City of Saint Petersburg (125)	71. Altai Krai (362)
3. Moscow Oblast (210)	72. Krasnoyarsk Krai (363)
4. Kaliningrad Oblast (241)	73. Republic of Khakassia (364)
5. Pskov Oblast (273)	74. Altai Republic (365)
6. Kaluga Oblast (278)	75. Tuva Republic (366)
7. Tver Oblast (279)	76. Sakha Republic (367)
8. Leningrad Oblast (280)	77. Magadan Oblast (369)
9. Smolensk Oblast (281)	78. Chukotka Autonomous Okrug (371)
10. Tula Oblast (282)	79. Kamchatka Krai (372)

Source: OECD calculations based on data described in Annex 1.A1.

Box 1.4. Regional market potential

Many studies have highlighted the core-periphery nature of economic development: while regions in a central location may attract investments and workers, regions in peripheral locations may suffer from industrial decline and dependence on national transfers. It is sometimes argued (though unproven) that globalisation may be opening new opportunities for more peripheral places. A market potential indicator assesses regional attractiveness from an economic geography view. It is a measure summarising, for a given region, the proximity to economic demand from other locations. Empirical studies have computed indicators for market potential at national level and found significant and robust correlations with wages, labour reallocation across industries, firm location choices and migration flows.

Relying on its rich dataset on regional GDP and population for OECD and selected non-OECD countries, the OECD has recently constructed indicators of market potential at regional level (see Annex 1.A1). This is the first effort to develop regional market potential for a fairly comprehensive list of regions from OECD and non-OECD countries: regional market potential is computed for more than 400 regions in 29 countries, accounting for more than 75% of 2012 world GDP; the rest of the world is entered into the data as whole countries. It should be noted that the inclusion of places like Argentina, India, Iran and Turkey as entire countries tends automatically to increase their "weight": it is the hierarchy among regions that is more telling. The detailed construction of the indicator is described in Annex 1.A1.

Source: OECD calculations based on data described in Annex 1.A1.

Nevertheless, Krasnoyarsk is, in a global perspective, one of the most remote locations on earth. Fortunately, its position appears to have improved substantially over the recent past, owing chiefly to the shifting centre of gravity of the world economy towards China and the wider Asia-Pacific region: Krasnoyarsk Krai ranks in the *top quintile* of the 409 regions covered in terms of increase in market potential over the period 1995-2010. This on-going shift creates new opportunities for the Krai and the Agglomeration. However, waiting for the world to change is unlikely to be a satisfactory strategy, and the potential advantages for Krasnoyarsk stemming from the rise of Asia remain just that – potential. Much must be done to realise them. Overcoming the barriers posed by remoteness involves optimising transport networks and connectivity.

As noted above, longer distances and concomitant higher transport costs have two major implications for tradable producers in geographically remote regions, both of which reflect the role of competition:

- Constraints on accessibility constitute a form of protection for producers. Other things being equal, local producers enjoy a competitive advantage in such places, since would-be importers face higher costs. However, other factors often overwhelm this advantage, since local producers in a small, remote market may not be able to realise the economies of scale needed to compete with imports. Even if they do, the result is likely to be higher prices for local consumers, including not only households but also firms reliant on locally produced inputs.
- Long distances and high transport costs make it harder for local producers to enter larger, external markets. To export, they need a productivity advantage great enough to offset this disadvantage: being as good as their rivals is not good enough. They have to be better. Otherwise, they may have little incentive to innovate and increase productivity, as well as their ability to expand output and employment. Firms oriented towards such distant markets need to achieve this productivity edge in spite of the costs outlined above, which result from weak competition among input suppliers and providers of non-tradable services.

Taken together, these two factors imply that transport costs reduce the scope for specialisation according to comparative advantage, one of the critical drivers of gains from trade.

For Krasnoyarsk, this points to the importance of addressing transport bottlenecks in general and of further reform in the rail and air transport sectors, in particular. Upgrading much of the country's long, stringy road network would also help. Krasnoyarsk's industrial structure and firm demography represent a mixed blessing in this regard. On the positive side, the Agglomeration benefits from the presence of several large, internationally active companies, like the aluminium producer RusAl. In that sense, its ability to export successfully is not in doubt. On the other hand, the dominance of very large firms may make it more difficult to strengthen competition in local product markets, which is also a necessary measure to counter the effects of remoteness, particularly in new or emerging sectors.

The different dimensions of peripherality call for different responses

Peripherality has two distinct dimensions. The first is simple physical distance to major markets. This matters (Box 1.2): distance increases travel times and shipping costs, which must be borne by the buyer (in the form of higher prices) or seller (in the form of lower margins). Yet straight-line distance is not all that matters: maritime transport is far cheaper and more flexible than overland transport, and it requires less dedicated infrastructure (Table 1.3). Consequently, access to the sea is a crucial variable – southern Chile and coastal China are far less remote from North American and European markets than, for example, Brazil's Amazonian regions or China's interior, respectively, even though these are physically closer to the main markets. Where overland distances are concerned, the quality and layout of infrastructure is clearly critical.

Table 1.3. **Transport and connectivity**

	Modes of transport				
	Fixed route?	Set-up costs	Cost/kg/km	Speed	Best distance
Road	Yes	High	Medium	Medium	Short
Rail	Yes	High	Medium	Medium	Medium
Air	No	Low	High	Fast	Long
Ship	No	Low	Low	Slow	Long
		Network connectivity			
Telecommunications		Presence, speed, penetration			
Personal knowledge		Direct contact, benefits of agglomeration and physical proximity			
Common media		Shared language and values			

Source: Freshwater, D. (2011), "How should we think about 'peripherality'?", presentation to the NORA Region Conference, Copenhagen, 5 April.

The implications of this reality for Krasnoyarsk are clear. Maritime access is currently very limited, though this may change (see below). Air freight tends to make sense only for products with very high value to weight and, in particular, for perishable products, where speed of delivery is a key priority. Overland transport is far cheaper but depends on the quality of the available infrastructure, as well as on the routes available. As noted above, the Russian Federation's road and rail networks pose problems on both counts. Moreover, since transport costs for raw materials tend to be lower than those for manufactured goods, high transport costs tend to reinforce the specialisation in raw commodities and constitute yet another barrier that producers of higher-value manufactures must overcome in order to compete. This is not an insuperable obstacle – manufacturing exporters in the Agglomeration like the aluminium-alloy wheel producer SKAD have demonstrated their ability to compete even on overseas markets. However, even they acknowledge the difficulties involved, particularly owing to the need to rely on road freight rather than rail. The guaranteed rail delivery time to St. Petersburg, at 30 days, makes it impossible to rely on the railways, even if one might expect most rail shipments to arrive somewhat faster. Fortunately, both the Baikal (M53) and Yenisei (M54) motorways – the two major roads crossing Siberia – run through the city of Krasnoyarsk. Yet the road network is poor and, in the view of many firms in Siberia, tightening regulation of the trucking industry is making it harder to remain competitive while relying on road freight (Kichanov, 2013).

Given the problems with competition on the rail network described above, it is difficult to tell whether or not the prevailing structure of freight tariffs is economically warranted or not. Local critics of Russian Railways insist that the tariff structure exaggerates the cost differential between bulk commodities and manufactures, artificially favouring the export of unprocessed raw materials. It is difficult to assess such a claim, but the unfinished state of railway reform in the Russian Federation at least leaves open the question of whether a more competitive rail network could help Krasnoyarsk and other Siberian cities to compete on national and international markets.

A further issue concerns the development of Siberia's rail infrastructure. The city of Krasnoyarsk sits on the Trans-Siberian Main Line, the primary overland rail route between Europe and East Asia. The authorities currently plan a USD 17 billion upgrade of both the Trans-Siberian and the Baikal-Amur Mainline, Siberia's other major rail line, which will increase freight capacity by almost 50% over the coming five years. This represents a significant potential opportunity for Krasnoyarsk. Critics have expressed some scepticism about the ambition of the project, since currently only about 1% of cargo traffic between Europe and East Asia passes through Siberia, and around 90% of commercial freight worldwide travels by sea (Bloomberg News, 2013; Nasyrova, 2013; Chernyshov, 2013). However, even if the upgrade does not lead to the projected growth in transit volumes from Europe to the East, the upgrade could make it easier and cheaper for Krasnoyarsk to trade with foreign markets. This will depend, of course, on the structure of tariffs but also on the success with which the project upgrades the rail-to-port connections in Russia. Currently, for example, a container is held at customs in the Far East port of Vladivostok for 13 days. It then takes a further four to five days to be processed through the port. In Singapore, by contrast, a container is held for about two days and processed through port on the same day it is released. Ultimately, this project probably matters more to Krasnoyarsk than a proposed Siberian High-Speed Rail (HSR) network. The HSR is far more relevant for passenger use and unlikely to be a profitable way to deal with freight exports. Krasnoyarsk's future thus probably depends more on rail reforms and the upgrading of freight lines than on the development of HSR.

As will be seen, there are also serious efforts under way to develop Krasnoyarsk's potential as an aviation hub in Eurasia, a role that could grow substantially as technology opens the way to routine air traffic directly over the North Pole. Traditionally, aircraft have avoided flying over the North Pole, because doing so involved an extended period of navigation without any contact with the ground. The advent of systems like GPS is changing this and could lead to significant traffic from North America to Southeast Asia, for example, over the North Pole and across Siberia.

The second dimension of peripherality is the degree of economic connectedness. Lack of economic integration not only reduces current trade opportunities, it reduces the ability of agents in a place to identify new opportunities. Thus, there are costs in both static and dynamic perspectives. To take a trivial example, one might note that Australian wheat farmers, though located in a very remote place, are extremely well connected – they are deeply integrated into international grain markets and very well informed about what is happening on them. By contrast, the residents of many small towns along the US Appalachian mountain chain, which are among America's poorest places, are physically very close to some of the world's biggest factories and consumer markets, but they are poorly linked to those markets and thus largely disconnected from activities taking place only a short distance away.

The Agglomeration enjoys a relatively strong position with respect to this second dimension of peripherality. The presence of a number of large companies operating on international markets, the existence of a significant science base and the overall high human capital levels of the population serve to ensure that the city and its hinterland, though physically remote from the major centres of gravity of the world economy, are nonetheless well connected and integrated with the national and international economies. Telecommunications infrastructure is relatively good and, while data on the ICT assets of the Agglomeration are lacking, the estimate of 95 computers per 100 Agglomeration residents in 2011 compares favourably with even the most advanced industrial countries and no doubt reflects, at least in part, the presence of a significant science base in the region in the field of satellite communications. The main priority of the Krasnoyarsk authorities in the field of telecommunications is the construction and development of multi-purpose fibre-optic networks (communications, television, Internet, control and information system, etc.) and expansion of the networks of cellular operators.

Both the Krai and the Agglomeration face a particularly clear competitiveness challenge

Low-density economies located far from major markets tend to face a number of common problems (for a summary, see Freshwater, 2012). First, and perhaps most important, the principal sources of growth tend to be exogenous to the region and are mediated to the regional economy via its export base (Box 1.5). Since they can only produce a limited range of the goods and services they need, such regions are of necessity oriented to exports of one sort or another, unless they benefit from on-going income transfers. Otherwise, they cannot afford to import the goods they need from other places. Secondly, local markets tend to be thin, with weak competition. As noted above, this constitutes both a form of protection from external competitors, as well as a constraint on firm growth. Partly for this reason, firm populations in such places tend to be dominated by SMEs, but these are often low-growth firms. Thirdly, the economic structures of such places often have specific features:

- Production is concentrated in relatively few sectors, since it is impossible to achieve "critical mass" in more than a few activities. Whatever the respective roles of the primary, secondary and tertiary sectors, a narrower economic base implies greater vulnerability to sector-specific shocks, whether positive or negative. In a very large, dense economy, the greater range of activities typically offers a greater degree of resilience.
- Most employment is in services, but this tends to be mainly low-end consumer services, with relatively low levels of employment in high-end business services (these tend to predominate in very large cities) and comparatively large employment shares in the primary sector.
- Most manufacturing tends to be "mature" in product-cycle terms. There are important exceptions to this rule, but cutting-edge manufacturing tends to be concentrated in large cities and to shift into more rural places where one or both of two conditions hold. The first is that proximity to some primary resource is important (e.g. the structure of transport costs is such that it is better to produce close to the resource rather than to the consumer market).[14] The second is that the technology is mature enough that producers' main concern is cutting production costs – in short, production often shifts to more distant places when sectors are in decline. Where the latter motivation prevails, the tendency is to favour rural areas with good connections to major markets but low labour and real estate costs.
- Low density economies are, almost by nature, characterised by limited diversification of economic activity. Smaller places cannot achieve critical mass or economies of scale in many activities. This also means that local producers often face thinner markets for their inputs – a lack of redundancy in markets can mean that weakness in one part of a supply chain harms other firms in the chain. It is not so easy to replace a supplier who fails or is under-performing in terms of quality or price. Low levels of diversification thus imply heightened vulnerability to external shocks, particularly those affecting the "export base" sectors.
- On average, human capital levels are higher in denser places. There are, to be sure, many exceptions to this rule, but rural places tend to have workforces with weaker skills. They are also more likely than other places to have significant out-migration of skilled workers and a consequent ageing of the local workforce.

Box 1.5. Export base models

While export base or economic base models are often criticised, they remain an important tool for regional economics. The fundamental assumption of export base models is that there are two types of economic activity in a community. Some part of the local economy is oriented to creating goods or services that are sold to other regions, while other parts of the local economy are oriented to providing goods and services to be consumed within the region. While both types of activity are important, the distinction is central to the logic of the model.

Few economies are able to produce locally all the goods and services that the residents want or firms need as inputs. These have to be purchased from external sources. The basic sector of the local economy is the part that sells its output externally and generates the revenue needed to do this. The idea is particularly powerful in less dense places because they tend to be small, specialised in the production of a limited number of goods and services, and hence in a position where more of what resident firms and families consume has to be imported. Unless the community receives on-going income transfers (owing, for example, to remittance flows or the presence of a large elderly population in receipt of pension benefits), it has to generate enough export revenue to pay for its imports. In large urban areas, by contrast, a far higher share of final demand can be met from local sources so the internal dynamics of the economy are both more complex and more dominant.

The second part of export base theory deals with the role of the non-basic, or local, component. Production sold for local demand is important because it may be an intermediate input in the production of an export good or because it is consumed by workers in an export activity. Thus, a firm producing lumber that is sold to another firm that produces chairs for sale overseas is a key part of the production process. But export base theory differentiates the two functions. If there were no demand for chairs, there would be no local demand for lumber. Conversely it may be possible for the chair manufacturer to import wood. Most importantly, if chair sales increase or decrease, there is a direct effect on the sales of the lumber firm.

The share of basic and non-basic activity can be determined in a number of ways. Some activities, such as tourism, are inherently basic, because by definition tourism involves customers from some other place who buy a tourism experience. Other activities, such as dry cleaning, are almost entirely non-basic: it is unusual for people to bring their clothes from one community to another to be cleaned. Still others may be harder to classify. Retail firms may sell some goods locally while others are exported. By segmenting economic activity on the basis of sales or employment into the two categories, it is possible to determine the share of non-basic and basic activity.

The ratio of non-basic to basic activity provides a simple multiplier. If exports increase by some amount, then total economic activity will increase by the multiplier times the increase in exports. The simple development strategy for a low-density region or community consists in the first place of increasing exports and in the second place in ensuring that there is adequate capacity in the non-basic sector to support the expansion of the economic base. The logic of the model suggests that some sectors/firms are more important than others, because in a sense they are the locomotives that power the local economy. Other firms, while important (and sometimes vital), do not cause the train to move. Their efficiency is nonetheless critical, since it can impinge directly on the competitiveness of export-oriented firms, which may rely on them for inputs and non-tradable services.

Source: OECD (2011b), *OECD Territorial Reviews: NORA Region 2011: The Faroe Islands, Greenland, Iceland and Coastal Norway*, OECD Publishing, Paris, http://dx.doi.org/10.1787/9789264097629-en.

In consequence of many of these factors, such places tend to have lower levels of productivity, except in the primary sector, and limited entrepreneurial activity. Entry rates for new firms are typically lower than in denser places. Other things being equal, cities offer new firms a richer "eco-system" in which to develop. The opportunity costs of failure in big, dense economies tend to be lower (resources released in the event of a failure are easier to reallocate to other uses) and, in part for that reason, the cost of capital tends to be lower as well.[15] Survival rates for new firms, though, are often higher in less dense economies, because entrants have to be fairly productive in order to overcome the barriers to entry (OECD, 2012c). In general, levels of patenting and formal research and development also tend to be low, though such economies can be surprisingly innovative in ways that traditional innovation indicators do not capture.

The considerations listed above do not all apply in equal measure to Krasnoyarsk Krai, still less to the Krasnoyarsk Agglomeration, itself the densest concentration of people and activity in Eastern Siberia. For example, both the Krai as a whole and the Agglomeration have relatively high levels of human capital and, as regards innovation, they benefit from the presence of an important science base in and around the city of Zheleznogorsk, which is a closed administrative-territorial formation (ZATO) in view of its importance to national security. Zheleznogorsk is not covered in this review – no data on the city are available and the OECD team was unable to visit it – but it is nevertheless important to the Agglomeration's economy and, in particular, its innovation potential. Many in Krasnoyarsk would like to develop an innovation cluster on the basis of Zheleznogorsk, with its nuclear and space sciences, but this will require finding some way to allow deeper economic engagement between the city and the surrounding agglomeration without compromising the security concerns of the federal authorities.

More generally, the Agglomeration benefits from the extent to which the science base of Krasnoyarsk reflects its economic needs, which is reflected in the data presented above on the award of higher degrees. One of the consequences of Soviet location and science policies is that much of the science base that the Russian Federation inherited from the former USSR is poorly adapted to the current needs of the economy, at national or regional levels. In some places this implies the need to sustain sometimes costly science infrastructure that may very well pay substantial dividends in the long run but that is of little direct economic benefit in the short to medium term, especially for regional economies (see OECD, 2006 for a discussion). In Krasnoyarsk, however, there is a substantial education and research base linked to the region's specialisation, which should make it easier for the authorities to link its knowledge assets to commercial activities. This issue will be explored in greater depth in Chapter 2.

It is also the case that Krasnoyarsk's economic base has proven to be quite robust. While employment in industry fell substantially in the early 2000s, as a result of a shake-out in manufacturing, it has been relatively stable in recent years, and the primary sector remains an important exporter to Russian and global markets. The problem is that the primary-sector firms often have limited forward and backward linkages in the Agglomeration's economy: deepening these is likely to be important to any drive to diversify economic activity in Krasnoyarsk. A further problem is that the economic base, though fairly strong and certain to remain rooted in the Krai, is very exposed to external markets. In recent years, the external environment has generally been rather good for the primary sector, but this cannot be taken for granted. The evidence suggests that real commodity prices for both energy and non-energy commodities are subject to long super-cycles, which entail decades-long deviations from long-run price trends. Recent work by Jacks (2013) suggests that the current set of super-cycles likely to be at, or close to, their peak. If this is so, an extended period of depressed prices could be in the offing. Even if it is not, Jacks' analysis, based on data covering the period from 1850, provides a healthy reminder that the price cycles for raw commodities can be very long and can turn at unexpected moments.

Nevertheless, many of the above-listed characteristics are all too familiar to policy makers and firms in Krasnoyarsk and they point to the very fundamental reality that an export-oriented economy located far from the major centres of demand faces an exceptional competitiveness challenge, particularly in manufacturing sectors. As noted above, it implies that tradables producers require an edge in terms of efficiency to offset the handicap of distance – they need to be that much better than their rivals; being just as good may not be enough. Moreover, the limited scope for pursuing economies of scale in many sectors suggests that producers in the non-resource tradable goods sector need other sources of competitive advantage, e.g. focusing on unique qualities of products, where scarcity can add value.

The challenge of diversification

Krasnoyarsk's industrial base, resting as it does on several important primary resources, is solid. In that sense, both the Krai and the Agglomeration are in a stronger position than many, perhaps most, of Russia's non-metropolitan regions. Nevertheless, this economic base will not, on its own, deliver the kind of high-productivity employment needed to assure the long-term prosperity of the population as a whole. The discussion thus returns to where it began: the question of economic diversification. The Krasnoyarsk Agglomeration needs to diversify the range of competitive tradable activities taking place there, while still husbanding its traditional strengths. Economic diversification is, in essence, about identifying one or more new and profitable niches in the international division of labour. While cutting-edge innovations might meet this challenge, for many economies, all that is needed is to discover new potential for producing established products profitably.

This is no mean feat. It is difficult to know *ex ante* what new activities might be competitive, given the cost structure of the economy, if only because the existing set of market prices in an economy reveal nothing about the potential profitability of alternative (as yet hypothetical) allocations of resources (Rodrik, 2004). Moreover, entrepreneurs moving into new (to the economy) sectors must often compete directly with established producers elsewhere, even before they have achieved critical mass or reached the levels of productivity they might be capable of attaining. As described above, this challenge is even more daunting in geographically remote, low-density places. Producers in such places who are oriented towards external markets must often cover higher transport and capital costs and then compete on distant markets with rivals who source inputs and services in much deeper, more competitive markets.

As will be seen, diversification efforts are likely to involve a great deal of trial and error; they cannot generally be determined and planned *ex ante*. This implies that the outcomes of successful diversification policies will be difficult to predict, so policy makers should resist the temptation to try to define the production structure towards which they believe the economy should evolve. The emphasis should be not on pre-determined "strategic sectors" but on fostering the emergence of new activities, some of which will fail and others of which will take root. Given Krasnoyarsk's starting point, this is likely to involve, to some extent, helping industrial producers to move up the value chain, thus diversifying on the basis of existing strengths. However, the particular directions this evolution will take are impossible to foresee, and other new activities are also likely to take off, given the right conditions.

The example of Finland is instructive. Its comparative advantage in forestry products is long-standing and obvious, but most of its other competitive strengths are not: not even the most well-informed economist could have foreseen its development of strong comparative advantages in such products as lifts, satellite navigation equipment, off-shore drilling equipment or – to name the most famous of all – cellular telecommunications. In 1990, the last of these products would hardly have merited a mention in any industrial strategy for Finland; ten years later, they were a cornerstone of Finnish growth, and a decade after that the country as a whole felt the fall-out from the rise of the iPhone, the eclipse of Nokia being as unexpected as its rise. Yet new sources of growth rapidly began to emerge based on the human capital and infrastructure associated with the telecoms sector. Finland thus continues to adjust, its success a product not of anyone's ability to predict, let alone direct, the productive structure of the economy, but of a set of transversal, sectoral and regional policies that create conditions favourable to innovation and entrepreneurship.[16]

The chapters that follow are therefore focused on some of the ways in which actors in the Krasnoyarsk Agglomeration can work to offset these disadvantages, in particular by:

- creating the most favourable environment possible for entrepreneurship, innovation and business development;
- improving connections between the enterprise sector and the region's science base, not least by finding ways to make more of the innovation potential of the ZATO Zheleznogorsk without compromising national security;
- strengthening competition and deepening product and labour markets, in particular by enhancing internal connectivity within the Agglomeration, as well as its external connections to the rest of the world;
- making the most of potential agglomeration economies by strengthening co-ordination of transport, labour market interventions and skills policies across the Agglomeration, as well as housing, land-use planning and service provision – in short, governance of the Agglomeration.

Notes

1. The term "Dutch disease" originated in connection with the Netherlands' development of natural gas deposits in the 1970s and usually refers to a situation in which a country suddenly discovers large natural resources, the extraction of which increases the equilibrium exchange rate and thereby puts pressure on the competitiveness of the other tradables sectors in the economy. In the Russian context, the discovery of natural resources as such is not the source of the problem. Rather, it is the fact that their full weight in the economy made itself felt only at the start of the transition, when the relative prices of primary raw materials, which had been held at artificially low levels under central planning, soared, as did resource exports. The subsequent boom in commodity prices in the early 2000s reinforced the problem. This exposed large differences in productivity between sectors in the Russian Federation. (The name "Dutch disease" is, in fact, rather unfortunate, as the Netherlands ultimately handled such a situation comparatively well.)

2. Ultimately the exchange rate is a reflection of the relationship between tradable and non-tradable prices in the economy, and the problem of sustaining (or achieving) competitiveness in non-resource tradables has been observed even in places like Greenland, which do not have their own currency (Paldam, 1997).

3. Regions have increasingly complained that the federal resources provided to finance recent federal mandates have been insufficient, placing a steadily increasing burden on regional budgets; some rating agencies agree with this assessment. For a recent discussion, see *Vedomosti*, 12 December 2013.

4. Particularly in a dynamic sense: many large resource-sector firms have high levels of productivity; the issue is how much pressure they face to improve their productivity performance.

5. Geography is a big part of the challenge here. The problem is not merely the Russian Federation's vast size and relatively dispersed settlement pattern but also the fact that it is far slower, more expensive and more difficult to build durable, good-quality roads over permafrost.

6. In July 2013, the head of the Federal Anti-Monopoly Service, Igor' Artem'ev, described the RZhD publicly as "a typical Soviet monopoly" that operated "at the expense of its customers" (OECD, 2014a).

7. The other PGMs are ruthenium, rhodium, osmium and iridium.

8. These and other data exclude the city of Zheleznogorsk, which is a closed administrative-territorial formation (ZATO) located within the Agglomeration. It remains a closed city on account of the sensitivity of the nuclear and space science assets that are located there.

9. Net inflows into Russia from abroad are included in the data, but figures tend to be low because migration mostly occurs internally between different areas of the county.

10. With the exception of Mana and Sukhobuzim Districts, differences in the ratio of working-age to total population are very small: the communities with more elderly people also tend to have fewer children. In 2010, the ratio of working-age to total

population in all segments of the Agglomeration except those two fell between 73.1% and 76.8%; the respective figures for Mana and Sukhobuzim were 67.3% and 70.1%.

11. In the estimates of gross value added (GVA) by major sector, the "budget sector" (sector 6) typically accounts for no more than about 1% of total value added, as against a figure of around 11% for the Russian Federation as a whole. This is too low an estimate to be credible and reflects the difficulty of estimating this sector's contribution to GVA.

12. See, for example, OECD (2012b): Skåne's innovation strength in pharmaceuticals and healthcare far exceeds its role as a producer in those sectors.

13. On some specifications, it ranks lower still, on others somewhat higher, since much depends on the weights assigned to overland and maritime distances. Economic history and theory both point to the importance of access to the sea, but it is not clear just how great the disadvantage of landlocked location should be. See Annex 1.A1 for a discussion.

14. This depends on processing technologies, transport costs and the structure of demand, all of which may change over time. Thus, most crude oil was refined near to the wellhead prior to 1940, but the low cost of crude-oil transport subsequently led to a shift whereby crude was moved all over the globe and most oil was refined close to the final consumers of the refined product.

15. Lenders must always consider the potential value of collateral: in a denser economy, it is likely to be higher because deeper markets imply greater opportunities for reallocation of assets. To take a simple example, if a borrower builds a plant in a large city and then goes out of business, the building and grounds are likely to be easier to re-sell advantageously than if he builds the same plant in a small town, where it may stand empty and derelict for a long period.

16. Markets will always produce surprises: as Hayek (1988: 76) famously observes, "The curious task of economics is to demonstrate to men how little they really know about what they imagine they can design."

Bibliography

Ahrend, R. (2006), "How to sustain growth in a resource based economy? The main concepts and their application to the Russian case", *OECD Economics Department Working Papers*, No. 478, OECD Publishing, Paris, http://dx.doi.org/10.1787/622880627053.

Behar, A. and A. Venables (2010), "Transports costs and international trade", in: A. De Palma et al. (eds.), *Handbook of Transport Economics*, Edward Elgar, pp. 97-115.

Blonigen, B. and W. Wilson (2006), "New Measures of Port Efficiency Using International Trade Data", *NBER Working* Paper, No. 12052, February.

Bloomberg News (2013), "Polar Sea Lane Finds Favor as Suez Security Doubts Grow", Bloomberg News, 12 September 2013, http://www.bloomberg.com/news/articles/2013-09-11/sea-levels-may-rise-69-centimeters-until-2100-on-ice-melt (accessed 10 December 2013).

Boulhol, H., A. de Serres and M. Molnar (2008), "The contribution of economic geography to GDP per capita", *OECD Economics Department Working Papers*, No. 602, OECD Publishing, Paris, http://dx.doi.org/10.1787/242216186836.

Chernyshov, S. (2013), "Pora lozhit'sya na rel'sy", *Ekspert-Sibir'*, No. 12, 25-31 March.

Clark, X., D. Dollar and A. Micco (2004), "Port efficiency, maritime transport costs and bilateral trade", *NBER Working Papers*, No. 10 353, March.

Combes, P.-P. and M. Lafourcade (2011), "Competition, market access and economic geography: Structural estimation and predictions for France", *Regional Science and Urban Economics*, No. 41, pp. 508-524.

Corden, W. and J. Neary (1982), "Booming sector and de-industrialisation in a small open economy", *Economic Journal*, Vol. 92, No. 368, pp. 825-848, December, Royal Economic Society.

De Sousa, J., T. Mayer and S. Zignago (2012), *Regional Science and Urban Economics*, No. 42, pp. 1 037-1 052.

Disdier, A. and K. Head (2008), "The puzzling persistence of the distance effect on bilateral trade", *Review of Economics and Statistics*, No. 90, pp. 37-48.

Dunford, M. (2009), "Regional development models", in: *International Encyclopedia of Human Geography*, Vol. 12, pp. 192-201.

Duranton, G. and D. Puga (2004), "Micro-foundations of urban agglomeration economies", *Handbook of Regional and Urban Economics*, in: J.V. Henderson and J.F. Thisse (ed.), *Handbook of Regional and Urban Economics*, Edition 1, Vol. 4, Chapter 48, pp. 2 063-2 117, Elsevier.

Egger, P. and A. Lassmann (2012), "The language effect in international trade: A meta-analysis", *Economics Letters*, No. 116, pp. 221-224.

Fally, T., R. Paillacar and C. Terra (2010), "Economic geography and wages in Brazil: Evidence from micro-data", *Journal of Development Economics*, No. 91, pp. 155-168.

Financial Times (2013), "Chinese cargo ship sets sail for Arctic short-cut", *Financial Times*, 11 August, http://www.ft.com/cms/s/2/05daa11e-0274-11e3-880d-00144feab7de.html#axzz3Q7k1hOjZ (accessed 15 June 2014).

Freshwater, D. (2012), "Modernising rural economies", presentation to the VIII OECD Rural Policy Conference, Krasnoyarsk, Russian Federation, 4 October.

Freshwater, D. (2011), "How should we think about 'peripherality'?", presentation to the NORA Region Conference, Copenhagen, 5 April.

Fridland, A. (2013), "O structure zatrat na aviaperevozki i effektivnosti predlagaemih mer", presentation to the Transport Union of Russia, Moscow.

Fujita, M., P. Krugman and A. Venables (1999), *The Spatial Economy: Cities, Regions, and International Trade*, MIT Press, Cambridge.

Gaddy, C. and F. Hill (2003), *The Siberian Curse: How Communist Planners Left Russia Out in the Cold*, Brookings Institution Press, Washington, DC.

González, A., L. Iacovone and H. Subhash (2013), "Russian volatility: Obstacle to firm survival and diversification", *World Bank Policy Research Working Papers*, No. 6 605, September.

Granville, C. (2013), "Russia's courts: A C", In K. Barysch (ed.), *Three Views on Modernisation and the Rule of Law in Russia*, Centre for European Reform, London.

Gros, D. and A. Steinherr (1995), *Winds of Change: Economic Transition in Eastern and Central Europe*, Longman, London.

Hanson, G. (2012), "The rise of middle kingdoms: Emerging economies in global trade", *Journal of Economic Perspectives*, No. 26, pp. 41-64.

Hanson, G. (1998), "Regional adjustment to trade liberalization", *Regional Science and Urban Economics*, No. 28, pp. 419-444.

Harris, C. (1954), "The market as a factor in the localization of industry in the United States", *Annals of the Association of American Geographers*, No. 64, pp. 315-348.

Hayek, F. (1988), *The Fatal Conceit: The Errors of Socialism*, University of Chicago Press, Chicago.

Head, K. and T. Mayer (2014), "Gravity equations: Workhorse, toolkit, and cookbook", in: *Handbook of International Economics*, Vol. 4, Elsevier.

Head, K. and T. Mayer (2011a), "Gravity, market potential and development", *Journal of Economic Geography*, No. 11, pp. 281-294.

Head, K. and T. Mayer (2011b), "Illusory border effects: Distance mismeasurement inflates estimates of home bias in trade", in: Brakman, S. and P. van Bergeijk (eds.), *The Gravity Model in International Trade: Advances and Applications*, Cambridge University Press.

Head, K. and T. Mayer (2004), "The empirics of agglomeration and trade", in: V. Henderson and J.F. Thisse (eds.), *Handbook of Regional and Urban Economics*, Vol. 4, pp. 2 609-2 669.

Head, K., T. Mayer and J. Ries (2010), "The erosion of colonial trade linkages after independence", *Journal of International Economics*, No. 81, pp. 1-14.

Hillberry, R. and D. Hummels (2008), "Trade responses to geographic frictions: A decomposition using micro-data", *European Economic Review*, No. 52, pp. 527-550.

Hummels, D. (1999), "Toward a geography of trade costs", mimeo, University of Chicago, Chicago, IL.

Hummels, D. and G. Schaur (2012), "Time as trade barrier", *NBER Working Papers*, No. 17 758, January.

IEA (2012), *World Energy Outlook*, OECD Publishing, Paris, http://dx.doi.org/10.1787/weo-2012-en.

IEA (2011), *World Energy Outlook*, OECD Publishing, Paris, http://dx.doi.org/10.1787/weo-2011-en.

IMF (n.d.), *Primary Commodity Prices*, http://www.imf.org/external/np/res/commod/index.aspx (accessed June 2014).

IMF (2013), *World Economic Outlook Database*, www.imf.org/external/pubs/ft/weo/2013/02/weodata/index.aspx.

Institute of Economy and Transport Development (IERT) (2012), *The Reference and Analytical Paper on the Railway Infrastructure Development in the Regions of the Russian Sea Ports Until 2015*, Institute of Economy and Transport Development, Moscow.

Jacks, D. (2013), "From boom to bust: A typology of real commodity prices in the long run", *NBER Working Papers*, No. 18 874, March.

Kichanov, M. (2013), "Eto pokhozhe na shutku", *Ekspert-Sibir'*, No. 12, 25-31 March.

Limão, N. and A. Venables (2001), "Infrastructure, geographical disadvantage, transport costs and trade", *World Bank Economic Review*, No. 15, pp. 451-479.

Lloydslist (n.d.), http://directories.lloydslist.com/ (accessed 25 November 2013).

Martin, R. and P. Sunley (2006), "Path dependence and regional economic evolution", *Journal of Economic Geography*, No. 6, pp. 395-437.

Mayer, T. and S. Zignago (2011), "Notes on CEPII's distances measures (GeoDist)", *CEPII Working Paper 2011-25*.

Mikhailova, T. (2004), "Essays on Russian economic geography: Measuring spatial inefficiency", PhD Thesis, Department of Economics, Pennsylvania State University, August.

Nasyrova, E. (2013), "Role of Russian Railways logistics in transit development on Asia-Europe axis", *Gudok*, No. 19.

OECD (2014a), *OECD Economic Outlook: Statistics and Projections* (database), http://dx.doi.org/10.1787/eo-data-en.

OECD (2014b), *OECD Productivity Statistics* (database), http://www.oecd.org/std/productivity-stats/.

OECD (2014c), *OECD Economic Surveys: Russian Federation 2013*, OECD Publishing, Paris, http://dx.doi.org/10.1787/eco_surveys-rus-2013-en.

OECD (2014d), *OECD Regional Statistics* (database), http://dx.doi.org/10.1787/region-data-en.

OECD (2013a), *Inventory of Estimated Budgetary Support and Tax Expenditures for Fossil Fuels 2013*, OECD Publishing, Paris, http://dx.doi.org/10.1787/9789264187610-en.

OECD (2013b), *OECD Territorial Reviews: Antofagasta, Chile 2013*, OECD Publishing, Paris, http://dx.doi.org/10.1787/9789264203914-en.

OECD (2012a), *OECD Territorial Reviews: The Chicago Tri-State Metropolitan Area, United States 2012*, OECD Publishing, Paris, http://dx.doi.org/10.1787/9789264170315-en.

OECD (2012b), *OECD Territorial Reviews: Skåne, Sweden 2012*, OECD Publishing, Paris, http://dx.doi.org/10.1787/9789264177741-en.

OECD (2012c), *OECD Territorial Reviews: Småland-Blekinge, Sweden 2012*, OECD Publishing, Paris, http://dx.doi.org/10.1787/9789264169517-en.

OECD (2011a), *OECD Economic Surveys: Russian Federation 2011*, OECD Publishing, Paris, http://dx.doi.org/10.1787/eco_surveys-rus-2011-en.

OECD (2011b), *OECD Territorial Reviews: NORA Region 2011: The Faroe Islands, Greenland, Iceland and Coastal Norway*, OECD Publishing, Paris, http://dx.doi.org/10.1787/9789264097629-en.

OECD (2009), "OECD Economic Outlook interim report", OECD, Paris, April.

OECD (2008), "Territorial grids of OECD member countries", OECD, Paris, available at: www.oecd.org/gov/regional-policy/43428422.pdf.

OECD (2006), *OECD Economic Surveys: Russian Federation 2006*, OECD Publishing, Paris, http://dx.doi.org/10.1787/eco_surveys-rus-2006-en.

Paldam, M. (1997), "Dutch disease and rent seeking: The Greenland model", *European Journal of Political Economy*, Vol. 13, No. 3, September.

Portugal-Perez, A. and J. Wilson (2012), "Export performance and trade facilitation reform: Hard and soft infrastructure", *World Development*, No. 40, pp. 1 295-1 307.

Redding, S. and A. Venables (2004), "Economic geography and international inequality", *Journal of International Economics*, No. 62, pp. 53-82.

Rodrik, D. (2004), "Industrial policy for the twenty-first century", *Faculty Research Working Papers Series*, John F. Kennedy School of Government, Harvard University, November.

Santos Silva, J. and S. Tenreyro (2006), "The Log of Gravity", *The Review of Economics and Statistics*, No. 88, Vol. 4, pp. 641-658, November.

Schuur, E. et al. (2008), "Vulnerability of permafrost carbon to climate change: Implications for the global carbon cycle", *BioScience*, Vol. 58, No. 8, pp. 701-714.

SFU (2012), "Background report for the OECD Territorial Review of Krasnoyarsk", Siberian Federal University, Krasnoyarsk, Russian Federation, November.

Sutela, P. (2005), "The political economy of Putin's Russia", *BOFIT Russia Review*, No. 3, March.

The Economist (2007), "Guyana: Looking south. Bridging a divide of language and history", 11 January, www.economist.com/node/8525813.

Timmer, M. and I. Voskoboynikov (2013), "Is mining fuelling long-run growth in Russia? Industry productivity growth trends since 1995", GGDC Research Memorandum.

Villeret, G. (n.d.), Population Mondiale, http://www.populationmondiale.com/#sthash.Q0cEA96C.dpbs (accessed 25 November 2013).

World Economic Forum (2013), *Global Competitiveness Report 2013-14*, World Economic Forum, Geneva, available at: http://www10.iadb.org/intal/intalcdi/PE/2013/12834.pdf

World Bank (2014), *Diversified Development: Making the Most of Natural Resources in Eurasia*, The World Bank, Washington, DC.

World Bank (2009a), "Adapting to climate change in Europe and Central Asia", The World Bank, Washington, DC, 1 June, available at: www.worldbank.org/eca/climate/ECA_CCA_Full_Report.pdf.

World Bank (2009b), World Development Report 2009: Reshaping Economic Geography, The World Bank, Washington, DC.

Annex 1.A1
The regional market potential indicator

Introduction

The role of geography in explaining economic performance is receiving increasing attention. Many studies have highlighted the core-periphery nature of economic development: while regions in a central location may attract investments and workers, regions in peripheral locations may risk industrial decline and dependence of national transfers. This is becoming more important as recent studies using highly disaggregated data are showing that trade may be highly localised over short distances (Hillberry and Hummels, 2008). On the other hand, globalisation is opening new opportunities associated to increase in productivity and South-South trade (Hanson, 2012). Connectivity among regions is often viewed as a way to generate inclusive development while preserving productivity gains (World Bank, 2009b).

One indicator intending to assess this regional attractiveness is the market potential. It is a measure summarising the proximity to demand from a given location. Empirical studies have computed this indicator for national economies and found significant and robust correlations with wages, labour reallocation across industries, firm location choices and migration flows. This annex explains how the OECD has calculated such an indicator for regions. The regional market potentials computed in this dataset correspond to more than 400 regions in 29 countries, accounting for more than 75% of world GDP in 2012 (IMF, 2013). This annex presents the details on the method of calculation, sources of data employed, potential usages and limitations.

Conceptual framework

Understanding the role of interactions between economies has been explored for a while. Harris (1954) considers that such interactions are more important than factor endowments (natural resources, labour abundance). He emphasises the role of accessibility to large markets by combining in a single indicator a proxy for market size and a proxy for transport costs. Taking gross domestic product (GDP) as a measure of market size and bilateral distance, the market potential proposed by Harris for a location *i* would be:

$$HMP_i = \sum_j GDP_j / Dist_{ij} \quad (1)$$

where the subscript *j* denotes potential destination markets. The reason for using distance comes from the intuition that trade costs between producer and consumer are increasing in distance. A more general interpretation would be that important economic interactions affecting competitiveness like knowledge transfer are strongly localised. Note that bilateral distance ($Dist_{ij}$) is dividing GDP, which implicitly assumes that distance is reducing the accessibility in a linear way. Moreover, the impact of distance is the same for all markets with an absolute elasticity of 1. This indicator has been used to explain industrial or firm location choices. Subsequent studies have made several refinements to this measure. Three are of particular interest for the construction of our indicator: internal distance, distance decay and trade-costs components.

Paradoxically enough, it is essential to incorporate a measure of internal distance – the distance from a region to its own market,[1] and more importantly, to define a proxy for its own accessibility. One alternative is to propose an ideal shape of regions and compute the average distance between two points. For example, if the shape is a disk, the land area is enough to compute the average distance through the following formula:

$$dist_{ii} = \sqrt{\frac{area_i}{\pi}} \quad (2)$$

As a consequence, internal trade costs are larger the larger a region's land area. Head and Mayer (2011b) note that this equation is assuming that population is uniformly distributed across the disk. Redding and Venables (2004) and Gros and Steinherr (1995) among others, multiply the internal distance by a factor of 1/3 to take into account that population is actually agglomerated and the average distance is lower. Head and Mayer argue that the factor 2/3 represents better an economy in which production in sub-national regions is concentrated in a single point at the centre of the disk and that consumers are uniformly distributed across the disk.

The distance-decay function is a second concern. The original measure proposes that bilateral distance is reducing the market potential with an (absolute) elasticity of 1. In some works, it is assumed an elasticity of 0.5 (Gros and Steinherr, 1995). This elasticity can be measured using trade gravity equations.[2] A meta-analysis of 1 467 estimates by Disdier and Head (2008) found a mean value of 0.9.

Finally, the literature has introduced many other factors affecting trade costs and thus market potential, such as sharing a common language or a common border, being a landlocked region, being part of a custom union, and so on. In the particular case of estimating market potential for sub-national units, it is also important to distinguish between markets within the country and abroad because important "border effects" have been identified in the empirical literature. Two empirical strategies have been followed. The first estimates trade gravity equations where these additional trade costs enter as dummies (for instance, whether two partners share a common language or not). The regression coefficients are then used as weights.[3] The second, preferred for regional analyses, allocates weights arbitrarily and performs a sensitivity analysis. Gross and Steinherr (1995), for example, compute a gravity index to assess the evolution of the regional integration of Russian regions with European and Asian nations. They propose the following indicator:

$$MP_i = \underbrace{\sum_{j \neq i} GDP_j \frac{GDPpc_j}{GDPpc_{max}} d_{ij}^{-0.5} u_{ij}}_{\text{Non-local } MP_i} + \underbrace{b * GDP_i \frac{GDPpc_i}{GDPpc_{max}} d_{ij}^{-0.5}}_{\text{Local } MP_i} \quad (3)$$

This market potential index address the considerations mentioned above.

- An elasticity of 0.5 results in a much lower impact of physical distance.

- It incorporates additional trade costs through the parameter u_{ij}. This is a dummy variable that takes values of 1.2 when the partners are Russian regions and 1 for the others relationships (Russian partner with a country or among countries).[4]
- This version includes a term for the internal market, that we term local market potential. Its specification uses an internal distance d_{ii} as the only trade cost. This distance is defined as in equation (2), but is multiplied by a factor of 1/3 like in Redding and Venables (2004), which supposes a highly agglomerated region (producers and consumers are very close within the region making the distance "smaller").
- Finally, this indicator introduces a weight b defined as:

$$b = \frac{\sum_i Non\text{-}Local\ MP_i}{\sum_i Local\ MP_i} \quad (4)$$

This forces the weight of the internal and external markets to be equal. In practice, the weight is higher than 1, reflecting a potential non-linear reduction in trade flows when shipments must cross a national frontier (the so-called "border effect" in gravity equations). Finally, the proxy for market size combines the GDPs as in the original equation (1) with a ratio of GDP per capita. This ratio is the GDP per capita in the destination market deflated by the highest GDP per capita among all countries/regions.[5]

Extensions to the basic model

The original Gros-Steinherr (1995) market potential in equation (3) assumes a distance elasticity of 0.5 and an internal distance weighted by a factor of 1/3. As already discussed, recent studies suggest that an elasticity of 1 and a factor of 2/3 could better fit trade flows. In addition, it is possible to refine the estimation by introducing a national border effect (the parameter u_{ij} in equation (3)) and additional trade costs for international markets. The literature on trade gravity equation suggests three variables:[6] common language, colonial link and contiguity. In addition, the literature on trade facilitation and logistics highlights the importance of ports. Taking into account these considerations results in four variants of the market potential.

The three additional variables for international trade costs have been weighted[7] using coefficients found in empirical work. In the case of common language, we employ the average coefficient of 0.44 found in a meta-analysis by Egger and Lassmann (2012). For the other variables, there is no consensus.[8] However, a meta-analysis by Head and Mayer (2014) considers 266 regressions and finds mean and median coefficients of 0.66 and 0.52. The latter is also the simple mean of the estimates reached by Santos Silva and Tenreyro (2006), Head, Mayer and Ries (2010) and De Sousa, Mayer and Zignago (2012). Regarding the colonial link, the average and median coefficients are 0.75 and 0.84.[9] The effect of colonial link may also be decreasing over time. This is what Head, Mayer and Ries (2010) have found using trade flows for a long span of time. Their results suggest that the effect stabilises around a 25% of additional trade with respect to the situation of never having a colonial link. This corresponds to a coefficient of 0.22, which is employed in the analyses here.[10]

It is also possible to refine further the indicator by incorporating a measure of access to ports. Several studies have shown that landlocked status, port efficiency and trade facilitation strongly affect trade performance (Limão and Venables, 2001; Portugal-Perez and Wilson, 2012). Incorporating access to ports may better characterise the market potential for regions in remote countries (like Australia, Chile or South Africa), or regions landlocked but well connected by inland ports (like many states in the United States). The specification of the function is, however, more challenging than for the other trade costs. The traditional measure of bilateral distance among capitals should be broken into two components. The first is the distance covered by land (by railway or road) and the second the ship transport (by the sea or river). This allocation is quite difficult, as many regions may have several alternatives and combinations of overland and sea routes. Computing all these possibilities is time-consuming and requires data not publicly available (see Hummels and Schaur, 2012, for more details on this approach). A simpler method inspired in Blonigen and Wilson (2006) is to select the closest ports for origin and destination. This allows to compute the geodesic distance between the regions and ports (the overland distance) and the geodesic distance between both ports (the overseas distance),[11] and then adjust both distances by parameters in the distance-decay function.

There is some guidance on the parameters from the empirical literature. As already explained, the parameter ranges between -1 and -0.9 when using the traditional measure of bilateral distance among capitals. In the case of overland and sea transport, different freight costs and different distance-decay functions for trade may apply. To better understand the relationship between trade and distance in these cases, researchers separate the effect into two elasticities. The first corresponds to the impact of freight rates on trade. A recent survey by Behar and Venables (2010) reports values between -2 and -3.5. The second elasticity refers to the impact of distance on freight rates. The literature systematically finds that transport by sea is cheaper than by land. Hummels (2001) has found coefficients of 0.2 for sea transport, 0.275 for road transport and 0.39 for rail transport.

Multiplying both elasticities gives an estimation of the elasticity of trade with respect to distance that we use in the specifications of market potential. For example, for sea transport, such elasticity ranges between -0.4 and -0.7, well below the coefficient of -0.9 issued from the meta-analysis by Disdier and Head (2008). Among many possible explanations, this gap could be attributed to the more expensive land transport. If we let the first elasticity (trade with respect to freight rates) equal among modes of transport, it is the second elasticity (freight rates with respect to distance) that determines the contribution of each mode. Taking the average of Hummels' elasticities for rail and road modes (0.33), we observe that the overland elasticity is 50% higher than the elasticity for sea transport (0.2). If we set the total impact of trade with respect to distance to -1 and assume that both modes can account for all the effect, we get a proportion of 60% for overland and 40% for overseas. To compute distances between regional and country capitals to the closest port, we use the information on latitudes and longitudes of ports in the Lloyd's list.

Data

Regional data

The first source of data is the *OECD Regional Database* with information at sub-national level for all OECD countries and a selected group of eight non-OECD countries. This information includes GDP, population and land area for regions in

42 countries at the first hierarchical sub-national level (TL2). The non-OECD countries are: Argentina, Brazil, the People's Republic of China, Colombia, India, Indonesia, the Russian Federation and South Africa. The information is available starting in 1995 for most of the countries but with many gaps. Actually, two OECD countries (Iceland and Israel) and one non-OECD country (Argentina) have too few observations to include them in the regional analysis. The remaining 39 countries contain data for more than 600 regions, with important gaps, between 1995 and 2010. The most important cases among OECD countries concern New Zealand and Switzerland (series shorter than four years). Among non-OECD countries, Indonesia has no data on regional land areas. All these cases are also discarded. Chile[12] and Greece[13] have minor issues requiring some adjustments but can be included. The Turkish series stops in 2001.

China, India and the Russian Federation deserve special attention. In the case of China, the vast majority of the regions (31 out of 34) have complete series for the period 2004-09. As the market potential measure requires a square matrix, the best choice is to consider only this period to build the Chinese regional market potentials. India has 30 out of 35 regions with all the data required to compute the market potential for the period 2000-08 as shown in Table 1.A1.1. Three other regions (IN08, IN21, IN26) have one or two missing years that will be extrapolated. Unfortunately, five regions must be excluded from the analyses due to data limitations. This affects not only Indian market potential but (to a lesser extent) other countries, as these five regions are also potential destination markets for all countries and regions of the world. Russian regions have important gaps in three regions (the Nenets, Khanty-Mansi and Yamalo-Nenets Autonomous Districts) for which an extrapolation is made. One region (Chechnya) is discarded from the analysis. The end of the period for most of the countries is established in 2009. A limited number of countries have regional data in 2010. Specifically, three OECD countries (Canada, Korea and the United States) and two non-OECD countries (Brazil and the Russian Federation).[14]

Country data

The same data required at regional level are also needed for the rest of the world, aggregated at country level. These data are taken from the World Bank dataset World Development Indicators (WDI). A total of 174 countries have all the data needed to compute market potentials. In some cases, minor imputations are made to include them (Table 1.A1.1).

Geographic data

Bilateral distances between capitals can be computed using latitudes and longitudes. At country level, CEPII offers a bilateral dataset for 225 countries (Mayer and Zignago, 2011). In the case of the regional units, latitudes and longitudes were taken from the World Gazetteer (WG)[15] (one of the original sources used to generate the CEPII dataset). This website gathers geographic and population information for the largest cities and towns in many countries. Unfortunately, the WG information can only be matched with the *OECD Regional Database* using the names of regions.[16] Differences in naming required a match region by region. The exercise included all regions of all 42 countries in the OECD dataset, in order to make this information useful for other future purposes. The matching was very good in all cases.[17] Additional information to refine trade costs like dummies for common language, colonial link and contiguity among countries are also available at country level in Mayer and Zignago (2011). Data on ports comes from Lloyds's list.[18] This directory provides latitudes and longitudes for almost 3 000 ports in

192 countries or territories. The advantages of this dataset are the focus on commercially relevant ports and the availability of some information on port characteristics, like the presence of railway, dry-docks, facilities for containers, services of repair and maintenance, etc.

Table 1A1.1. **Special cases in the World Development Indicators dataset**[1]

Country	Data available	Gaps	Status	Action taken
Afghanistan	2002-10	1995-2001	Left-censored	
Libya	1999-2009	1995-98; 2010	Left- and right-censored	
Qatar	2000-10	1995-99	Left-censored	Not considered for the entire period
Sao Tome and Principe	2001-10	1995-2000	Left-censored	
Timor-Leste	1999-2010	1995-98	Right-censored	
Barbados	1995-2009	2010	Right-censored	
Djibouti	1995-2009	2010	Right-censored	Extrapolation for 2010
Iran	1995-2009	2010	Right-censored	
Iraq	1997-2010	1995-96	Left-censored	Extrapolation for 1995-96
Argentina	1995-2006	2007-10	Right-censored	Inclusion of IMF data for 2007-10[2]

Notes: 1. In addition, 19 small countries and islands do not have GDP data and one country (Jamaica) has only information for one year. 2. Data come from the *World Economic Outlook Database* which provides GDP in current prices, GDP deflator and PPP conversion rates. The original source for GDP is Haver Analytics. We reproduce here a note provided in the World Economic Outlook dataset: "Private analysts are of the view that real GDP growth was significantly lower than the official estimates in 2008 and 2009. However, the difference between private and official estimates of real GDP growth has narrowed in 2010."

Notes

1. The fact that industries contribute to the regional GDP creates obvious endogeneity issues if local GDP is employed. See the survey by Head and Mayer (2004) for the empirical treatment of this problem.

2. This is valid for a general class of trade models. One of the main assumptions behind this result is that trade costs are modeled as an *ad valorem* tax equivalent (iceberg costs). While this may be valid for some trade costs (e.g. tariffs), many others are subject to non-linearities (shipment costs), making per-unit costs more realistic in many cases.

3. Because of data limitations, this strategy has been used mainly to study country-level market potentials (Redding and Venables, 2004; Head and Mayer, 2011a; see Fally, Paillacar and Terra, 2010, for an exception using regional trade data).

4. It also takes values of 1.1 for "regional groupings" of countries, but the specific list of countries/regions included in this category is not provided in the text.

5. The absence of trade data at sub-national levels for enough countries makes the choice of the second method more attractive.

6. The literature has also considered other variables like migration flows, institutional quality, tariffs, non-tariff measures, affiliation to WTO or regional trade agreements, sharing a common currency, etc. Unfortunately, endogeneity problems cast doubts on the effects found in the literature for these variables, making their inclusion in the market potential measure much more involved.

7. In virtually all empirical applications, these three variables enter in a log linear relationship, i.e. the log of trade is regressed on dummies for common language, shared border and colonial link. As a consequence, in the market potential equation (3), the weights should enter exponentially.

8. The coefficient associated to sharing a common border (contiguity) varies widely from 0.37 (Santos Silva and Tenreyro, 2006), to 0.55 (Head, Mayer and Ries, 2010), to 0.67 (De Sousa, Mayer and Zignago, 2012). We chose these three studies because they have several important methodological advantages: they include exporter and importer fixed effects to control for unobservable determinants of trade flows and implement an estimation that addresses many potential biases, including the high number of zero trade values flows (the method is "Poisson Pseudo-Maximum Likelihood" described in detail in Santos Silva and Tenreyro, 2006).

9. The meta-analysis is much less informative here, as it is based on 60 regressions only.

10. Given the log-linear relationship in gravity equations, the effect is measured like this: $100*[\exp(.22)-1]= 24.8\%$.

11. It can also be a distance over a river. In practice, most of the cases are transport through the sea. Moreover, we did not find estimations in the literature for the transport costs over a river. We assume that the elasticity for river and sea transport is the same.

12. Information was not available for any region in 1995 and not available for two regions (CL14, CL15) for the whole period.

13. Information was not available for 2009-10.

14. Data are also available for Indonesian regions on GDP, but as explained before, surface data are not available.

15. Villeret, G. (World Gazetteer) (n.d.), Population mondiale, www.populationmondiale.com/#sthash.Q0cEA96C.dpbs (accessed 25 November 2013).

16. A dummy variable identifies regional capitals in the WG dataset but it is often at a lower spatial level than TL2.

17. The cases of Leningrad Oblast, Moscow Oblast and Bogota deserve a comment. Each of these cities is a capital for two regional units. The choice was to take the geographic coordinates in WG for one of the cases and geographic coordinates in Wikipedia for the other cases. In every case, bilateral distances are very small for obvious reasons.

18. Lloyds List (n.d.), http://directories.lloydslist.com (accessed 25 November 2013).

Chapter 2

Mobilising and developing human potential in the Krasnoyarsk Agglomeration*

This chapter focuses on the policies needed to help make the most of the Agglomeration's human potential, particularly by promoting entrepreneurship, human capital formation and innovation. It examines the business climate in the Agglomeration, which is fairly strong overall by Russian standards, before looking at its performance with respect to innovation and entrepreneurship, which have been disappointing. It presents a number of recommendations for creating a more integrated, Agglomeration-wide approach to skills and labour market policy, and at the potential for local action to stimulate more innovation.

* The statistical data for Israel are supplied by and under the responsibility of the relevant Israeli authorities. The use of such data by the OECD is without prejudice to the status of the Golan Heights, East Jerusalem and Israeli settlements in the West Bank under the terms of international law.

As noted in Chapter 1, diversification is not a *sine qua non* for growth in the Russian Federation, the Krai or the Krasnoyarsk Agglomeration, and one should not exaggerate the potential for diversification of activity in the Agglomeration except perhaps over the very long term. The economy is very likely to remain heavily dependent on its existing strengths and these are considerable. The case for working towards further diversification is two-fold. First, it will reduce somewhat the vulnerability of the economy to commodity-price cycles. Secondly, it will create new opportunities for high-productivity employment. Perhaps the chief difficulty with heavy reliance on extractive industries is that they are very capital-intensive but do not employ much labour. The risk is that a mining or oil-producing region has a small number of extremely high-productivity jobs in the core sector and the high-value business services linked to it, and a much larger number of jobs in relatively low-productivity proximity services. This is not a very satisfactory picture for policy makers or the public. Given Krasnoyarsk's population and human capital, it would represent a waste of both economic and, perhaps more important, human potential. The point of a diversification strategy, therefore, is less to bring about a fundamental shift in the sectoral structure of the economy than to create new opportunities for people with skills and talent to employ them productively in and around Krasnoyarsk.[1] This chapter thus explores policies to mobilise and develop those talents, focusing on three areas: entrepreneurship, human capital formation and innovation.

Two other initial observations may be relevant for Krasnoyarsk:

- For a place as small as the Krasnoyarsk Agglomeration, a fair degree of specialisation is inevitable – it cannot hope to achieve "critical mass" in many sectors. Krasnoyarsk's diversification ambitions should thus be tempered by recognition of this limitation, as well as the conditions affecting diversification efforts in Eastern Siberia that are described in Chapter 1.
- Diversification is not a natural process. It rarely takes place without significant policy intervention (Hausmann and Rodrik, 2003). This makes things rather more complicated because such assistance most often fails to deliver. To put it bluntly, the most successful economies in the world since 1945 have pursued policies that were extremely heterodox from the perspective of conventional economics, but most economies that pursued heterodox, interventionist policies performed very poorly.

It is clear, then, that diversification poses a serious challenge for policy, and one might argue that Russia's efforts to develop new non-resource tradable sectors are simply a case of fighting the country's comparative advantage. For Krasnoyarsk, however, the challenge looks more manageable: while the region's small population limits the scope for diversification, it also limits the need. The emergence of new, competitive activities on a fairly modest (by global standards) scale could make a significant difference in terms of productivity, resilience and quality of life, particularly if allied to sound management of the region's resource wealth.

Chapter 1 has already described many of the barriers to diversification in Russia overall, as well as those that are particularly relevant to Krasnoyarsk. This chapter therefore focuses on policy responses to some of these barriers and on the main building blocks of a strategy to enhance productivity and promote a degree of diversification in the Krasnoyarsk Agglomeration. It begins by looking at what can be done to create a business environment that is conducive to experimentation and entrepreneurship. The discussion then turns to policies concerned with human capital and the labour market before shifting the focus at last to innovation.

Creating a favourable climate for entrepreneurship

Structural policy reforms can create a much better environment for diversification

At micro level, there are a host of policies that can foster or impede the emergence of new sectors and activities. For a start, reducing the burden of product-market regulation (PMR) could directly address some of the anti-competitive barriers that impede the entry and growth of new firms and activities. While there has been significant progress here in recent years, the OECD's PMR indicators suggest that barriers to entrepreneurship remain high by the standards of most OECD countries, though they are lower than those found in many emerging markets. Overall, only 25% of Russian employment is in small and medium-sized enterprises (SMEs), compared to an average of 50% in OECD countries, and SMEs' share in value added is estimated at just about 20% (Interfax, 2012). This reflects the dominant role of large, often state-owned, enterprises,[2] the poor business climate and poor access to financing. Attitudes towards entrepreneurship also matter. The latest Global Entrepreneurship Monitoring (GEM) review puts the Russian Federation last among 69 countries in terms of willingness to start a business (GEM, 2013), apparently a reflection of perceptions of the business environment and the potential returns to entrepreneurship. Nevertheless, there have been some positive steps in recent years. Restrictions and red tape have been reduced, as reflected in the improvement in OECD PMR indicators for Russia (Figure 2.1). The share of firms reporting that licencing, tax and court administrations were significant obstacles to their business in 2011 also fell significantly compared to 2008 (World Bank, 2013).

Figure 2.1. **Regulatory reform progress, 2008-13**

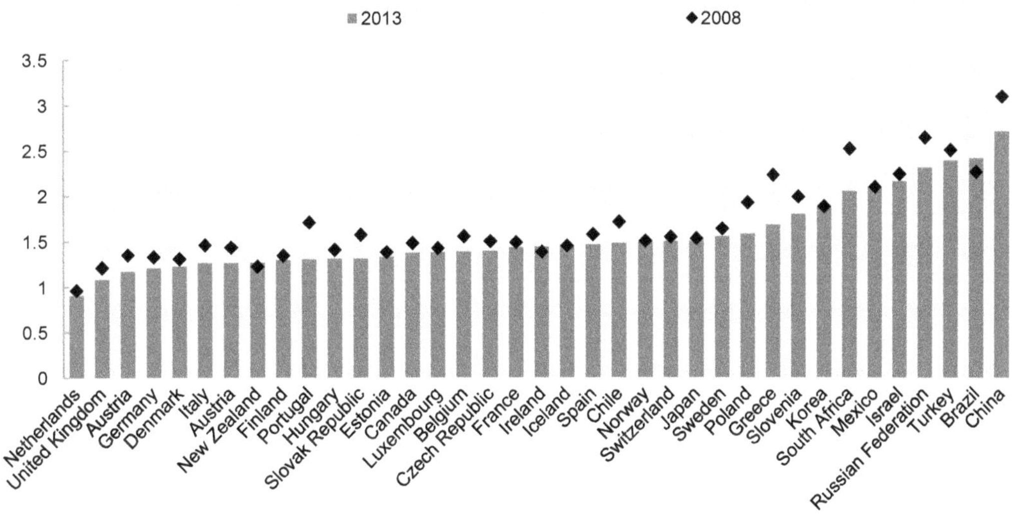

Note: Countries omitted where product-market regulation for 2013 had not yet been calculated as of January 2014.

Source: OECD (2013a), *OECD Product Market Regulation Statistics* (database), http://dx.doi.org/10.1787/pmr-data-en.

Russia has taken a number of steps to reduce the administrative burden on start-ups and SMEs, including the creation of "one-stop shops" for handling administrative procedures, reductions in licencing requirements and streamlined processes for claiming the zero VAT rate. However, there was no progress introducing a "deemed clearance" regime (OECD, 2014). The Ministry of Economic Development is currently working on simplifying the registration process for both legal entities and sole proprietors. The National Entrepreneurial Initiative "Improvement of Business Climate", initiated at the end of 2011, includes 11 roadmaps to make business processes simpler, faster and cheaper. Work on preparing seven roadmaps has been completed and the process of implementation in pilot regions has started.

Regulatory impact assessment (RIA) was introduced in 2010 in an effort to avoid imposing excessively costly regulations on firms. It will be extended to customs and tax regulations and to the regional (2014) and municipal levels (2015), where many barriers to business entrepreneurship originate (European Bank for Reconstruction and Development, 2012). However, a recent OECD assessment of RIA implementation finds that so far, it is relatively weak (OECD, 2014). There is still a lack of methodological clarity and many RIAs are of poor quality and fail to conform to the guidelines set. For the most part, RIA is in the hands of the institutions drafting regulations, with only a final check by the Ministry of Economic Development. There is still a need for capacity building, particularly (but not only) at regional and local levels, and also for facilitating access to information for non-state actors. Thus, RIA is not yet the kind of tool that it could be for promoting a better business environment, but a great deal has been done in the last few years, and work on improving and embedding RIA continues.

As noted in Chapter 1, one of the problems with economic volatility is that it tends to favour incumbents relative to entrants, even where the former are less productive. The same is true of weak competition: strengthening competition in product markets should, over time, create a context more favourable to diversification. Not only potential competition policy reforms, which tend to be fall under federal jurisdiction, but also some infrastructure investments – over which the Krai and the municipalities of the Agglomeration have more of a say – should be considered in this light. Improved connectivity can strengthen competition and deepen both product and labour markets. This is one reason the present review places such emphasis on internal and external connectivity. Of course, enhanced connectivity brings with it not only new opportunities but also new competitive threats. While many incumbent firms may struggle to meet this challenge and the ensuing structural change may be painful for some communities, such a development is to be welcomed, since a model based on weak connectivity and *de facto* protected markets is, by definition, self-limiting. For regional and local policy makers, this suggests a need for integrated development strategies that help prepare individuals and firms for the new competitive conditions, not least by improving human capital and reducing barriers to private-sector development (OECD, 2009a).

There is also much that governments at all levels can do to help firms and entrepreneurs in the non-resource tradable sectors to compete more effectively as markets become increasingly integrated and competitive. In particular, steps to improve the performance of non-tradable sectors can be critical, since producers of tradables depend on them for services. An inefficient non-tradable sector is a real competitive handicap. At national level, this may involve reforms to major network infrastructure sectors, such as those currently under consideration by the government. At regional and local levels, it may include measures to improve the performance – and reduce the cost – of local utilities and public services.

Human capital and institutional quality are the key variables

Finally, there are two cross-cutting issues that have profound implications for Krasnoyarsk's ability to stimulate entrepreneurship and innovation, as well as to raise productivity. The first is human capital. A large body of work suggests that human capital is among the key determinants of regional performance and, in particular, that reducing the share of low-skilled people in the workforce probably matters more for a region's growth than increasing the share of high-skilled people in the workforce. The drag effect on growth of large pools of unskilled or low-skilled labour is substantial (OECD, 2013b). This is, moreover, the kind of challenge that must be addressed at regional and local level, for the following reason. Very highly skilled labour tends to be quite mobile: if attractive opportunities for such individuals exist in a place, it will probably be possible to attract highly qualified professionals to occupy them. By contrast, less skilled workers are less mobile – and yet their presence is often essential to employing very high-human capital individuals. If the skills required by local firms and industries are not generated locally, shortages may result, even in the presence of high levels of un- or under-employment. Interaction between technical and vocational institutions and industry in updating training content, equipment and facilities, as well as providing career guidance and introducing new programmes and cost-effective delivery approaches, has become a key feature of technical and vocational systems across the world. This is most efficiently done at the level of the functional labour market – i.e. the Agglomeration (OECD, 2012a). Subsequent sections of this chapter thus explore human capital and labour-market challenges in depth.

The second issue is institutional quality. There has been great deal of work in recent years on measuring the quality of institutions and the variation across countries (see Kaufmann and Kraay, 2008, for a review), as well as considerable debate about the relationship between institutional quality and economic performance. It is now fairly widely accepted that there is a link between the two (e.g. Woolcock, 1998; North, 1990; Acemoglu, Johnson and Robinson, 2001, 2005; Easterly and Levine, 2003; Dollar and Kraay, 2003; Rodrik et al., 2004). That said, there remains controversy over the nature of the causal links between them. While some have argued strongly that better institutions contribute to better economic performance, institutional quality may also be a product of economic performance (i.e. it may be endogenous to the economic process)[3] or both may be driven by some third factor – most likely, human capital. In fact, these are not mutually exclusive views and the relationship is thus likely to involve a number of direct and indirect causal links.

This is an area where Russia undeniably faces particular challenges. Its rank of 64th out of 148 on the World Economic Forum's (WEF) Global Competitiveness Index for 2013-14 leaves the country very much in the middle ranks globally. This ranking reflects Russia's perceived strengths with respect to such factors as macroeconomic conditions and market size. However, the WEF survey of Russian executives finds that these advantages are largely offset by institutional weaknesses: the Russian Federation ranked 121st in the WEF index of the quality of institutions, 126th on goods market efficiency and 121st on financial market development. Corruption, tax rates, tax regulations and inefficient bureaucracy were ranked as the most problematic factors to doing business, with corruption in first place by a substantial margin. The contrast between the WEF's high rating of Russia on key economic endowments and its very low ratings on institutional factors underscores the price that the country continues to pay for weak institutions: its undoubted strengths are simply not being fully developed. It is important to stress the importance of institutional weakness in the context of entrepreneurship and diversification. As noted in Chapter 1, weak institutional environments are far more damaging to newer and smaller firms than to established incumbents (*cf.* Charron, Lapuente and Nistotskaya, 2012).

These findings coincide with other external assessments of governance in Russia, which point to progress over time but still underscore its weaknesses *vis-à-vis* both Eurasian peers and the most advanced OECD countries (Table 2.1). Transparency International's Corruption Perceptions Index ranked the Russian Federation 127th among 177 countries in 2013. Problems with the rule of law also find expression in the World Bank's "Doing Business" indicators, which rank the Russian Federation 92nd out of 189 countries overall, with particularly low scores for investor protection, obtaining construction permits, access to credit and getting electricity. Trading across borders was also found to be especially difficult. While the World Bank finds that Russia has made impressive progress in some areas, such assessments point to how much more remains to be done.

Table 2.1. **Governance indicators, 1996-2012**

Percentile ranks

	Russian Federation			Poland	Sweden	Ukraine
Indicators	1996	2004	2012	2012	2012	2012
Voice and accountability	40.9	30.3	19.9	81.0	99.5	39.8
Political stability	12.0	7.7	20.9	83.4	90.0	41.7
Government effectiveness	32.7	43.9	40.7	71.8	98.6	31.6
Regulatory quality	39.2	50.0	38.8	78.5	99.0	28.7
Rule of law	23.4	19.1	23.7	72.0	99.1	26.1
Control of corruption	15.6	25.4	16.3	71.8	99.0	15.8

Note: A higher score denotes a better rank.

Source: World Bank (2013), "Governance Research Indicator Country Snapshots", The World Bank, Washington, DC, http://data.worldbank.org/data-catalog/worldwide-governance-indicators (accessed 14 December 2013).

Human capital and institutional quality are linked. The frequently observed correlation between indicators of institutional quality and such factors as income and education suggests that poor quality of government is not merely a product of elite greed; in many cases, the weakness of public institutions is linked to lower levels of human and physical capital, as well as poorer technology (La Porta et al., 1999; Botero, Ponce and Shleifer, 2012; Chong et al., 2012). In short, public institutions in many places have low productivity for the same reasons that private firms in those places do. Moreover, the evidence suggests that increasing income and education are also associated with greater demands for voice and accountability and greater capacity for good (public or private) management (Almond and Verba, 1963; Dahl, 1971; Diamond, 1992; Hadenius, 1992; Helliwell, 1994). Thus, it would appear that governance and growth are good for each other, and that education is good for both.

Seen in a Russian context, Krasnoyarsk's business environment has important strengths

The latest round of the Business Environment and Enterprise Performance Survey (BEEPS) conducted by the World Bank and the European Bank for Reconstruction and Development in 2011-13 provides some basis for a more detailed benchmarking of the business environment in the Agglomeration against other regions of the Russian

Federation (Box 2.1). The number of respondent firms per region in the most recent round was typically around 120 but was lower in some places than others. In Krasnoyarsk, 89 firms responded, all of them situated in the Agglomeration. Thus, while numbers are too small to permit a high level of confidence about small differences in the precise results, they are broad enough to permit meaningful comparisons on a broader scale. The discussion that follows thus draws on a number of issues addressed by the BEEPS data which met two criteria:

- At least 75 firms in Krasnoyarsk answered the question. Response rates for some survey items were far lower, with the likelihood of selection bias affecting the responses that were received. Only a few questions with low response rates are considered, and the potential unreliability of these results is noted.
- The results in Krasnoyarsk differed significantly from the all-Russian or Siberian Federal District (SFO) average and/or responses from a group of peer regions selected for consideration alongside Krasnoyarsk.[4] Since the surveyed firms in these regions were likewise concentrated in or around the main urban centres, comparisons with the Agglomeration are not inappropriate. By contrast, many smaller federal subjects are omitted, precisely because the utility of benchmarking the Krasnoyarsk Agglomeration against smaller, poorer places is not apparent.

Box 2.1. The Business Environment and Enterprise Performance Survey (BEEPS)

The Business Environment and Enterprise Performance Survey (BEEPS) is a joint initiative of the European Bank for Reconstruction and Development (EBRD) and the World Bank Group (World Bank). The survey was first undertaken on behalf of the EBRD and the World Bank in 1999-2000, when it was administered to approximately 4 100 enterprises in 25 countries of Eastern Europe and Central Asia (including Turkey) to assess the environment for private enterprise and business development. Subsequent rounds were conducted in 2002, 2005 and 2011-13, in an increasing number of countries. The fifth round, in 2011-13, covered approximately 15 600 enterprises in 30 countries, including 4 220 enterprises in 37 regions of the Russian Federation. Some 89 enterprises in Krasnoyarsk Krai were surveyed, all of them in the Agglomeration. The latest round includes an innovation module, covering product, process, organisational and marketing innovation, as well as management practices in manufacturing enterprises with at least 20 employees (50 employees in Russia).

The BEEPS survey universe consists of the majority of manufacturing sectors (excluding extraction), retail and residual stratum that includes most services sectors (wholesale, hotels, restaurants, transport, storage, communications, IT) and construction. This corresponds to firms classified with ISIC Rev 3.1 codes 15-37, 45, 50-52, 55, 60-64 and 72. Only formal (registered) companies with five or more employees are eligible for interview; there are no restrictions on their age. In some larger economies such as Russia, Turkey and Ukraine, the survey design allows stratification by some of the sectors with the largest contribution to employment and value added. Firms with 100% government/state ownership are no longer eligible to participate in BEEPS (see Enterprise Surveys, 2009, for fuller information on sampling methodology).

The BEEPS is answered in face-to-face interviews by business owners and top managers. Sometimes the survey respondent calls company accountants and human resource managers into the interview to answer questions in the sales and labour sections of the survey. Due to sensitive survey questions addressing business-government relations and bribery-related topics, private contractors, rather than any government agency or an organisation/institution associated with government, are hired by the EBRD and the World Bank to collect the data. Confidentiality of the survey respondents and the sensitive information they provide is necessary to ensure the greatest degree of survey participation, integrity and confidence in the quality of the data. Surveys are usually carried out in co-operation with business organisations and government agencies promoting job creation and economic growth, but confidentiality is never compromised.

Source: European Bank for Reconstruction and Development (n.d.), "BEEPS: About", http://ebrd-beeps.com/about (accessed 12 December 2013).

Figure 2.2 gives a snapshot of the main obstacles firms face in the business environment. Krasnoyarsk stands out with respect to two: access to finance and access to land. Electricity also appears to be somewhat more of a problem than elsewhere, but it still ranked seventh among Krasnoyarsk's firms' concerns. Several things suggest that the business environment in the Agglomeration is, overall, rather good by Russian standards. First, it is important to remember that firms responding to this question were asked to name their biggest barriers – not to say how great those barriers were. In fact, in response to more detailed questions on access to finance, respondent firms in Krasnoyarsk did not paint a grimmer picture than firms elsewhere. Respondents were asked to rate the difficulty of access to finance on a scale from 0 to 4, with 0 being not a problem at all and 4 being a very severe problem: the average response in Krasnoyarsk, at 1.5, was slightly higher than for the SFO (1.3) but right in line with the Russian average. The corresponding figures for access to land suggest a more serious problem, at least in relative terms: it, too, was 1.5, but the corresponding averages for the Russian Federation and the SFO were far lower, at 0.9 and 0.7 on average, with only St. Petersburg, among the comparator regions, recording a higher score. As is clear from Figure 2.2, corruption is still seen as a significant barrier to business, but it is not as high on the agendas of firms in Krasnoyarsk as it is elsewhere in Siberia.

Figure 2.2. **Main obstacles in the business environment reported by responding firms**

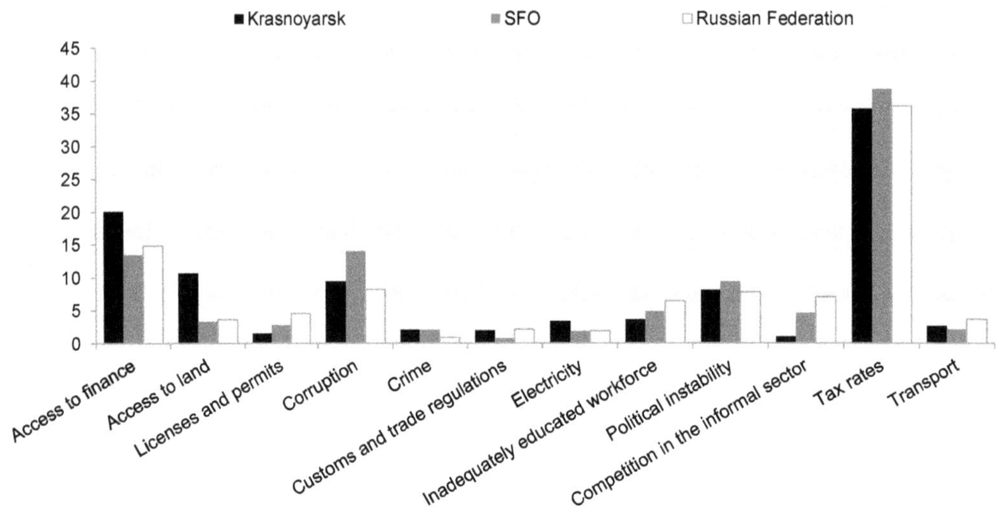

Source: World Bank/EBRD (2013), *Business Environment and Enterprise Performance Survey 2013*, http://data.worldbank.org/data-catalog/BEEPS (accessed on 14 December 2013).

There are other indications in the BEEPS data that the business environment in Krasnoyarsk, though not without significant problems, is comparatively healthy by Russian standards. For one thing, Krasnoyarsk firms really do appear to have far less difficulty dealing with licences and permits than firms in most other places in the Russian Federation, as Figure 2.2 would seem to suggest. Almost none (0.8%) reported that informal gifts or payments were requested in conjunction with the issuing of licences and permits, as against a country-wide average of 10.1%. Response rates were also in many cases very low with regard to these questions, making it difficult to draw firm conclusions even in the most general terms, but there were much higher response rates (close to 85%) on general questions pertaining to informal payments and gifts made to federal, regional and local officials: on these questions, Krasnoyarsk also comes out significantly below the Russian and Siberian averages. In other words, it appears to suffer less from corruption than most of its peers, a conclusion which is (partially) consistent with the overall assessment underlying Figure 2.2. There is a partial paradox, in that informal payments expressed as a share of total annual sales are about double the national average, and respondents in Krasnoyarsk are far more likely than most to report informal payments in connection with tax inspections. However, the response rates for these two questions are far lower, so selection bias may well be at work. It is also possible that official corruption is rarer but involves larger sums.

Respondent firms also reported an exceptionally low level of involvement with the courts – only 14.9% had been involved in litigation as a plaintiff or defendant within the last three years, as compared to figures of 26.7% for the SFO and 32.3% for the Russian Federation as a whole. This might imply an unusually low level of trust in the courts and thus a reluctance to use them, but responses to questions concerning the fairness, impartiality and probity (lack of corruption) of the courts, Krasnoyarsk respondents were close to the Siberian and Russian averages. In fact, Krasnoyarsk respondents were slightly more positive in their assessments. On the 0-4 scale used to rate the courts as an obstacle to doing business, Krasnoyarsk firms were outliers on the very low side. The average figures across the country were typically in the 0.3-0.7 range, with a national average of 0.5, suggesting that the courts are rarely seen as much of a problem; the corresponding figure for Krasnoyarsk was 0.1, suggesting that almost no firms at all see them as a barrier. This is good news indeed.

The Krasnoyarsk Agglomeration is also one of Russia's stronger local markets

In addition to offering a business environment that, in some important respects, appears to be better than average for the Russian Federation, Krasnoyarsk as a city also has some potentially important assets when it comes to attracting or retaining talent. While its location and climate on balance represent competitive drawbacks, as is clear from Chapter 1 (and from the data on out-migration from the region), a recent comparison of 100 major Russian cities highlights some strong points that should not be overlooked (Kolesova, 2013).[5] In particular, Krasnoyarsk ranks in the top fifth among major Russian cities in terms of the population's purchasing power (deflating local incomes to reflect local price levels) and in the top 10% in terms of the quality of its built environment. Despite its remote location, it ranks near the top in terms measures of external connectivity, as well. Nevertheless, given its location, climate and environmental conditions, the Agglomeration remains at somewhat of a disadvantage in the competition to retain firms and talented individuals. It must therefore do more than its more favourably located rivals to stimulate entrepreneurship and innovation and to retain firms and talent. Being as good – or even a bit better – is not enough. As will be seen, there is considerable potential for the constituent units of the Agglomeration to build on their undoubted strengths by working together to create a more competitive, attractive Krasnoyarsk and, in particular, to create the best possible conditions for entrepreneurs and innovators.

Even with sound macroeconomic and structural policies, policy intervention may be needed

Even if Russia effectively addresses the macroeconomic challenges described in Chapter 1 and the institutional agenda identified above, this may not result in much diversification of activity. Sound framework institutions are a necessary condition, but by no means a sufficient one, because there are significant market failures involved that may point to the need for public intervention:

- The usual arguments for intervention rest on (static or dynamic) technological externalities (learning-by-doing that is external to firms).
- More serious may be the information externalities concerning the cost structure of the economy (Hausmann and Rodrik, 2003). Entrepreneurs entering new (to the economy) activities generate information (available to government, markets and other entrepreneurs) about the cost structure of the economy. The externality exists whether or not the venture succeeds. If a new activity proves an unprofitable flop, the failed entrepreneur will bear the cost, but others will benefit from the information generated by the entrepreneur's attempt to enter a new field. On the other hand, if the new venture is a success, the entrepreneur will share the value of her/his discovery with other entrants, unless s/he is able to restrict entry.[6] While cutting-edge innovations may benefit from patent protection, the discovery that a certain good established in world markets can profitably be produced at home will not. The modifications required to adapt the relevant technology to domestic conditions are unlikely to amount to something patentable or monopolisable.[7] In addition, the "discoverer" (unlike the producer of a cutting-edge innovation) will be competing with established suppliers from the beginning.
- The other major externality concerns co-ordination. Many activities require simultaneous, large-scale investments to be profitable. An emerging activity may fail unless upstream and downstream investments are co-ordinated.[8] In established industries, the private sector is often quite capable of co-ordinating such operations, but if the private sector is not organised – and in a nascent sector, it is unlikely to be – then a co-ordinating role for government may be required.

The foregoing implies that diversification into new activities may be harder in cases where infrastructure requirements and/or economies of scale or scope naturally create *de facto* barriers to entry and possibly also exit. The importance of impediments to exit should not be overlooked, as they can deter entry if ventures are perceived to be risky.

In the context of the Krasnoyarsk Agglomeration, it is important to highlight the extent to which the challenges and opportunities identified by this analysis are place-based.

- Lychagin et al. (2010) highlight the extent to which knowledge spillovers, though often large, decay quickly over distance. Their work focuses on innovation but their conclusions should be equally true of self-discovery, where the knowledge gained often concerns specific local conditions and may in large part be tacit or imperfectly formalised and transferable.[9] In the case of Krasnoyarsk, much of this knowledge may be connected to sectors like metallurgy, where the Agglomeration could have potential to expand processing activities efficiently on the basis of local expertise and experience.
- The co-ordination failures identified above often arise precisely because of the need for up- and down-stream suppliers to operate in close geographic proximity – or, indeed, where key inputs are non-tradable (Rodrik, 1996). Krasnoyarsk's location reinforces this point, since entrants in new sectors are working in thinner markets: in denser places, it might be easier to connect with potential suppliers and customers. Thinner markets also make exit more difficult

and this may deter entry or restrict access to financing. If a venture fails, redeploying the assets and facilities involved may be harder in a remote, low-density location than in or near a large conurbation like Greater Moscow. This will affect the cost of financing.

- The technology-transfer literature highlights the extent to which successful transfer depends on adaptation to local conditions that involves a large amount of tacit knowledge. Hausmann and Rodrik (2003) illustrate a number of examples in which local adaptation and co-ordination were critical to successful adoption of foreign technologies (or where their absence contributed to failure). Tacit knowledge increases the need for close relationships along the supply chain (Pack and Westphal, 1986).
- Self-discovery is of necessity a bottom-up process, so there should be advantages in being able to address the co-ordination and information externalities closer to where they occur. While it is true that national governments are typically better equipped to intervene, in terms of resources and authority, the information needed for effective action is often local. If lower tiers of government often suffer from capacity gaps, national governments often face information gaps.

So what does the foregoing imply for the development of the Agglomeration?

- The information externalities point to the need for policies that encourage entrepreneurs to explore new (to the local/regional economy) activities. In theory, this could be done via some sort of subsidies for non-traditional activities. In practice, such subsidies would be very difficult to administer – the information and monitoring requirements would be onerous indeed. Trade protection or restrictions on entry would likewise raise serious practical problems – especially since they would be, in essence, firm-specific (it is the initial investor, not the copycats, who should reap their benefits). Support for access to finance might be the most obvious place for policy makers to begin, particularly as it has been identified by firms as an important barrier in Krasnoyarsk.
- Co-ordination externalities need not be costly to the budget to address, since the logic of the problem is that if the simultaneous investments are made, they will end up being profitable (unless some other externality is at work). Rodrik et al. (2004) point to the potential for designing *ex ante* subsidies that need not be paid *ex post* (e.g. an investment guarantee). The key task of development for the authorities in the Agglomeration may be information revelation and co-ordination rather than the provision of subsidies or tax credits.
- When addressing both sets of externalities, interventions should logically target new activities, rather than sectors per se. Indeed, there is a strong argument for moving policy making away from a sectoral approach altogether. The boundaries between sectors are in many cases increasingly fuzzy, particularly in advanced fields like high-tech manufacturing and knowledge-intensive services. Moreover, the development of increasingly complex global value chains, in which production processes are unbundled across the globe, means that – even in more "traditional" sectors – it makes more sense to think in terms of tasks or activities than entire sectors.[10] The challenge in the age of globalisation is less to push into sectors on the international stage, as countries once sought to do, than to integrate

into global value chains at whatever levels their endowments make them competitive (Baldwin, 2006; OECD, 2013c).

Such interventions are fraught with risks of their own

If policy intervention is required, steps must be taken to minimise the likelihood that it will fall victim to the pathologies that so often render industrial policy ineffective, if not destructive. The Russian Federation's own recent history furnishes plenty of examples of diversification initiatives that led to little or no results – or that simply fuelled rent-seeking by established interests. Clearly, sound governance is a *sine qua non*, but even this will not, on its own, be sufficient to avoid waste and rent-seeking. The cross-country literature suggests a number of important lessons here:

- Distorting prices to "push" resources into more advanced sectors (e.g. via import-substitution on Latin American lines) is likely to be a bad idea, for two reasons (Rodríguez-Clare, 2005). First, such policies are often based on the idea that cluster economies – the knowledge spillovers, labour pooling and proximity of specialised suppliers that can arise from concentration of production in a specific location – are an intrinsic characteristic of an industry. They are not: the same industry could generate spillovers in some places and not in others, or at some stages of development and not at others.[11] Secondly, the benefits of clustering are unlikely to be realised unless the economy enjoys a comparative advantage in the sector. Rodríguez-Clare concludes that "industrial policy is not about 'creating comparative advantage', but about achieving the high productivity that comes from a cluster in the sector where it has a comparative advantage" (Rodríguez-Clare, 2005: 13).
- Cluster economies of this kind are linked to technologies (including organisational and transactional "technologies" no less than production technologies) rather than to specific industrial sectors. The activities targeted, moreover, should have the clear potential to generate positive externalities (spillovers, demonstration effects, etc.).
- Process matters more than specific outcomes, because outcomes are inherently unknowable *ex ante*. Of course, policies should be evaluated for their contribution to growth/diversification – criteria for success and failure must be clear – but the key point is that outcomes cannot be identified with precision in advance. If the point is to promote discovery, one cannot know *ex ante* what one will discover. The purpose of policy should therefore be to stimulate experimentation, creating incentives for firms and the government to learn more about underlying costs and opportunities. A few successes are likely to pay for a large number of failures, as long as the mechanisms in place ensure that failures are allowed to fail, and quickly.[12]
- The approach to policy itself, moreover, should be experimental.[13] Discovering the best ways to foster discovery will involve some trial and error. Even failures can have some value, to the extent that they generate useful information and learning. Indeed, there should be plenty of mistakes – the key is not to avoid mistakes but to avoid persisting in them. A policy of stimulating decentralised experimentation should mitigate the market failures while retaining the benefits of decentralised search.

- Sunset clauses are needed. Support for new activities should not be open-ended and resources should not be tied up for long in support of activities that are not taking off.
- Close collaboration between public and private sectors is required – which also implies a need for transparency, clear procedures and effective accountability (i.e. for sound institutions of public governance). This should help to reduce the risk of political capture, rent-seeking and corruption. Avoiding a sectoral focus for policy should also make it less likely that instruments will be captured by special interests representing those whose behaviour they aim to alter.

The emphasis on experimentation here points to a final and very important conclusion: the outcomes of successful diversification policies will be difficult to predict, so policy makers should resist the temptation to try to define the production structure towards one which they believe the economy should evolve.

Support for SMEs is substantial but could be streamlined

Entrepreneurial activity in the Agglomeration is steadily increasing, and small and medium enterprises (SMEs) are particularly prominent in construction, trade, transports and communications. While the share of large farms in the agricultural sector is greater than in the rest of the Russian Federation, a reverse situation is noticeable in the industry sector, reflecting the perspectives of firm creation in the small business ecosystem. On the available data, entry on the market appears to be significantly higher than exit (12% of new businesses are registered each year in the Krasnoyarsk Krai, while 6.4% are liquidated, although some of this differential may reflect a failure to wind up firms that are moribund. The corresponding figures for the Agglomeration are more favourable (14% and 5.5%) and volatility is higher. Independent entrepreneurial activity accounts for 10% of employment (SFU, 2012). Altogether, SMEs at the end of 2011 accounted for 17.2% of total employment in the Krai and close to 25% of the regional GDP. Some 74% of these small companies are concentrated in the Agglomeration (69% in the city of Krasnoyarsk). Most of them are engaged in wholesale and retail trade (31%) and real estate (19%). Only 12% are operating in the processing industries. Small business turnover per capita is similar to the Russian average but higher than the average for the Siberian Federal District.

Assistance to small and medium-sized enterprises is part of the 2011-13 SME Development Programme in the Krai and the city. This includes earmarked subsidies for municipalities, partial compensation for interest on bank loans, subsidies for the purchase of equipment, participation in fairs and exhibitions and reimbursement for energy conservation investments. Financial support is channelled to SMEs by the Krasnoyarsk Regional Agency for Small and Medium Enterprises. A number of organisations can also provide advice and services to small businesses (incubators, chamber of commerce, industry associations, trade unions).

A number of observations can be made regarding this policy apparatus:

- The policy is fragmented. There is a proliferation of programmes and initiatives thus leading to micro support. This also complicates entrepreneurs' task when searching for support.
- Financial means are limited. Though the policy effort has grown rapidly since 2008, it started from very low levels.

- SME policy mainly targets the financial dimension of SME activities. It does not attempt to influence SME behaviour, emphasising inter-firm co-operation or to upgrade social capital.

In that context, the SME sector is underperforming. The size of the SME sector is modest (17% of employment). Service-based and mining-related small companies are few in number. Moreover, SMEs have weak absorption capacities and their innovation potential cannot be fully tapped. Given that SMEs are increasingly considered as the driving force behind new products and processes, Krasnoyarsk's innovation performance will improve if SME dynamics are significantly reinforced. This will require launching a comprehensive SME plan and the mobilisation of appropriate financial means.

The Antofagasta (Chile) multi-dimensional *Región Fértil* Initiative (Box 2.2) is certainly a best practice for a remote mining region. It would be useful to use it as an inspiring experiment.

Box 2.2. The *Región Fértil* initiative

Región Fértil is an organisation composed of local enterprises, public organisations academic institutions and media operating under the sponsorship of the regional government. The purpose of Región Fértil is to "join all forces" in order to transform the region and the city into an innovation and entrepreneurship capital of Chile. The idea is to build an ecosystem capable of boosting to its maximum potential each and every public and private initiative within the region, both current and future.

The first results (2011-12) include the creation of structures to promote entrepreneurship and enterprise creation. This includes: *i)* AIESEC: a student association (allied to UCN) aiming at creating networks; *ii)* De-Pe (*De Emprendedores, Para Emprendedores*) a training programme disseminated by Start-up Chile for local entrepreneurs; *iii)* First Tuesday Antofagasta (i.e. monthly meeting) to promote entrepreneur networking; *iv)* Atacama-7, a club of 450 entrepreneurs that co-operates to develop their expertise and aims to strengthen business exchanges; *v)* TEDx Atacama business sessions derived from TED (technology, entertainment, design)[1]; and *vi)* Atacama Emprende: a capital risk award financed by CORFO.[2]

Energy, astronomy, mining and waters are the entrepreneurial areas chosen for the first stage of this initiative, that in future could be duplicated in other regions of the country. Antofagasta was selected as the key zone to start these projects based on the premise that with mining, innovations with great dynamic potential could be generated, bringing along with them a diversified economic and productive supply.

In the first stage, 100 projects will be selected, 10% of which should be dynamic, high-growth ventures. The winners will have access to seed funds from the Exploration Fund (SSAF) administered by Fundación Chile.[3] As well as access to these funds, the selected projects will be admitted to the Entrepreneurs Platform, which provides different services to empower business ideas and to support scaling up.

The objective of the action plan 2013 is to move forward along five axes:

1. strengthening entrepreneurship through greater access to local, national and international clients
2. reinforcing the social entrepreneurship culture and creating an urban environment conducive to its diffusion
3. improving the innovation culture, increase mediating vehicles diffusing new innovation business models such as TED, Tech Ranch Austin, 3 M technology platforms, and developing access to new agents of innovation (Innocentive,[4] Start-up Chile, AIESEC)

Box 2.2. The *Región Fértil* initiative (*cont.*)

4. creating a local market for innovation in order to attract talents from the rest of Chile and from abroad
5. disseminating initiatives and assessing them in order to ensure that they really impact cultural change.

Notes: 1. TED is a knowledge-sharing platform. It is a participatory and informal programme that brings experts from the TED community and industry together to work on projects that require different points of view. TED Atacama organises sessions around TED conferences in co-operation with Gulliver (an Antofagasta-based collaborative learning community aiming at accelerating innovation) and the FCAB. 2. Fundación Chile, together with Región Fértil, have organised Atacama Emprende to promote ventures that help to improve and empower the zone. A CHP 180 million seed fund will be available to finance development projects. 3. Fundación Chile is the largest private non-profit organisation for the promotion of innovation in Chile. Founded in 1976 by the Chilean government and the US ITT corporation, its core mission is to transfer state of the art technologies, management techniques and human skills to natural resource intensive sectors in alliance with local and global knowledge networks. Fundación Chile has developed an original and effective model for transferring technologies and developing innovative responses to economic opportunities. It creates new companies and joint ventures, carries out R&D, adapts foreign technologies and fosters the creation of technological consortia and the diffusion of technologies to SMEs. 4. Innocentive is based on a simple idea: if a firm cannot solve a problem on its own, why not use the reach of the Internet to see if someone else can come up with the answer? Companies, which Innocentive calls "seekers", post their challenges on the firm's website. "Solvers", who number almost more than 200 000, compete to win cash "prizes" offered by the seekers. Around 900 challenges have been posted so far by some 150 firms, including big multinationals such as Procter & Gamble and Dow Chemicals.

Source: Région Fértil (n.d.), www.Regionfertil.com (accessed 15 December 2013).

In that context, it is suggested to focus on a set of measures that are:

- Linked with human capital formation. Entrepreneurship thrives not only because opportunities for firm creation emerge but also because people have been trained for that objective and because they are willing to face the challenge. In other words, training for entrepreneurship is crucial at secondary and even more so at tertiary level education to prepare young brains for that job. It would be recommended to review the different entrepreneurship-related curricula in the different universities and technical schools in the city and to consider the ways to upgrade and amplify them. The German experience might be contemplated (see Box 2.3).
- Integrated within a concerted policy effort to support SMEs and the creation of new firms at the central level. The Krai lacks nevertheless a long-term entrepreneurship strategy that can articulate efforts to support underdeveloped venture capital, remedy to the entrepreneurial gap and strengthen SME dynamism. The private sector could be incentivised to take part in a specific innovation fund that would support innovative SMEs. The central level could also be called upon to revisit its support to entrepreneurs and the message could be voiced to Moscow by the local and regional authorities as well as by private interests.

Box 2.3. The Brandenburg Institute for Entrepreneurship and SMEs: Building critical mass in entrepreneurship education

The Brandenburg Institute for Entrepreneurship and SMEs (BIEM) is the entrepreneurship institute of the regional development agency and nine public higher education institutions, including universities and universities of applied sciences. The BIEM was founded in 2006 as a registered non-profit organisation. One of its main objectives is to reinforce, complement and co-ordinate the entrepreneurship support activities offered by Brandenburg's higher education institutions by pooling resources and enhancing collaboration and exchange. The BIEM helps to achieve the "critical mass" needed to realise projects with wide-ranging impact.

The annual budget of EUR 100 000 is financed by the European Structural Funds, the Ministry of Economics of Brandenburg and other project-related revenues (e.g. fees for services). The BIEM has eight employees. Each partner organisation runs additional projects and employs additional personnel.

The BIEM's activities include entrepreneurship education, start-up support, entrepreneurship research and networking with business support organisations and other universities. It focuses on the expansion and better integration of entrepreneurship education into curricula, including innovative teaching methods, broad communication of activities, and an expansion of co-operation beyond the BIEM's core partners (e.g. involvement of university staff and external experts, agencies and companies). Partnering higher education institutions benefit from rising numbers of students participating in entrepreneurship education activities and an increase in the number and variety of courses available for their students.

Higher education institutions have established "entrepreneurship location managers/animators" (*Standortmanager*), who act as "one-stop-interlocutors" for would-be entrepreneurs. This structure contributes to building stronger linkages between the university's internal and external support services and to integrating entrepreneurship education and start-up support services.

Other projects include "Entrepreneurship ACs", that evaluate entrepreneurial potentials and learning needs before start-up and match them with adequate mentoring during start-up, "Team Competency Lab" that focuses on team building and coaching at the BTU Cottbus or "GO:Incubator" at the University of Potsdam.

In 2009, the BIEM generated 370 initial consultations to would-be entrepreneurs. In addition, 203 were referred to external business support structures and 86 business start-ups were supported. The key elements for the institute's success is the multi-dimensional co-operation between all higher education institutions and their external partners, the involvement of higher education institutions in regional leadership and a phase approach to entrepreneurship.

Source: OECD (2009b), *The Impact of Culture on Tourism: Universities, Innovation and Entrepreneurship: Criteria and Examples of Good Practice*, OECD Publishing, Paris; Brandenburgisches Institut für Existenzgründung und Mittelstandsförderung e.V. (n.d.), www.biem-brandenburg.de (accessed 10 December 2013).

Strengthening and making better use of Krasnoyarsk's human capital

In Russia, the importance attached to education by the state and citizens is a positive legacy of the Soviet era. It is one reason why the country has a higher proportion of university graduates in the population and the workforce than does any OECD country (OECD, 2011a). The human resource picture in Krasnoyarsk is not much different from the rest of the Russian Federation. The quality of primary and secondary education in the Agglomeration (proxied by the performance on the Unified State Examination) is above average for the country.

Within that context, the Krai and city governments are increasingly promoting a strategy that aims to better tap the human potential of the region and its central urban agglomeration. Given the remoteness of the Krai and its low population, the supply of the right mix of skills is crucial for the regional and city economies. It is important to note that although enrolment levels are favourable, they conceal a relatively fast decline in the number of students being trained in vocational education institutions (see below). Students in Krasnoyarsk increasingly prefer tertiary education regardless of professional orientation. Given that vocational training institutions are usually the most sensitive to industry needs, gaps in the labour market between supply and demand tend to persist. The deficits of skills for a number of professions could hamper the growth of the economy all the more, as attracting talents from other regions remains difficult and costly.

It is therefore important that the public authorities and the education institutions have sufficient room for manoeuvre to adapt education policies to local conditions. The reform of higher education is an important item on the political agenda of the Russian Federation. There is obviously a need to instil a certain degree of decentralisation, so that universities will be in a position to set up development plans more in line with the needs of the regional and local economies and to increase their international links. Vocational education and training (VET) programmes should also include more elements of workplace training. This will require more partnerships with employers and unions in order to ensure that the content of the VET are relevant for the labour market.

Demand for higher education has grown steadily

The share of people with higher education in the city of Krasnoyarsk has increased steadily over the last decade and remains higher than both the Russian average and the Krai level (Table 2.2). The share of population with secondary vocational education is similar to the rest of the country, but significant disparities are noticeable in the Agglomeration.

Table 2.2. **Educational attainments of the population**

Share of population with	Secondary vocational education		Higher education	
	2002	2012	2002	2012
Russian Federation	27.1	30.3	16	22.7
Siberian Federal District	27.3	30.7	14	19.9
Krasnoyarsk Krai	27.6	31.3	14.4	20.2
City of Krasnoyarsk	27.5		22.6	
Rest of the Agglomeration	18.6-33.7		6.4-14.7	

Source: SFU (2012), "Background report for the OECD Territorial Review of Krasnoyarsk", Siberian Federal University, Krasnoyarsk, Russian Federation, November.

Higher education (HE) enrolment in the Agglomeration is the main reason for its education performance, together with the better quality of the primary and secondary education in the city. Candidates in the USE score better marks on average every year in nearly all disciplines than their counterparts in the Krai or in the rest of the Russian Federation.

While the number of students in HE institutions in Russia is declining, in line with demographic trends, it continues to rise in the Krai and in the Agglomeration, albeit at a slow and unsteady pace (Table 2.3). This has been facilitated by the growth of education spending in the Krai budget. Educational expenditure amounted to 31.3% of the general budget in 2011, up from 20.8% in 2000. The number of students enrolled in vocational education, however, has fallen rapidly. Similarly, there was a sharp decline in the number of students in public specialised secondary institutions in the Krai, from 62 100 in 2000 to 48 400 in 2010. This has been only very partially offset by an increase in tertiary education enrolment. Postgraduate programmes are focused on engineering, biology and economics, reflecting to some degree Krasnoyarsk's economic specialisation, with relatively stable numbers of participants.

Table 2.3. **Enrolment in higher education**

Thousands of students

Year	Russian Federation	Krasnoyarsk Krai	City of Krasnoyarsk
2000	4 270.8	94.4	85.5
2005	5 985	120.1	105.2
2010	5 848	121.8	106.5

Source: SFU (2012), "Background report for the OECD Territorial Review of Krasnoyarsk", Siberian Federal University, Krasnoyarsk, Russian Federation, November.

Krasnoyarsk hosts one of the major concentrations of higher education east of the Urals

Tertiary education is provided by 30 higher education institutions (HEIs) of various types. The Siberian Federal University (SFU) is home to more than 3 000 faculty teaching 41 000 students. It also manages no fewer than 402 programmes of further professional education for enterprises and company specialists and managers, including 14 programmes of further qualifications to basic higher education (Box 2.4). Other universities include the Krasnoyarsk State Pedagogical University (KGPU), the Siberian State Technical University, the Siberian State Aerospace University (SibGAU), the Krasnoyarsk State Medical University and the Sukhachev Institute of Forestry of the Siberian Division of the Russian Academy of Sciences.

Box 2.4. **Siberian Federal University**

SFU is the largest university in the Russian Federation east of the Urals, with more than 400 professors and more than 1 500 assistant professors. It is home to 19 institutes that provide education in more than 170 fields and training areas. A wide range of specialties – from technical to humanitarian – is offered. Its scientific journal is published in five thematic series. The annual turnover raised by its R&D and paid services reaches RUB 800 million.

More than 60 collaboration agreements have been signed with Russian and foreign universities and research centres. About 200 foreign students study at the university annually and around 200 visiting professors teach and conduct joint research there, 50 of them from the leading universities of the Russian Federation, England, Germany, Spain, the United States and other countries.

The university is training more than 1 000 students in the fields of communication, translation and economy at the university's military department and military centre. SFU is also forming as a supporting element for Krasnoyarsk's future social and intellectual Agglomeration infrastructure.

SFU was created in 2006 by merging four local HEIs. It is a federal university (Box 2.5), ranked 12-14th in the total National Rating of Universities compiled by Interfax and the radio station Ekho Moskvy. It is 7-8th on "innovations and entrepreneurship" and 6-10th in the section "education". It was also ranked 14th among Russian universities in the international "Web of Science" rankings issued by Thomson Reuters. Today, it has about 70 agreements with strategic partners and employers. In recent years, the university has been pursuing the policy of close co-operation with large Russian and international companies operating in the Krasnoyarsk territory. Such co-operation includes the organisation of summer internships, the involvement of company specialists in educational processes, and the establishment of joint research and production centres like that created with Krastvetmet at the Gulidov Nonferrous Metals Plant. The partners of the university support talented students and postgraduates by awarding 315 personal scholarships for a total of RUB 12 million.

Box 2.5. **Federal universities in the Russian Federation**

Seven regional universities have received the status of federal university. This marks them out as leading teaching institutions in the Russian Federation, with a view to increasing their contribution to the development of the regions in which they are located. They are charged with better integrating education, science and business in a number of thematically defined priority areas. The first two federal universities were selected in Southern Russia and in Siberia (SFU) in 2006. In 2009, a further five were created in other federal districts. USD 600 million has been earmarked for this programme.

Source: OECD (2011a), *OECD Reviews of Innovation Policy, Russian Federation 2011*, OECD Publishing, Paris, http://dx.doi.org/10.1787/9789264113138-en.

Specialists are also being trained in the Krai in 59 institutions of secondary vocational education and in 11 institutions of elementary vocational education. Despite the great number of these institutions, there are more students in HEIs and the gap is expanding. Vocational institutions have been attracting fewer and fewer students since the beginning of the last decade (Table 2.4).

Table 2.4. **Distribution of students in Krasnoyarsk Krai's higher education institutions and secondary vocational institutions**

In %

Year	Industry and building	Agriculture	Transport and communications	Economy and law	Public health	Education	Culture and art
Higher education institutions							
2001	53.6	12	...	7.0	3	23.6	0.8
2009	44.2	12.8	3.4	12.5	3.2	22.3	1.6
Secondary vocational education institutions							
2001	46.3	12.2	11.6	11	9.4	7	2.5
2009	44.8	13.3	10.1	12.2	8.8	8.4	2.4

Source: Popodko, G. and O. Nagaeva (2012), "A change in the structure of training of qualified specialists for providing sustainable development of the region", *Journal of Federal Siberian University*, Krasnoyarsk, Russian Federation.

The skills distribution is changing and skill shortages have emerged in some sectors

The distribution of graduates among disciplines has changed in recent years in response to:

- Trends in demand from business and the public sector. For example, the share of highly skilled and skilled workers fell from 39.5% in 1989 to 30.6% in 2009 because of the relative growth of services, introduction of new technologies and closing up of a number of large industrial firms (Popodko and Nagaeva, 2012). The need for highly qualified specialists and people with a tertiary education has also increased.
- Student demand for "fashionable" specialities that are not necessarily in demand in the region. Cultural preferences (e.g. for management rather than technical professions) also appear to have played a role in the changes.

As a consequence, the proportion of students enrolled in industry- and building-related HE curricula declined from 53.6% in 2001 to 44.2% in 2009, while those studying economy and law increased from 7% to 12.5% (relative terms). Figures have remained stable for agriculture, health, culture and education, and they increased substantially, albeit from very low levels, in transport and communication, to reflect the importance of logistics in the region and also for culture (Table 2.5). Similar trends are observed in institutions of secondary vocational education, though at a reduced pace. However, these institutions are more focused on training students to satisfy industrial needs. Humanities and social sciences are a smaller part of their curriculum.

Table 2.5. **Projected shares of graduates from Krasnoyarsk's higher education institutions by specialisation**

Specialities	2009	2010	2015	2020	2025
Industry and construction	44.2	41.2	38.4	38.0	37.0
Agriculture	12.8	13.9	15.3	16.1	16.5
Transport and communications	3.4	3.6	3.9	4.1	4.2
Economics and law	12.5	14.4	15.7	15.4	14.4
Public health	3.2	3.7	4.0	5.0	5.0
Education	22.3	22.3	21.7	21.0	21.0
Culture and arts	1.6	1.0	1.0	1.4	1.9

Source: SFU (2012), "Background report for the OECD Territorial Review of Krasnoyarsk", Siberian Federal University, Krasnoyarsk, Russian Federation, November.

There are shortages of graduates in a number of occupations. These deficits are due to: *i)* an unbalanced distribution of educational institutions over the territories; *ii)* inefficient use of human resources; and *iii)* lack of attractiveness of workplaces for highly skilled specialists, given the considerable geographic differences within the Krai. Figure 2.3 shows that in 2010 the number of graduates clearly exceeded the number of job vacancies for humanities, education and teaching, and economy and law. At the same time, a reverse gap was observed for transport, while there appeared to be a better balance of supply and demand for IT, high-tech and food-processing technologies.

Figure 2.3. **Job opportunities and the supply of graduates, 2010**

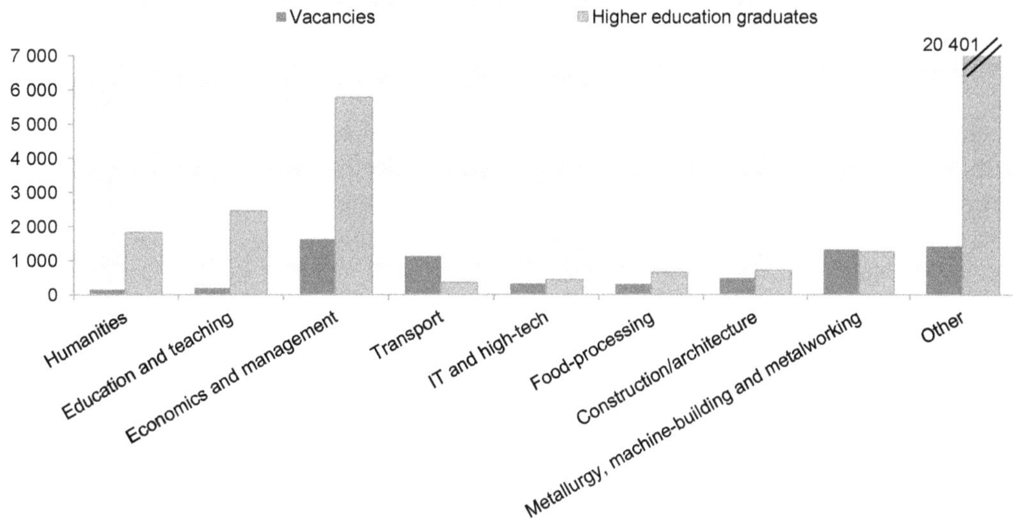

Source: SFU (2012), "Background report for the OECD Territorial Review of Krasnoyarsk", Siberian Federal University, Krasnoyarsk, Russian Federation, November.

This is in any case a very rough lower-bound estimate of labour market gaps. Employers insist that graduate qualifications often do not correspond to declared requirements and stress the lack of experience (70%) and skills/job mismatches (28.7%). They also emphasise the inability of young people to work in a team, to build relations with colleagues, their weak ability for self-training and their excessive ambitions (SFU, 2012). At the same time, some employers value the personal qualities of graduates more than their professional skills. The regional labour market has been thus far characterised by a high need for workers (about 76% of the general demand). It accounted for 67% of job opportunities at workplaces with part-time employment during the decade. Personnel shortages have been reported in the following sectors: transport, metallurgy, energy and construction. Professions in demand include engineers, nurses, doctors, accountants and technicians. The system of "professional orientation" is thus called upon to bridge the gap between the population's demand for professional education services and the labour market requirements. Social partners have an important role to play to improve the market adjustment.

The share of graduates with a degree in construction and industry is projected to decline

Projections have been made using a factor model elaborated by the Krasnoyarsk Office of the Research Institute of Labour (Table 2.5). The most striking feature of the projection is that the steadily declining share of industry and construction will mostly be offset by rises in the share of graduates with agricultural specialisations. Modest increases in transport and communications, economics and law, and public health are also anticipated. The analysis accompanying the projections suggests that in the area of services training, programmes will have to be expanded. In certain branches of the economy, such as the oil and gas complex, forestry, the food industry and road construction, the need for specialists is far from being covered locally and will necessitate appropriate investment. The education system will also need to be made more efficient. A support system will be needed in order to give grants and scholarships to motivate students to enter these fields (Popodko and Nagaeva, 2012).

Labour market policies

In the city and the Agglomeration, labour market policies are increasingly concerned with addressing perceived skills mismatches and the need to attract talents from the rest of the country, as well as to retain talent in Krasnoyarsk that might otherwise move away. The strategy at the level of the Krai and the Agglomeration is to stabilise framework conditions and to ensure the fine-tuning of skill demand and supply. The creation of the Agglomeration framework has resulted in embryonic co-ordination between the constituent municipalities but no common policy has been established. The difficulty of satisfying the demand for qualified specialists and training them has resulted in a number of young people leaving the regions in order to seek education elsewhere. Vocational training remains an important issue. A number of training programmes are funded by large firms, notably in the engineering and metal industry sector and more training centres have been established since 2010 or so, but the system is still fragmented.

General labour market environment

As noted in Chapter 1, labour-force participation in the Agglomeration is quite high by OECD standards. There has also been some convergence of labour-force participation rates across the Agglomeration's constituent units – in 1999, the variation was from around 61% to about 83%; by 2011, all elements of the Krasnoyarsk Agglomeration reported labour-force participation rates between 65% and 70%. Over the intervening period, the Krai economy was able to take advantage of its rich endowment in oil, gas and metal and of the natural resources boom to bring down unemployment (Table 2.6). Over the period, long-term unemployment has continuously been less important in the city (in relative terms) (7.2% of unemployed in 2010) than in the rest of the country (17%). The youth share of total unemployment has been moderate (9.2% in the city) and below the Russian average (16.6%), pointing to the relatively greater efficiency of local labour markets. Figures for the Krai are nevertheless quite less satisfactory (around 22% for both parameters). The positive trends in the city can be attributed to the steady growth that has prevailed in recent years, apart from a brief downturn when the global financial crisis first hit. It is also the result of migration processes that took place within the Krai in favour of the core city or other parts of the Federation. Moreover labour market policies and skill supply have been improved.

Table 2.6. **Unemployment rates in and around Krasnoyarsk**

Year	Russian Federation	Siberian Federal District	Krasnoyarsk Krai	Krasnoyarsk Agglomeration	City of Krasnoyarsk	Rest of the Agglomeration
1999	13%	14.9%	14.4%	12.9%	12.4%	8.5-29.9%
2005	7.6%	9.4%	9%	7.1%	7%	3.2-18%
2012	6.5%	7.8%	6.2%	5.4%	5.5%	1.9-9.1%

Source: SFU (2012), "Background report for the OECD Territorial Review of Krasnoyarsk", Siberian Federal University, Krasnoyarsk, Russian Federation, November.

Mobility is relatively low within the Krai. Labour market conditions do not enhance mobility. People working in big corporations nevertheless have more chances to move. Graduates are mainly interested in settling in the Agglomeration. Students often start to work in jobs that do not correspond to their education (engineering, pedagogy, construction), and many of them choose in the end to complete a second education. As noted in Chapter 1, most migration in and out of the Krai is from Krasnoyarsk Agglomeration (close to 90% of arrivals – with the city itself accounting for all but about 7 percentage points of that). The higher the urban share of population in a municipality, the more it attracts migrants from elsewhere in Russia or abroad. Migration in rural places is usually outwards, to other places in the Krai.

Krasnoyarsk has been working towards a more integrated labour market strategy

Krasnoyarsk Krai has designed a labour market strategy that emphasises the forecasting and monitoring of recruitment needs. The Krai Ministry of Education and Science has elaborated a planning model for this task in co-operation with researchers from SFU. This is based on the reported needs of enterprises and on human resources trends. It aims at improving the quality and appeal of workplaces, encouraging mobility (externally and within the region) and promoting the return to employment of the inactive population. An important challenge is to use the most up-to-date information about labour market conditions and workforce availability and to anticipate structural changes on the demand side. The model takes into account training and distribution of specialists and the alignment of skill demand and needs, as well as the upgrading of qualifications. A system of career guidance is integrated, but uniform regional management of human resources only started to function in 2011.

The creation of regional technology platforms in a number of industrial sectors will help to better connect business and HEIs, as well as vocational and other educational institutions. This should render the adjustment between companies' labour demand and the local employment supply smoother in these sectors. The Krai has also adopted a strategy for the development and modernisation of professional education over the period to 2020, with the assistance of the World Bank. The strategy is expected to provide a more balanced system of skills supply and demand and to reduce disparities in education quality. Finally, since the Krai shares competencies with the federal government over labour market programmes, it was able to pass a regional law on employment in 2012. This law targets employment assistance and is allowing a better adjustment to users' needs.

Labour market integration is important to the development of the Agglomeration

It should be borne in mind that one of the main motivations for creating the Agglomeration was its potential to enlarge the urban labour market and to attract skilled labour. It is expected that the Agglomeration will generate economies of scale and provide greater opportunities to obtain advanced expertise. As seen in Chapter 1, labour market conditions vary widely across the Agglomeration's constituent units. For example, wages in the city of Krasnoyarsk are, on average, 1.5-2.0 times higher than those on the periphery of the Agglomeration. This could reflect a bias towards lower productivity sectors on the periphery of the Agglomeration and few job opportunities with relatively important employment demand. In 2011, employment in Divnogorsk and Sosnovoborsk was down by about one-third on the level of 1999, whereas the corresponding decline in the city of Krasnoyarsk was just around 8%. Employment in Sukhobuzim rose by 17.8% over the period. In that context, commuting from the periphery to the city of Krasnoyarsk increased over 2000-12. There was substantial growth in the number of commuters from Sosnovoborsk (34%), Emelyanovo (11.8%) and Berezovsk (10%) but a decline for those living in Divnogorsk (-6.9%) or Sukhobuzim.

Since the creation of the Agglomeration in 2008, no common labour market strategy has been elaborated, though there have been a number of scientific publications dealing with the topic. Professional training activities are also increasingly planned at this level, for example in the engineering sector. At the level of the Krai, labour market management targets the quality of working places, workforce management, employment support system and social partnerships. It is less focused on commuting issues: thus, while Krai-level policies establish a framework for the region, work at Agglomeration level may be needed to address obstacles to intra-Agglomeration mobility and labour market integration.

Vocational training has been undergoing major changes

Programmes for human resources training involve Krai ministries and employers at primary and secondary vocational education institutions in a number of sectors, including metallurgy, transport, construction, forestry and related industries, as well as housing and communal services. Retraining programmes with involvement of specialised branches (mining, metallurgy) attract about 300 participants per programme, e.g. in technological management in Zheleznogorsk, as well as in other Krasnoyarsk Krai districts, such as in Krasnoyarsk for representatives of SMEs. These programmes are often funded by companies. Demand for such programmes is high and topics change each year. These training programmes can be attended by the unemployed. The right to participate is assessed by specialised agencies on the basis of standardised tests. "Clients" can be coached to re-orient their careers.

Though limited in scale, such retraining appears to be a success. Initially, employment rates after training were between 60% and 70%, but they have risen to around 99%.

The training system nevertheless faces a number of challenges:

- to adjust to the demands of a more diversified economy
- to compete with universities for a shrinking share of school graduates
- to cope with an overall lack of resources and to upgrade/replace outdated training technologies
- to optimise the network of institutions spread over a large territory.

In order to relieve the tension on the labour markets for a number of professions, the Krai Ministry of Education and Science has taken steps to restructure the secondary vocational education and training system. Some assessment and diagnostic studies have been completed. It strives to produce graduates with skills more relevant to the local labour markets. International experience (see Box 2.6) shows that interactions between vocational institutions and industry are crucial in updating training contents, equipment and facilities as well as providing career guidance and introducing new programmes. The reform being implemented in the Krai needs to prioritise partnerships between business and the public sector. Universities have also started to provide some type of continuous training programmes. They could be more active in this field given the right incentives.

Box 2.6. International models to target training to business needs

The policy systems that govern private-sector involvement in training vary widely from country to country. The "dual system" of private engagement in technical training, adopted in Austria, Germany and Switzerland, delegates the responsibility for curriculum and assessment to a coalition of labour representatives, businesses and educators. Business associations then manage the system by monitoring the quality of training provided by firms (Gill and Dar, 2000). However, this dual system relies heavily on the ability of business to see that it has an interest in paying for the training of vocational graduates. The need to hold down unit labour costs may undermine the viability of too much reliance on the private sector. Much also depends on the degree of actual or anticipated turnover in the labour market, since employers are more likely to be ready to invest in training for workers they expect to retain for the longer term.

A second model of private-sector involvement relies on a strong network of relationships between educators and employers. Manufacturing labour in Japan has historically come from high schools with a strong network of relationships with hiring managers in industry; in this manner, high school staff can place their most accomplished students preferentially. This system, however, relies on the ability of high school staff to evaluate correctly the skills of their graduates and their fit with industry needs. This is particularly hard in times of rapid structural or technological change. Furthermore, communication remains unidirectional and often fails to allow for industry input into curricula.

A third model, "Human Resource Development" (HRD), focuses on encouraging firm-level training through government policies. HRD strategies, pursued for example in South Korea, Malaysia and Singapore involve the taxation of firms, with the resulting revenues available for use within the firm to train workers within their own companies (Gill et al., 2000).

The Swedish model of the "triple helix" aims to create a dynamic relationship between academia, industry and government. Whilst this tri-partite relation was initially focused on fostering innovation and creativity amongst the high-skilled, its insights (and those of its successor, the "quadruple helix", which brings civil society into the picture) provide a useful basis for thinking about communication, and potential synergies in the provision of appropriate education and skills, accessible to all.

Source: OECD (2012a), *OECD Territorial Reviews: The Chicago Tri-State Metropolitan Area, United States 2012*, OECD Publishing, Paris, http://dx.doi.org/10.1787/9789264170315-en.

Thanks to the priority national project "Education", high-technology centres have been established with state support. Educational institutions are located in Krasnoyarsk, Divnogorsk, Sosnovoborsk and Zheleznogorsk. They supervise a more modern type of educational programme. In 2012, three more centres opened (for the wood industry, railway transport and IT), bringing the total to 12. There are also a number of corporate education and training centres (e.g. the Vankor oil field centre run by Rosneft). Large companies often partner with HEIs such as SFU. They sponsor academic exchange and educational activity programmes, including training services.

The number of secondary and tertiary vocational education institutions has diminished in the last ten years. Nevertheless, the level of graduates from secondary vocational institutions did not change and the number of specialists with tertiary education increased by 15.7%. At the same time, the need to better train employees is urgent, since 35% of tertiary graduates and 40% of graduates of secondary vocational institutions are reckoned to be unprepared for employment on completion of their studies (SFU, 2012). One of the main objectives of labour market policy is to reduce the gap between the content of education and professional training and the demand of local industries. To achieve this goal, dialogues between employees and training institutions are encouraged e.g. in the Krasnoyarsk Polytechnic Institute.

The need for supplementary and more efficient training effort is confirmed by the BEEPS data. They show that Krasnoyarsk Krai underperforms in formal training compared to many regions in the Russian Federation and notably the neighbouring ones in the Siberian Federal District. Only 24.8% of the companies interviewed and operating in the Krai provided formal training to their full-time employees during 2012. This figure is significantly lower than that reported for Omsk (48.2), Tomsk (58.1) or Kemerovo (57.6). As a consequence, the proportion of employees receiving training is the lowest among the 15 Russian regions studied, though this seems to characterise more the production employees than the non-production ones.[14] However, the BEEPS data do not show the inadequate education of the workforce as a major issue for employers in the region.

Efforts are under way to adapt public employment services to local needs

There has been progress in making public employment services better able to respond to the needs of local markets. Until 2012, employment service activities were pretty much exclusively federal competencies and were financed by special federal funds. Professional training, internships, etc., were federal responsibilities. Since 2012, though, the subjects of the Federation have more responsibilities in this sphere. The Krai Ministry of Finance can now support such programmes. There are also new programmes targeting doctors, teachers and other social sphere workers, especially to support rural service provision, offering them favourable conditions for rent or mortgages, child-care support and the like. Employment centres have also been modernised. For example, recruitment procedures now involve Skype interviews organised with competitors living in distant communities of the regions – a simple but very effective step, given the distances involved. Most training programmes are designed and implemented by specialised agencies. Within the framework of the employment agency, 9 000-10 000 persons (mostly senior) are retrained every year.

In order to favour internal mobility, the Krai has developed programmes to foster a better inter-territorial distribution of the labour force, given that job opportunities often emerge in Krasnoyarsk and newly developed areas, whereas the labour force is located in other parts of the Agglomeration. The Krai also evaluates the quality of labour forces and the demand of employers and offers professional training.

The Krai and the city have started to elaborate a policy of retention and to set up programmes directed towards the migrants who use the Krai as a transfer point in their move towards the West. International migration now accounts for 30% of overall migration growth in the Krasnoyarsk Agglomeration. Another programme has been launched to encourage the settlement of Russians living abroad. As a result, around 1 000 people have moved back to Krasnoyarsk, mainly from Belarus and Kazakhstan, but some from as far afield as Australia. The resettlement is focused on the city of Krasnoyarsk, Sosnovoborsk and the Mana and Sukhobuzim Districts. These initiatives should probably not discriminate non-Russian people outside the Federation. In other words, an initiative to attract highly skilled people from abroad would be welcome.

Even if expenditures on labour market policies tend to receive more financial support from the budget than previously, they still need to be strengthened. On the one hand, restructuring of large firms has accelerated in recent years and several plants have been closed in the Agglomeration. On the other hand, the wage-setting system in the Russian Federation and in the Krai is largely at the discretion of employers. Low-paid jobs are numerous, allowing many relatively uncompetitive activities to survive. Structural adjustment is therefore still relatively slow. Active labour market policies may contribute to upgrading the stock of skills, enhancing employability and encouraging SME competitiveness, subcontracting practices and firm creation. Training programmes play a pivotal role in that context. Partnerships between firms and public institutions need to be further developed to tailor skill acquisition to business needs. Enterprise involvement in advising on curriculum design and offering placement should also be encouraged (OECD, 2011b).

Innovation

Krasnoyarsk's innovation system is not performing up to its potential

The latest round of Business Environment and Enterprise Performance Survey (BEEPS) data gathered by the World Bank and the EBRD cast light on innovation activity in Krasnoyarsk. On the whole, they suggest a fairly high degree of conservatism in Krasnoyarsk firms. As is clear from Figure 2.4, self-reported firm responses on patents, the introduction of new products and services, and the adoption of new management and/or production methods all suggest a relatively low level of innovation among firms, despite the presence of a strong science base at the heart of the Agglomeration.[15] The respondent firms in Krasnoyarsk were also more than five times less likely to report spending – either internally or via outsourcing – on research and development.[16] This is consistent, in fact, with an economy in which markets are relatively thin and competition weak. It is also, perhaps, unsurprising in a place where, for reasons of geography (climate, location, etc.), it may be difficult to realise the full potential of innovative ideas locally. Innovations born in Krasnoyarsk may well be implanted in production elsewhere, particularly if they are connected to the activities of some of the very large companies based in the Krai.

Other data and indicators reinforce this impression. Though growing over the period, domestic research and development (R&D) expenditures (EUR 177 million in 2010) remain low by international standards (0.9% of regional GDP) and even a bit below the average of Russian regions (1.1%). Investment in R&D is limited, especially in the business sector and HEIs, despite their capacities to take out patents and create spinoffs. University-industry linkages are weak by international standards. The Innovation Cities Global Index ranked the city of Krasnoyarsk 277th in 2012-13, behind not only Moscow (75) and St. Petersburg (84) but also Kazan (209), Yekaterinburg (238), Novosibirsk (252) and Samara (253). In that context, urban policy initiatives aiming at repositioning the city on a sound, long-term growth trajectory are increasingly welcome.

Yet as seen in Chapter 1, the Agglomeration contains significant innovation assets, including a substantial science base and high levels of human capital, by both Russian and international standards (see also Table 2.7). It is therefore not surprising that firms responding to the EBRD/World Bank BEEPS questionnaire were less likely than in most Russian regions to cite the inadequate education of the workforce as an obstacle to business operations. Perhaps for this reason respondent firms in Krasnoyarsk also appear to be far less likely than most others to provide formal training to permanent, full-time employees (Figure 2.5). There is an interesting contrast here with Tomsk, where workforce education is not seen as a problem, but where the great majority of firms provide training. In Novosibirsk, the opposite tendencies prevail – a relatively high level of dissatisfaction with the workforce and very low levels of training provision.

Figure 2.4. **Indicators of innovative activity among firms**

BEEPS responses, selected Russian regions

A. Proportion of firms introducing new products/services over the last three years

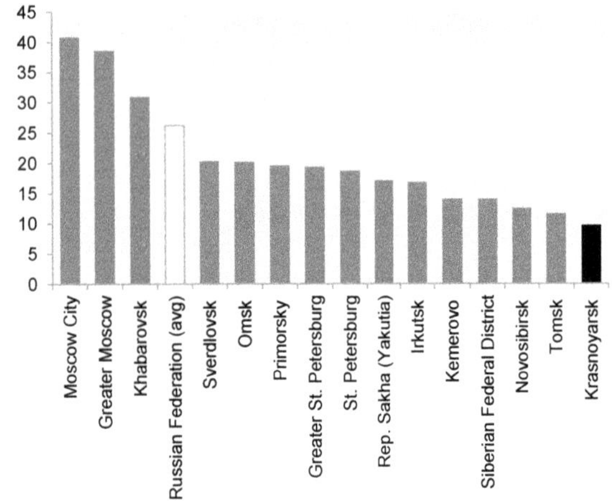

B. Proportion of respondent firms that has been granted a patent

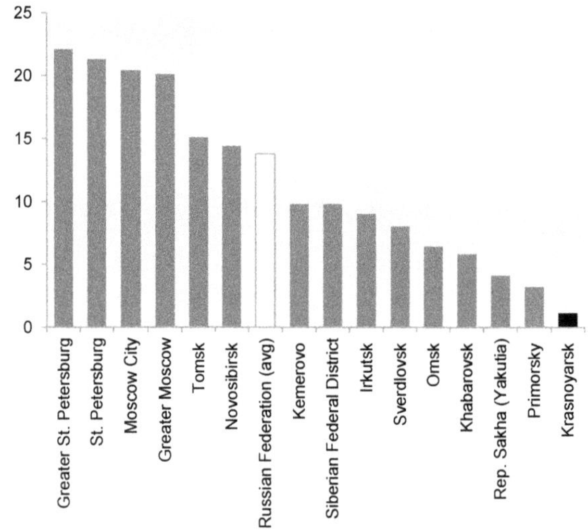

C. Share of firms reporting new method of supplying products/services to the local market

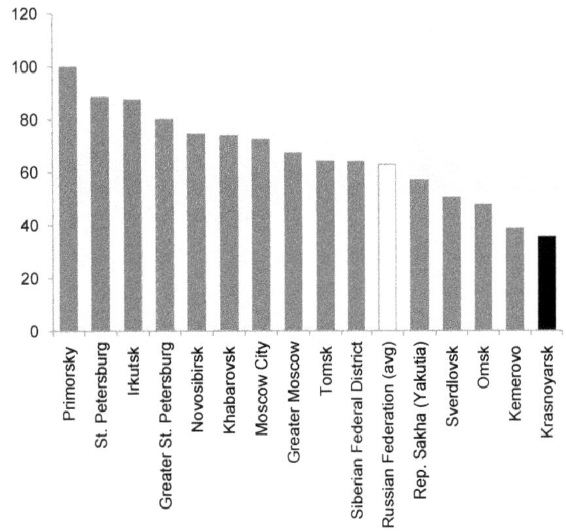

D. Share of respondent firms adopting new organisational or management practices or structures over the last three years

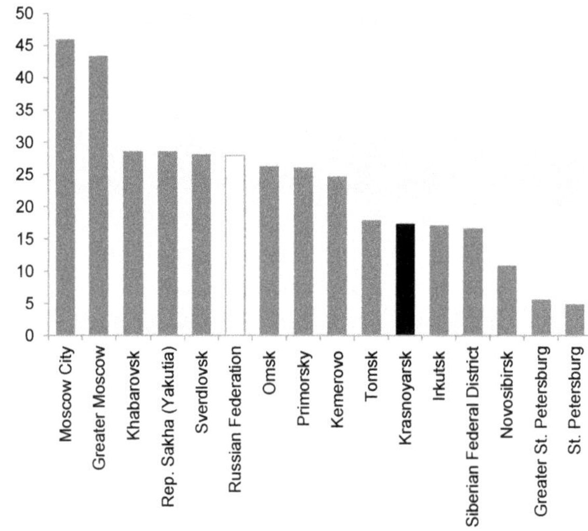

Source: EBRD/World Bank (2013), Business Environment and Enterprise Survey 2013, http://data.worldbank.org/data-catalog/BEEPS (accessed on 14 December 2013).

Table 2.7. **Indicators of innovation potential in selected Russian regions**

	Moscow City	Moscow Oblast'	Leningrad Oblast'	Novosibirsk	Tomsk	Tatarstan	Krasnoyarsk Krai
Population with tertiary education (%)	49.9	33.4	25.7	26.9	26	25	23.5
Employment in knowledge-intensive business services (%)	6.84	4.41	2.3	4.06	4.07	2.68	2.48
Business R&D/total R&D	25.5	14.9	18.87	12.41	15.51	27.78	11.23
Communication and R&D organisations/all firms (%)	0.63	0.75	0.45	0.48	0.77	0.66	0.83

Source: Kiselev, V. (2010), *Comparative Innovation Analysis of Russian Federation Regions*, Centre for Science Research and Statistics, Ministry of Education and Science, Moscow.

Figure 2.5. **Enterprise responses on workforce education and training**

BEEPS 2013 data for the Russian Federation and selected Russian regions

A. Respondent firms' assessment of inadequate education of the workforce as an obstacle to current operations (0 = no obstacle, 4= a very severe obstacle)

B. Share of respondent firms offering formal training to permanent, full-time employees

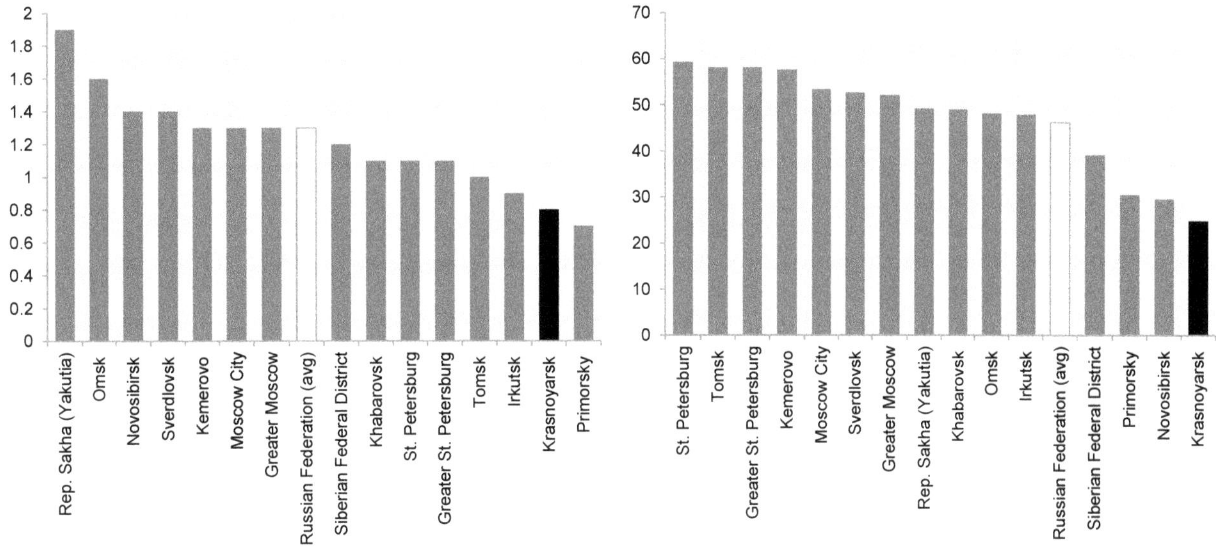

Source: EBRD/World Bank (2013), Business Environment and Enterprise Survey 2013, http://data.worldbank.org/data-catalog/BEEPS (accessed on 14 December 2013).

At present, the Agglomeration's innovation system is not realising its potential. In part, this reflects the difficulty of linking the Agglomeration's economy to the towns of Zheleznogorsk, which lies near the heart of the Agglomeration, and Zelenogorsk, which is not far from it (Box 2.7). These two towns were originally created as closed military research-industrial complexes, and they are now designated "closed administrative-territorial formations" (ZATO). The city needs also to build on its existing strengths and for this purpose to reinforce its SME sector. Finally, major Siberian cities compete with one another to attract international and domestic investment and have so far overlooked the possibilities of co-operation. Their common engagement in a number of clusters would significantly improve their competitiveness and their visibility on international markets.

Spurring innovation activity is an increasingly important policy goal

The Krai and the city have started to meet the challenge. At the sectoral level, the Krai authorities have started to establish and co-ordinate 13 technological platforms (energy, life support system, chemicals, solid mineral deposits, new materials, chemical engineering, metallurgy, ICT, translational medicine, food security, wood resources, renewable energy, educational technologies). This is part of a general effort to foster the competitiveness of the Krasnoyarsk Agglomeration, emphasising the economic specialisation of the local industries, the development of the business infrastructure and of the transport and communication means. Some sustainability elements have been introduced in the strategic exercise, but the whole procedure lacks consistency. Moreover, in early 2013, only a few platforms were operational.

Box 2.7. "Closed cities" in and around the Krasnoyarsk Agglomeration

Closed administrative-territorial formations (ZATOs) form a class of single-industry towns in Russia subject to special governance arrangements that are linked to the security implications of their research and/or industrial activities. Many are connected with the nuclear sector and fall under the overall aegis of the state nuclear energy corporation Rosatom. According to a Russian law adopted in 1992, the inhabitants of ZATOs on the territory of the Russian Federation that are included as part of towns and cities of regional subordination participate in the election of regional governors and local legislative authorities. ZATOs are financed and overseen by the federal authorities, and access to them can be restricted – particularly for foreigners. While some ZATOs are open to foreign investment, foreign citizens need special permission to enter them and some are closed to foreigners altogether. In 2012, there were 44 publicly acknowledged ZATOs in the Russian Federation with a total population of about 1.5 million people. Around three-quarters were administered by the Ministry of Defence, with the rest being administered by the Rosatom.

With a population of about 92 000, Zheleznogorsk, formerly known as Krasnoyarsk-26, was established in the early 1950s on the right bank of the Yenisei, north of the city of Krasnoyarsk. Initially created for the production of weapons-grade plutonium, Zheleznogorsk also became the primary centre for the production of Russian civilian satellites and one of its main employers is the Information Satellite Systems, the Russian Federation's largest satellite manufacturer and the prime developer of the GLONASS programme. GLONASS is a space-based satellite navigation system operated by the Russian Aerospace Defence Forces. It provides an alternative to Global Positioning System (GPS) and is the only alternative to GPS with global coverage and comparable precision. In addition, Zheleznogorsk's nuclear activities extended in civilian uses, particularly the production of plutonium, electricity and district heat using graphite-moderated water-cooled reactors, as well as the processing and storage of nuclear waste. The Mining and Chemical Combine (MCC) employs around 20% of the working population and accounts for over a quarter of the city's budgetary income. The MCC is responsible for 68% of the city's industrial output. Its main areas of work include the improvement of procedures and technologies for irradiated nuclear fuel processing, alternative forms of energy, decommissioning and clean-up of nuclear facilities and conversion programmes. This combination of nuclear and space specialisations form the basis for a strong production base for industrial and civil construction.

Somewhat further from the city of Krasnoyarsk is Zelenogorsk, formerly Krasnoyarsk-45, a ZATO city of about 68 000 on the banks of the Kan, about 180 km from its confluence with the Yenisei. Likewise under the supervision of Rosatom, Zelenogorsk was involved in uranium enrichment for the (then) Soviet Union's nuclear programme.

Source: Rosatom (n.d.), www.rosatom.ru/aboutcorporation/nuclearindustry/zato (accessed 10 December 2013).

One question to consider is whether the number of technology platforms is appropriate. Given that the Krai and the city have limited budgets for policy support, it is important not to distribute it too thinly among too many recipients. Support needs to be selective and addressed to a few areas of comparative advantages in order to diversify the sources of growth. It would seem advisable to strengthen the focus on:

- *Agriculture*. The Krai produces 42% of grain, potatoes and vegetables, 41% of milk, and 36% of meat and eggs in Eastern Siberia. Approximately 426 farms of various types of ownership and 4 797 communal farms are currently operating in the region. There are plans for the formation of a food ring around the city using innovative technologies to provide inhabitants with organic food and high-quality dairy products. Turning land resources available in neighbouring districts into agriculture, horticulture or cattle areas could also ensure a combination of small farms production and the organisation of product processing and large commodity production. There are also opportunities to export the production to other territories of the Russian Federation, provided that transport links improve.

- *Renewable energy.* Rushydro, headquartered in Krasnoyarsk, operates over 70 renewable facilities and co-ordinates the renewable energy technical platform. It intends to enhance its innovation capacities for a wide range of renewable energy technologies including non-conventional ones such as wind and solar energy. Experimentation has started in the Agglomeration for non-conventional sources. A solar cluster project has been setup by a group of Russian companies and the roadmap has been approved by Rosatom. Other pilot projects notably in the field of biomass could be envisaged; in the long run, they could help reduce energy and infrastructure costs in remote places across Russia. The Krai Ministry of Industrial Production and Energy has also allocated funding to a research centre at SFU to run a programme to evaluate the feasibility of applying renewable energy to regional needs.[17] Given the Polycrystal Silicon Research capabilities in MCC Zheleznogorsk, a new facility to produce photovoltaic cells is planned. New analysis will nevertheless be needed to assess the competitive potential of the different elements of the supply chain. The renewables sector has in many places been subject to boom-and-bust dynamics, not least those fuelled by ill-designed public support measures (OECD, 2012d).

- *Broadband.* Internet penetration is lower than average in the Siberian District but developing fast. Developing broadband is a way to break isolation of most settlements in the Krai. It has a high innovation impact in terms of economic and social development as the region works to build the information society. So far, this digital potential is underutilised to develop an Internet-based entrepreneurial community. A sound development strategy should encourage investment and employment creation in this sector (many plans with these implicit objectives have been launched in US states: e.g. in Florida, Wisconsin, etc.).

- *Subcontractors and service providers for the extraction sector.* Competitive mining cities in countries like Canada are typically home to a large number of companies servicing primary industries. Many local and international consultants are, for example, based in the Greater Vancouver area. They support the mining industry across British Columbia, as well as in other areas of Canada. For example, accounting firms also provide mining companies with assurance/audit, tax and advisory services, law firms advise on mergers and acquisitions, initial public offerings and joint ventures. Finally, analytical and metallurgy services are also critical for mining operations and a number of world laboratories are operational. These activities in the Krasnoyarsk Agglomeration could be further developed: the share of knowledge-intensive business services (KIBS) in the Agglomeration is low (Table 2.7). They are often still fulfilled by the large primary industries companies. Instilling more competition on these markets and encouraging the externalisation of the above tasks would help to increase the efficiency of the local resource-based economy.

Tourism has also been highlighted in some proposals and plans. However, expectations here should be rather modest. The Agglomeration has some assets with tourist potential, chiefly in the natural environment surrounding the city, which provides opportunities for hiking and climbing. Important economic events and fora regularly take place in Krasnoyarsk, thus contributing to the development of business tourism. Nevertheless, winters are long and much of the time too severe for mass ski resorts, travel to the region is rather expensive and summers are short. In addition, most jobs in tourism tend to be not only seasonal but relatively low-productivity employment. It is likely that the more profitable niches in the tourist sector are small – high-value "adventure" tourism (wilderness trekking, hunting, etc.) could be further enhanced but this would require significant infrastructure investment.

R&D performance is not commensurate with the Agglomeration's potential

Most of the public basic research in the Krai and the city of Krasnoyarsk is undertaken by Russian Academy of Sciences (RAS) Institutes from the Siberian branch (SB). Akademgorodok Krasnoyarsk is a scientific centre located in the west side of the city, home to more than 20 R&D institutes and organisations, the most prominent being the SB Institute of Forest, the SB Institute of Physics, the SB Institute of Computational Modelling, the Institute of Biophysics and the SB Institute of Chemistry.

While business is clearly the sector most concerned by innovation expenditures in the broadest sense, its involvement in R&D spending is comparatively small (Table 2.7). Given that large firms in Krasnoyarsk's primary sector are often headquartered outside the Agglomeration, research expenditures might be assigned to other locations. This would, however, also be true of other regions in Table 2.7, such as Tomsk, Tyumen and Tatarstan. Employment in KIBS is also low compared to the rest of the Siberian Federal District. Communication organisation and media companies are active in the Krai and mainly in the city of Krasnoyarsk. Only large firms are engaged in innovation expenditures.

Research output among HEIs is also relatively low, at least as measured by SCImago rankings (Table 2.8), and is largely concentrated at SFU, the largest HEI in Siberia. SFU has singled out six top-priority spheres of scientific and educational activity: engineering physics, chemistry of new materials and material science, bio-physical ecology and biotechnology, space and informational-communicative technologies, geo-technologies, regional technology and human capital management. There are also 13 enlarged groups of directions and specialties of personnel training. HEIs in Krasnoyarsk appear to be less engaged in R&D than their counterparts in Novosibirsk, Tomsk or Kemerovo. International co-operation in research is also less intense than in Tomsk's and Novosibirsk's state universities. The quality of publications is also lower (Table 2.8). The gap is not only significant with respect to other mining-oriented universities in foreign countries, such as the Laurentian University in Ontario (Canada) or Católica del Norte in Chile, but also with regard to specialised technological research universities such as the MISIS[18] in Moscow or the St. Petersburg State Polytechnic University. SFU is nevertheless rising in the rankings and has overtaken, among others, the Bauman Institute, a well-known Russian HEI whose R&D activities are especially centred on machine building, computer systems, robots and applied mathematics, i.e. a number of specialisations that are in line with those of SFU.

In the last five years, the efficiency of research activity of Krasnoyarsk scientists has been improving and SFU, in particular, has moved 100 places up the SCImago rankings over the last couple of years. This is also reflected in the Russian Index of Scientific Citations: the number of publications of SFU employees in Russian and foreign journals with the impact-factor rose from 439 in 2007 to 910 in 2011 and the institution itself climbed to 21st place in the rankings.

Table 2.8. **SCImago ranking of major Russian and other selected universities, 2013**

	Institution	Output	IC	NI	Q1	Spec	Exc	Leaders (%)
115	Lomonosov University	20 151	34.1	0.63	21.93	0.76	5.74	62.98
660	St. Petersburg State University	5 404	44.54	0.61	24.74	0.77	5.23	60.34
1 207	Novosibirsk State University	2 609	25.07	0.58	23.38	0.82	4.18	21.35
1 698	Kazan Federal University	1 547	36.46	0.45	20.75	0.81	3.22	63.61
1 803	Laurentian University (Canada)	1 407	35.32	1.04	47.48	0.62	11.31	61.05
1 815	St. Petersburg State Polytechnic	1 445	41.3	23.4	0.6	0.9	5.6	764
1 838	Lobachevskii State University	1 360	23.46	0.31	16.4	0.85	1.78	64.41
1 887	Tomsk State University	1 290	28.91	0.41	15.04	0.83	2.69	59.53
2 038	National U of S&T MISIS	1 108	26.62	0.53	18.32	0.94	3.69	64.53
2 080	Tomsk Polytechnic University	1 055	22.27	0.39	12.61	0.89	2.62	68.25
2 134	Universidad Católica del Norte-Antofagasta (Chile)	995	57.29	0.77	34.57	0.81	7.63	49.55
2 185	Siberian Federal University	932	23.28	0.45	16.63	0.8	2.35	39.59
2 281	Novosibirsk State Technical University	821	16.69	0.52	8.65	0.89	2.91	65.9
2 292	Bauman Moscow StateTech U	810	15.56	0.2	7.28	0.89	1.13	71.11
2 572	Irkutsk State University	506	26.09	0.39	17.19	0.85	4.06	56.72

Notes: The SCImago institutional ranking is a measure of scientific influence of institutions based on research output, international collaboration, normalised impact and publication rate. Output: total number of documents published in scholarly journals indexed in Scopus. Rankings in the table are based on this indicator. IC: international collaboration – an institution's output ratio produced in collaboration with foreign institutions. Q1: high-quality publications – ratio of publications that an institution publishes in the most influential scholarly journals of the world, those ranked in the first quartile (25%) in their categories as ordered by the SCImago Journal Rank (SJRII) indicator. NI: normalised impact is computed using the methodology established by the Karolinska Institut in Sweden where it is named "item-oriented field normalized citation score average". The normalisation of the citation values is done on an individual article level. The values (in percent) show the relationship between an institution's average scientific impact and the world average set to a score of 1, i.e. an NI score of 0.8 means the institution is cited 20% below the world average and 1.3 means the institution is cited 30% above average. Spec: the Specialisation Index indicates the extent of thematic concentration/dispersion of an institution's scientific output. Values range between 0 and 1, indicating generalist vs. specialised institutions respectively. Exc: the excellence rate indicates the amount (in percent) of an institution's scientific output that is included into the set of the 10% of the most cited papers in their respective scientific fields. Leaders: leadership indicates an institution's "output as main contributor", that is the percentage of papers in which the corresponding author belongs to the institution.

Source: SIR World Report (2012), "SCImago Institutions Rankings", data source: Scopus, www.scimagoir.com (accessed 10 December 2013).

The regional innovation system reflects the structure of the Krai's economy

The link between R&D activities and innovation performance in countries and regions is often far from clear. In some OECD regions (OECD, 2012c), highly productive R&D establishments may have few backward and forward linkages to the rest of the economy – thus, while the region can benefit from the presence of these high-value innovation activities, the fruits of this work are often deployed in production elsewhere. For example, pharmaceuticals research in Skåne (Sweden) may lead to important new developments, but there is little pharmaceuticals production there, so the new products developed in Skåne laboratories are likely to be produced somewhere else. The links between R&D and innovation performance can be significantly altered in a positive direction when synergies exist among the activities of the main players. This is a crucial parameter, given that in the present technological context isolated economic agents are increasingly unable to master the whole innovation process. In other words, new products and new processes are overwhelmingly the result of the co-operation of different organisations and firms. Partnerships are therefore critical and need a careful assessment.

In Krasnoyarsk, co-operative activities take different dimensions. Private companies order R&D work from research centres and laboratories. Leading scholars work as consultants, or even direct research projects undertaken by big private companies (e.g. Gazprom, Polyus, Rosneft, Norilsk Nickel or Rusal), which are conducted in the companies' facilities and wholly financed by them. Small enterprises are formed within universities, which specialise in R&D work for private companies. Collaboration with universities extends to the organisation of base departments of universities on the territories of partner companies. Some base departments and institutes (the Institute for Oil and Gas of SFU, for example) are created with financing from relevant companies (Rosneft in this case) with a view to training personnel that the companies need and also to undertaking applied research. This can work in the state/social sphere, too: 44 of the 69 departments of the Krasnoyarsk State Medical University are in clinical institutions. The Siberian State Aerospace University trains personnel in four basic departments and seven enterprises. SFU has 22 such departments linked to enterprises.

HEIs can also conclude contracts for the preparation of specialists for particular companies – by 2013, SFU had concluded 3 530 such contracts, and the Krasnoyarsk State Agrarian University was training students under 693 contracts. HEIs can conclude agreements with strategic partners to promote these forms of co-operation: the Oil and Gas Institute was created under a co-operation agreement with Rosneft. SFU has concluded 70 such agreements. Finally, some joint projects are undertaken by HEIs and companies with federal support: in 2010, Krasnoyarsk HEIs won four mega-grants for work on: *i)* resource-efficient building materials; *ii)* metallurgy (new, highly sophisticated aluminium alloys); *iii)* geological exploration technology; and *iv)* development of R&D infrastructure.

Nevertheless, the percentage of innovative firms that report co-operation with other firms or organisations is comparatively low across the Russian Federation (7% in 2008), particularly when compared to EU regions (26% for the low performing ones and more for the others). The Krasnoyarsk Krai figure is similar to the value of the indicator for the Moscow region. It is inferior to its value for Yaroslavl, Tatarstan, Ulyanovsk, Tyumen and Tomsk (Kiselev, 2010).

Collaboration is constrained in a number of ways. First, HEIs are not strongly research-oriented – for example, only 15% of SFU's budget goes to R&D (Institut Français des relations internationales, 2012) – and this limits the capacities for co-operation. Secondly, large mining and processing companies often undertake research in Moscow and co-operate with institutions in Moscow or St. Petersburg. In any case, their main source of technological upgrading lies in the purchase of new machinery and equipment, mainly from abroad. Thirdly, international links are underdeveloped. SFU has signed collaboration agreements with around 60 Russian and foreign universities and research centres, but many of them are co-operation frameworks and do not imply the implementation of specific joint projects. Finally, interactions with innovative SMEs are still marginal.

Table 2.9. **Innovation indicators, selected Russian regions**

	Moscow Oblast'	Leningrad	Tatarstan	Krasnoyarsk Krai	Novosibirsk	Tyumen	Tomsk
Patent	809	231	581	473.2	650.57	200.01	1 097
Innovative firms (%)	7.6	5.6	14.3	14	5.4	6.5	16
R&D/volume of goods	4.39	1.01	0.62	0.8	4.62	0.25	3.11
Innovative goods and services (%)	9.90	1.42	14.77	1.6	3.40	0.71	2.87
Export of innovative goods (%)	2.41	0.77	7.06	0.41	0.20	0.07	0.18

Source: Kiselev, V. (2010), *Comparative Innovation Analysis of Russian Federation Regions*, Centre for Science Research and Statistics, Ministry of Education and Science, Moscow.

Nevertheless, the capacities to patent and to create spinoffs are real. Patent applications are in line with the average performance of other polytechnics and state universities of the Siberian Federal District. More than 40% of the spinoffs formed in 2009-12 were generated by the universities, albeit with some government support. SFU and the Aerospace University in Zheleznogorsk have created around 44 firms (2009 figures), but this has not (yet, at any rate) led to much job creation. Another positive point for Krasnoyarsk is the relatively high share of innovative firms in the total firm population (Table 2.10). Though significantly below the EU-27 level (about one-quarter), this is one of the best scores in the Russian Federation. On some indicators, the Krai is doing significantly better even than the Leningrad region or the oil region of Tyumen. On some dimensions, it can be compared with Tatarstan, one of Russia's more active regions when it comes to innovation. Krasnoyarsk nevertheless encounters difficulties in translating its innovation effort into a significant volume of innovative products and services.

Comparison with other *oblasts* (provinces) in the Siberian District shows some clear differences between the Novosibirsk science city model and the Krasnoyarsk regional innovation system (RIS). In Novosibirsk, the RIS is very much research-based; researchers are three times more numerous relative to population than in Krasnoyarsk and internal R&D expenditures are 50% higher. However, its tech-push innovation model generates few new products and processes. Patent performance is only one-third greater, reflecting perhaps higher productivity by researchers in Krasnoyarsk. This also applies to the number of new technologies created through these patents. In Krasnoyarsk, the emphasis is clearly on engineering, production processing, automated monitoring, IT for production and integrated management. The import of technologies is also considerably more important in Krasnoyarsk (five times more in 2010). The Tomsk Oblast innovation configuration seems to deliver interesting results, with greater emphasis on business R&D, innovation infrastructures and co-operative projects, while Omsk is placed in an intermediary position between Novosibirsk and Tomsk (Table 2.10).

Table 2.10. **Innovation output in the Siberian Federal District, 2010**

	Krasnoyarsk Krai	Novosibirsk Oblast	Omsk Oblast	Tomsk Oblast
Share of innovative organisations (%)	10%	5.5%	7.3%	18.4%
Volume of innovative goods(RUB millions)	4 957	14 106	9 783	5 361
Number of created new technologies	1 937	2 483	4 165	1 818
Patents granted	383	505	205	331
Number of R&D workers per patent granted	8.6	18.1	7.6	9.9

Source: SFU (2012), "Background report for the OECD Territorial Review of Krasnoyarsk", Siberian Federal University, Krasnoyarsk, Russian Federation, November.

Policy can do more to stimulate innovative activity

Krasnoyarsk's modest innovative output is a matter of concern for the authorities. Several trends reflect a structural degradation over 2005-10 and need to be reversed – notably the decline in the volume of technological exports (only 5% of the total innovative goods in 2010) and the declining novelty of innovative products.[19] According to a 2010 business sector poll, obstacles to innovation are numerous. Economic factors with a negative effect included lack of funds (27.4%), limited state support (13.7%), the high cost of innovation activities (18.9%) and economic risk (10.8%). Production-related and institutional parameters were also cited, notably the low innovative capacities of companies (7.6%), the lack of qualified personnel (4.2%), uncertainties about intellectual property (5.1%) and insufficient legal framework (4.9%).

The region is starting to face these challenges. Here, the Krai Ministry of Investments and Innovation is the main policy actor in the region. It designs the regional innovation policy with the help of the Governor's Council for Innovative Development and the Innovation Council of Krasnoyarsk. It has recourse to a relatively large spectrum of initiatives and policy measures, including pecuniary incentives such as public procurements for research products, subsidies for commercialisation and purchase of equipment, partial funding of training expenses and indirect support through assistance for international co-operation and the organisation of public events (fairs, exhibitions, conferences) in order to diffuse knowledge and encourage market interactions. The budget for funding innovation at the level of the Krai is nevertheless limited to about RUB 737 million (EUR 18 million) for 2012-14.[20]

So far the policy has emphasised:

- *Innovation infrastructures.* The region is now developing the Krasnoyarsk Technopark, a RUB 3 billion project to give 50 000 m² of office, laboratory and production space for innovative businesses. Meanwhile, the Krasnoyarsk Regional Innovative Technology Business Incubator, or KRITBI, opened its doors in 2011. It now houses 92 residents, 27 on-site and 65 remote, and reported private investment of more than RUB 350 million for 2012. Its partnerships include Kazan's IT Park and Novosibirsk's Akadempark, based in Akademgorodok, and it is home to a Fablab digital production centre. Its objective is to attract new firms and talents to the city. There is also a city incubator (KCITBI).
- *Public-private partnerships.* Co-ordination between business, higher education and the public sector is encouraged within the framework of technological platforms. The aim is to establish 13 regional platforms. As of mid-2013, the elaboration process was mainly advanced for three of them: solid mineral deposits; information, telecommunication and space technologies; oil refining and energy industries.

Much of the funding for these programmes comes from the federal budget, and federal innovation policy is the backbone of all the regional and local initiatives. The relative weight of federal funds has also been increasing over time, to reach 45.7% of innovation spending in 2011. This policy is mainly organised through tax incentives and market procurements. Support is also given through federally targeted programmes, funds channelled through the Russian Foundation for Basic Research (RFBR) and a number of measures initiated by the Foundation for Assistance to Small Innovative Enterprise (FASIE),[21] such as the START programme.[22] Nineteen KRITBI projects received support within this framework in 2012. Particularly interesting is the federal programme supporting young researchers. Forty-five KRITBI projects benefited from this support in 2012. There is also a federal programme to fund scientific projects carried out in co-operation with leading foreign scientists. In the case of SFU, this federal money went to three projects in the field of biomaterials, bioluminescence and biogeochemistry. Though useful initiatives, these projects are nevertheless nurtured with relatively scarce resources (RUB 363 millions).

One important aspect of this federally supported regional innovation policy is the cluster programme. Twenty-eight clusters have been selected and a first group of 14 will receive financial support over 2012-17. One such cluster is located close to the city of Krasnoyarsk, at Zheleznogorsk; it concerns satellite activities. A number of other sectoral clusters, including mechanical engineering, instrument engineering, information and communication technologies, tourism, metallurgy, woodworking, construction, energy and chemicals, are targeted for Krai and city supports. Here, again, there is a danger of dispersion of effort: given the limited resources available, it probably does not make sense to support so many clusters locally. The Krasnoyarsk City administration has carried out several analyses on issues relevant to these clusters and identified development projects. A centre of cluster development will be established soon. It will offer R&D services with the assistance of HEIs, provide training and educational services and disseminate knowledge about the development of subcontracting procedures. It will also provide marketing advice and expertise to help the establishment of enterprises on foreign markets.

The implementation of this cluster policy raised nevertheless a number of questions because the sectoral cluster is not a well-delineated concept and cluster policies in many Russian regions have tended to confuse clusters with old Soviet-era territorial production complexes. As a result, they can easily become mechanisms for supporting incumbent enterprises in difficulty. Moreover, boundaries between sectors are blurring and changing fast, and public authorities typically lack the information needed to identify "priority" sectors in a world of increasingly complex global value chains. Specialisation now is often by task rather than sector (Baldwin, 2006). Broad networks (like technology platforms) that rely on light instruments look more promising than strong cluster policies.

The policy will need not only to be rebalanced but also consolidated. The business environment is not sufficiently conducive to research and development initiatives and to innovations. As shown by the case of Calgary (Box 2.8), a "mining city" similar in size to Krasnoyarsk, focusing on improving the tax regime for R&D investments and encouraging the development of venture development organisations has helped the city to achieve successful development.[23] The lessons that can be drawn from Krasnoyarsk's West Siberian neighbour, Tomsk, are not so different. The city is endowed with robust innovation infrastructures and intermediate institutions as well as proactive universities (Box 2.9). Facilitating the linkages with international firms is crucial and establishing an innovation-oriented special economic zone (SEZ) could be instrumental in that context.

Box 2.8. Calgary: A natural resources and mining city

Alberta is a land-locked province in Western Canada with a population of 4.0 million concentrated in the capital city of Edmonton (1.3 million) and the business hub of Calgary (1.5 million). Alberta's GDP is CAD 288 billion and its GDP per capita is 55% higher than the Canadian average. The oil and gas industry is a dominant sector in Calgary but the city area produces little to no oil and gas. Concentration of the oil industry in Alberta has made Calgary a leader in all aspects of energy: project design, exploration, production, finance, processing, transport, marketing and management. Calgary is home to the headquarters of major Canadian and global energy companies. Its employment structure is diverse, but talent is concentrated in oil and gas activities.

The city has the highest concentration of engineers and engineering technologies in the country. Calgary's employment is focused on the financial, scientific, technical, professional engineers and high tech that serves the energy industry with much of Calgary's employment quite focused on professional services. Calgary's finance and business industry has experienced significant growth, with 8 100 jobs created between 2003 and 2012, an increase of over 47%. Calgary's strategy aims at exploiting knowledge in the oil and gas platform to consolidate and diversify its industrial base. Examples of distinct industries spawned by needs from oil and gas include wireless telecommunications, GPS clusters and renewable energy. Calgary is trying to shift its business model from rent-seeking to productive entrepreneurship. One reason for the successful development of the city is its low tax regime. Alberta is the only Canadian province with a flat personal income tax (10%). It has also a scientific research and experimental development (SR&ED) tax credit programme which provides a refundable tax credit for corporations for SR&ED expenditures incurred in the province after 31 December 2008. Alberta's SR&ED tax credit is applied over and above Canada's federal SR&ED credit.

Source: Calgary Economic Development (2012), *Energy Sector Profile, 2012*, Calgary, Alberta, Canada; Alberta Treasury Board and Finance (2014), *Economic Outlook, March*, available at: http://www.finance.alberta.ca/publications/budget/budget2014/fiscal-plan-economic-outlook.pdf.

Box 2.9. The Tomsk regional innovation system

Tomsk exhibits similar geographical features with regard to Krasnoyarsk. It is adjacent to Krasnoyarsk Krai and the main centre of a sparsely populated territory well-endowed in oil and gas. It is nevertheless smaller and less rich in natural resources. The oil and gas industry employs 28% of the workforce and generates 60% of GDP. Nearly 200 large and medium companies form an industrial structure built around the exploitation of the oil and gas industry, petrochemicals, nuclear power, electro-mechanicals, metal working, woodworking and pharmaceuticals. In both a short- and longer term perspective, Tomsk's human potential is clearly a comparative advantage when compared to most other regions in the Russian Federation. Tomsk Oblast has a strong concentration of students and substantial research capability (150 researchers and 18 doctors of science or PhDs per 10 000 residents).

Tomsk hosts six state universities, two research institutes and 15 branches of universities headquartered in other cities and *oblasts*. It trains 85 000 students in more than 300 disciplines. Another 20 000 are trained by secondary vocational schools. Every fifth inhabitant of Tomsk is a student. The universities generate consolidated revenues from their educational services and scientific developments amounting to EUR 75 million a year. The Tomsk higher education system is organised around complementary high-quality organisations: a research pole with Tomsk State University (TSU), an academic innovation pole with Tomsk Polytechnic University (TPU) and an entrepreneurial pole, Tomsk University of Control Systems and Radio-electronics (TUCSR). Each university has a technology transfer office. A number of incubators have been set up relatively recently: there are now three at TPU and one at TSU. TUCSR organises a business plan competition prior to integrating new firms in its incubator. It also manages a network of spinoffs (106 in 2009).

Box 2.9. **The Tomsk regional innovation system** (*cont.*)

The Russian Federation provides the bulk of the support for R&D (about 90% of the volume of grants). The total number of grants of the Russian Foundation for Basic Research (RFBR) and the Russian Foundation for Humanities (RFRH) rose from 269 in 2002 to 470 in 2007. Combined with regional support, RUB 35 million was invested in basic R&D in 2007. Tomsk research organisations and R&D-based firms also benefit from the FTP, and 39 projects were being supported for 2007-12 with funds amounting to more than RUB 0.5 billion, a large share of which for nano-industries. Another important objective of federal support to the Tomsk Oblast is to encourage the formation of high-technology firms. FASIE is the key instrument. Its START programme supports 12 projects in the Siberian region, of which 5 are in Tomsk. Its UMNIK programme, which targets young scientists developing innovative R&D, has provided grants to 80 projects involving 220 students and researchers of the Tomsk Polytechnic University. FASIE has also already facilitated the creation of 20 companies, of which 10 by TPU in IT technologies, new materials, medicine and machine building.

Given the relatively small number of large innovative firms, the central government has tried to attract more international firms to the region, primarily through its tax incentives policy. A special economic zone (SEZ) was established in 2005, which had 45 resident companies in 2010, including several firms with foreign participation. More than 650 jobs have been created, and it supports 140 projects annually, mainly in the fields of ICT, new materials, nanotechnologies, biotechnology and medicine. The federal government and the municipalities have invested in the SEZ on a 74%/26% basis.

Source: OECD (2011a), *OECD Reviews of Innovation Policy: Russian Federation 2011*, OECD Publishing, Paris, http://dx.doi.org/10.1787/9789264113138-en.

The Krai's defence cities could be better linked to the rest of the Agglomeration

As noted above, Zheleznogorsk, situated 60 km north of Krasnoyarsk, is geographically a part of the Agglomeration. Zelenogorsk, somewhat further from Krasnoyarsk, still does not appear on most public maps. The authorities are well aware of the scientific and commercial potential of these two ZATOs, and Zheleznogorsk is especially important to the future of the Agglomeration (Box 2.10). For some time past, there has been a long-term vision of Zheleznogorsk as a city of high-tech production, acting as a centre for the design and development of innovative new technologies. Previous plans have focused on energy supply, employment creation and improving communications with the federal and regional authorities. Special attention has been given to small business. The city administration holds competitions for SMEs to help compensate for the interest they pay on commercial bank loans. The competition aims to reduce the cost of borrowing for small businesses in ZATO Zheleznogorsk. An incubator has been operating since 2004 and an industrial park will be completed over the 2013-17 period. However, the city's ZATO status does not facilitate the interactions with external actors. Satellite systems are dual technologies and defence industries increasingly rely on often more advanced civil technologies (electronics, materials). Their competitiveness is hampered by restrictive regulations with regard to import of technologies and co-operative exchanges with non-ZATO communities and firms.

Thus far, defence conversion has been promoted thanks to international programmes. The International Development Centre "IDC Zheleznogorsk", a non-governmental organisation founded in 1999, aims to provide business development services to the local community and to assist in creating jobs for specialists made redundant by the MCC. An offshore programming centre was created in Zheleznogorsk in 2002, with the support of the US programme NCI. Thanks to the IDC's provision of services for business plan preparation, market evaluation and risk analysis, more than 40 projects were completed and more than 1 000 people trained to run new innovative enterprises during 2000-10. While these initiatives are a step in the right direction, the whole policy addressed to Zheleznogorsk partially misses its target for a number of reasons:

- Limited public support to innovative activities. Regional and city budgets devote less than EUR 20 million to innovation within their programmes for 2012-14. As underlined above, the federal government is not adding much to this amount through its cluster policy.
- Bureaucratic obstacles and regulations. Because of closed city regulations, businesses face additional hurdles, when they want to invest in Zheleznogorsk. Special permission is required for investors and co-operation with public entities is more complex. Employees are submitted to travel and residency restrictions.
- Management rigidities. The national information satellite system in Zheleznogorsk has been selected as one of 28 national clusters eligible for support by the federal government. As a former Soviet defence combine, Zheleznogorsk does not really operate as a cluster. The whole system lacks flexibility and a co-operation friendly environment.

Box 2.10. Space and nuclear activities in Zheleznogorsk and Zelenogorsk

Founded in 1959, Reshetnev Information Satellite System, the largest satellite manufacturer in the Russian Federation (formerly called NPO PM) has built 27 different space systems and over 1 000 individual satellites. It designs and manufactures communication, TV broadcasting, navigation and geodesic satellites. The company also produces ground antennas. It is the main contractor for the GLONASS programme and produces the Ekspress series of communications satellites. The company is located in Zheleznogorsk and employs around 6 500 people. In contrast to launchers, the international competitiveness of these communication satellites is not yet well established. Wider use of GLONASS is hindered by the higher cost of GLONASS receivers and, according to some assessments, its inferior quality. Other satellites tend to be for military use only (Crane and Usanov, 2010).

Russia has a strong competitive position in the nuclear fuel cycle, especially in uranium conversion and enrichment. It has the world's largest enrichment capacity (40% of the global total) and much of it is located in or near Krasnoyarsk. Rosatom owns 100% of the electrochemical plant in Zelenogorsk as well as the Angarsk Electrolysis Chemical Complex, the Urals Electrochemical Combine and the Siberian Chemical Combine (Tomsk).

In Zheleznogorsk, the Chemical Company was established in 1958 as a testing station for liquefied rocket engines. It is an affiliate of the Federal Governmental Unitary Enterprise Krasnoyarsk Machine-Building Plant, which is managed by Rosaviacosmos. Its key areas of activity include testing of spaceships and rockets, utilisation of weapons, transport of special freights, cryogenic production, manufacture of polymeric products and wood-drying equipment, metal processing and assembling.

Source: CNCP (Closed Nuclear Cities Partnership) (n.d.), www.pe-international.ru (10 December 2010).

The challenge, then, is to better use the assets and liabilities of Zheleznogorsk and Zelenogorsk, while respecting the federal authorities' legitimate national security concerns in connection with these facilities. Here, the US experience may be relevant, particularly the experience of managing Oak Ridge National Laboratory (ORNL). Oak Ridge (Tennessee) was a closed city during World War II, when it played a central role in the early stages of the Manhattan Project – the development of the first atomic bomb. It shifted to civilian control in 1947. In 1959, the town was incorporated and a city manager and council form of government was adopted by the community rather than direct federal control. However, the ORNL itself remains an extremely sensitive federal installation. At present, the US Department of Energy runs the laboratory and is responsible for its security. Most interesting is the transfer of technology regime (Box 2.11) in which it operates. For both cities, it is important to facilitate the local and horizontal linkages with high-tech SMEs based in the federally managed facilities, and the universities and firms outside. It would be recommended to: *i)* alter the ZATO status and soften the present closed cities regulations; *ii)* set up a technology transfer policy modelled on the US CRADA system; and *iii)* rearticulate interventions within the framework of a sound niche-based strategy for the whole Agglomeration.

Box 2.11. Stimulating technology transfer and promoting integrated R&D: US initiatives

While the US Department of Defense (DoD) is continuously examining opportunities for using civilian R&D in place of DoD funded efforts, defence services also strive to spend a significant share of their research effort on projects with potential commercial applications. The Navy, Army and Air Force plan to improve co-ordination of research involving services, laboratories, industry and universities to leverage their limited research funds. Transfer of technologies activities cover the full spectrum of interactions, starting with the exchange of ideas between visiting researchers to contractually structured research collaboration involving the joint use of equipment and facilities. They include collaborative R&D agreements (CRADAs), patent license agreements and technical outreach.

Designed under the federal Transfer of Technology Act of 1986, which amended the Stevenson Wydler Technological Innovation Act of 1980, CRADAs are designed to allow technology transfer to the private sector, to speed up the commercialisation of technologies, optimise resources and protect the private companies involved. Under these agreements, federal labs and private sector collaborators share resources in collaborative R&D. The lab also assists industry, both on a reimbursable basis and in an informal manner by responding to requests for information. This framework also works for other related agencies such as the Department of Energy. A CRADA allows both parties to keep research results confidential for up to five years under the Freedom of Information Act. Private companies participating in a CRADA are allowed to file patents and they retain patent rights on inventions developed by the CRADA. The government gets a license to the patent. For example, Oak Ridge National Laboratory (ORNL) provides support on technology development in materials forming and processing and researchers at Los Alamos National Lab provide technical advice to small business. The government can thus assist industry informally, provide more formal consulting on a reimbursable basis, and grant licenses of technologies developed within the government.

Over the years, the DoD has seen a steady increase of CRADAs (in 2011, 2 500 were active and 700 new ones had been initiated during the year)[1], because DoD labs are looking to leverage private sector technologies, resources and funding through collaborative relationships. Efforts are now deployed to streamline licensing procedures and to improve public availability of patent license agreements and CRADAs through collaborative practices reviews, collecting lessons learnt and best practices and facilitating transfer of technologies through local and regional partnerships engagement. In addition, the Oak Ridge Manufacturing, Prototyping and Demonstration Center offers companies commercial expertise and demonstration equipment in a variety of manufacturing technologies.

1. These activities resulted in 800 patent applications in 2011 (600 in 2007).

Sources: US Congress, Office of Technology Assessment (1994), *Assessing the Potential of Civil-Military Integration: Technologies, Processes, and Practices, OTA-ISS-611*, US Government Printing Office, Washington, DC, September, available at: http://ota.fas.org/reports/9402.pdf; US Department of Defense (2012), "Strategy and action plan for accelerating technology transfer and commercialisation of federal research in support of high growth business", US Department of Defense, Washington, DC, 4 October, available at: www.nist.gov/tpo/publications/upload/DOD-Tech-Transfer-Plan.pdf.

Much can be done to strengthen inter-regional co-operation for innovation

Given its huge size, Siberia is home to many mono-cities. They have similar specialisation and often compete with one another. Novosibirsk, Tomsk and Irkutsk are all competitors for higher education and scientific research; Yekaterinburg, Omsk and Novosibirsk for mechanical engineering; Irkutsk and Kemerovo for energy systems; and Yakutia for access to natural resources. This competition has intensified as industrial restructuring has affected settlement patterns: as Siberia loses population and concentrates increasingly in capital- rather than labour-intensive activities, cities' futures depend more and more on competition for other functions within the urban hierarchy – for the status of regional centres, for the location of HEIs and federal facilities, etc. The designation of SFU as Siberia's federal university, for example, was undoubtedly a boost for Krasnoyarsk.

Unsurprisingly in this context, inter-regional and intercity co-operation in Siberia has remained underdeveloped. Some (limited) steps have nevertheless been taken. For example, the information satellite platform involves not only SFU and the Siberian State Aerospace University but also the Siberian branch of the Russian Academy of Sciences, the Tomsk Polytechnic University and Tomsk State University. However, such examples are few and the potential for development is enormous. EU initiatives such as the Interreg programme could serve as models for strengthening co-operation among the regions and cities of Siberia.

Such an approach would be welcome, since so far most of these cities have not built very strong links abroad and they still struggle to remain internationally competitive outside the primary sector. Co-operation has developed slowly with Europe and the United States since the 1990s. Over 2007-14, the EU/Russian Federation collaboration budget under the 7th Framework Programme amounted to only EUR 45 million and most of the money went to non-Siberian regions.

Given this environment, it would be particularly beneficial to exploit the potential for co-operation among Siberian regions and cities, particularly in research, education and workforce planning. These are areas where a degree of co-ordination could allow Siberian cities to realise some economies of scope and scale. Working through the Association of Innovative Regions,[24] Krasnoyarsk and its neighbours could also establish a platform for inter-regional innovation policy learning. To feed this learning process and reinforce its own ability to monitor and assess regional trends, the Federation could promote the harmonised development of statistics and other benchmarking instruments by the regions. Krasnoyarsk could also within this framework strive to promote the creation of another platform that would become the basis for joint innovation projects.

Conclusion

While the Krai and the city innovation policy may devote attention to a few high-tech segments, they need mainly to target a broad set of relatively traditional technologies linked with resource and production activities, i.e. metal processing, woodworking, energy, etc. that constitute the main comparative advantages of the territory. Productivity in these sectors is still well below the most advanced countries. Quality of services is so far underdeveloped and will also need to be upgraded. Greater efficiency in resource sectors would not only increase local competitiveness but also mitigate demographic issues and improve export performance. Synergies in the RIS should be more clearly encouraged through incentives, a clear focus on technological platforms and co-operative projects and the promotion of industry associations and fora. SMEs and entrepreneurship should also be more favourably prioritised given their active role in the innovation processes. Finally, new coalitions should be established with neighbouring Siberian *oblasts* and cities to take advantage of complementarities and to scale up the local innovation capabilities.

Notes

1. To some extent, this holds true for the Russian Federation as a whole, no less than the Agglomeration: as observed in Chapter 1, Russia is too large and populous to run on the primary sector alone. Resource extraction is unlikely ever to generate sufficient high-productivity employment to sustain the kind of living standards to which the country aspires, and the primary sector is not large enough to support a large workforce employed in low-productivity non-tradable activities.

2. When measured by the share of total net profits or market capitalisation, large firms still loom larger in the Russian economy than in many OECD and other countries. Sales data for 2010 confirm the dominance of large firms in the economy, with the total sales of the 10 and 50 largest firms being equivalent to almost 30% and 50% of GDP respectively (OECD, 2011a).

3. Higher levels of growth might lead to better institutional quality, through multiple channels. There is considerable evidence, for example, that the public sector, no less than the private, can benefit from the improvements in human capital and technology that growth can bring.

4. These were: Irkutsk, Kemerovo, Khabarovsk, Moscow City, Greater Moscow (including Moscow City and Moscow Oblast'), St. Petersburg, Greater St. Petersburg (including St. Petersburg and the surrounding Leningrad Oblast'), Novosibirsk, Omsk, Primorskii Krai, Sverdlovsk, Tomsk and the Republic of Sakha (Yakutia).

5. It should be noted that the Urbanika ratings are more interesting in their individual components than as an aggregate measure: the system of weights used to combine the 14 components into an integral rating is, in fact, highly problematic for two reasons. First, the rankings change abruptly from year to year, though it is hard to believe that the relative attractiveness of Russian cities changes so much over such a short period: thus, St. Petersburg fell from 5th to 19th over just 2 years (2011-13) and Yekaterinburg jumped 22 places over the same period. Moscow fell 41 places, to 48th, between 2012 and 2013, while Belgorod rose 25 places to rank 6th. Krasnoyarsk itself fell from 12th to 47th over 2011-13. Such movements are not very credible, given that conjunctural economic variables are not part of the picture. The second problem is simply that the movement of people and firms within the Russian Federation does not correspond to the rankings.

6. See Klinger and Lederman (2004) for evidence that the number of new products exported by a country is positively associated with the height of entry barriers. More burdensome regulation of business formation and market entry appears to contribute to a higher rate of self-discovery in exports. Ease of entry, which facilitates imitation, dissipates the rents that would otherwise accrue from self-discovery. Desjardins'

(2010) comparison of infrastructure improvements to tariff reductions should alert us to the need to think about infrastructure policy with some regard for its impact on self-discovery. The point is not that we would favour infrastructure bottlenecks to protect uncompetitive local producers but that the sequence and package of policies adopted could make a big difference in determining whether better infrastructure stimulated or impeded self-discovery.

7. Hausmann and Rodrik (2003) observe that some hugely valuable innovations – such as the discovery that Ethiopian seed-coffee could be planted in Central America – were not patentable at all.

8. Rodrik (1996) argues that co-ordination failures are especially likely where new industries exhibit scale economies and some inputs are non-tradable or require geographic proximity (these are most likely to be categories of specialised labour: a worker's investment in a particular skill depends both on demand for that skill and on the existence of complementary skills in the local economy).

9. Lychagin et al. (2010) focus on the United States. According to Rodríguez-Pose and Crescenzi (2006), a similar result is obtained for Europe: they find that in the EU-25 proximity is crucial for the transmission of economically productive knowledge. Spillovers show strong distance-decay effects: only the innovative efforts pursued within a 180-minute travel radius have a positive and significant impact on regional performance.

10. This can be difficult in a world in which data availability still dictates that a great deal of analysis takes place in terms of specific sectors; the reality is that the data categories reflect yesterday's economic realities.

11. This is similar to what happens when a poor country successfully courts a high-tech multi-national and then finds that the anticipated spillovers fail to materialise once the MNC is installed.

12. As Rodrik (2004) puts it, "the trick for the government is not to pick winners, but to know when it has a loser."

13. "Appropriate policies and institutional arrangements have a large element of specificity, and experimentation is required to discover what works locally.... Most first-order economic principles come institution-free. Incentives, competition, hard budget constraints, sound money, fiscal sustainability, property rights are central to the way economists think about policy and its reform. But these principles do not map directly onto institutional solutions" (Mukand and Rodrik, 2002: 3-4). Decentralised experimentation appears to have been important to China's success since 1979. See, *inter alia*, Naughton (1995) and Jefferson and Rawski (1994).

14. The production sectors are nevertheless particularly important in the Krai and the city of Krasnoyarsk, accounting for around 20% of the jobs and respectively 55% and 43% of the gross value added generated.

15. That said, response rates on innovation-related questions varied widely: response rates to the questions in Figure 2.1 panels A and D were 100% (N=89), while only 36 and 37 firms responded to the questions covered in panels B and C, respectively.

16. The Krasnoyarsk figure was also just under 40% of the SFO average. It should be noted, however, that this refers to the proportion of enterprises reporting such expenditure, not to the level of expenditure.

17. It is interesting to note that Tomsk Oblast is launching a project to electrify more than 20 settlements in the region using a wind/solar technology developed locally.

18. Interestingly, in the 1960s, part of the Non Ferrous Metals Institute were transferred to MISIS and the rest to Krasnoyarsk.

19. In 2010, the proportion of newly introduced products or products containing essential technological changes diminished by 27.2% compared to 2005.

20. Through the Krasnoyarsk Regional Fund (KGAU), they provide funds for co-financing of projects and researchers linked with regional priorities. These funds are nevertheless very limited and they target small enterprises. Forty-three scientific projects received RUB 68.7 million support (about EUR 1.5 million) in 2012.

21. The foundation is promoting science-based entrepreneurship through the provision of a wide range of support services, including direct financial aid. Its resources amount to 1.5% of the total R&D civil budget. Since its creation in 1994, it has supported about 10 000 firms.

22. START provides assistance to would-be innovators in two stages: seed money for prototype development, test, patenting, etc., and start-up support. Up to RUB 6 million can be granted over three years, with RUB 1 million the first year, RUB 2 million the second and RUB 3 million the third. There is no project selection in the first stage: all submitted projects can be funded; projects for the second stage are selected through competition. The support takes the form of fee-free, non-repayable grants (federal contracts). Over the 2004-10 period, more than 12 000 applicants benefited from START.

23. A VDO is a business-driven, public or non-profit organisation that promotes regional growth by providing a flexible portfolio of services, including: assisting in the creation of high-growth companies; providing expert business assistance to those companies; facilitating or making direct financial investments; and speeding the commercialisation of technology. The US Department of Commerce's Economic Development Administration (EDA) has emphasised the important role these organisations play in stimulating innovation-based regional growth. See, in particular, the EDA RIAN (Regional Innovation Acceleration Network) Programme.

24. At an Innovation Forum held in Tomsk in May 2010 the leaders of eight Russian regions decided to establish an Association of Innovative Regions. The founding regions are the Tomsk Oblast, the Republic of Tatarstan, the Novosibirsk Oblast, the Republic of Mordovia, the Perm Krai, the Krasnoyarsk Krai, the Kaluga Oblast and the Irkutsk Oblast.

Bibliography

Acemoglu, D., S. Johnson and J. Robinson (2005), "Institutions as the fundamental cause of long-run growth", in: P. Aghion and S. Durlafu (eds.), *Handbook of Economic Growth*, Elsevier, North Holland.

Acemoglu, D., S. Johnson and J. Robinson (2001), "The colonial origins of comparative development: An empirical investigation", *American Economic Review*, Vol. 91, No. 5.

ADB and the World Bank (2006), *Best Practices for Private Sector Investment in Railways*, prepared by TERA International Group, Inc., Final Report.

Alberta Treasury Board and Finance (2014), *Economic Outlook, March*, available at: http://www.finance.alberta.ca/publications/budget/budget2014/fiscal-plan-economic-outlook.pdf.

Almond, G. and S. Verba (1963), *The Civic Culture*, Princeton University Press, Princeton, NJ.

Baldwin, R. (2006), "Globalisation: The great unbundling(s)", Prime Minister's Office Economic Council of Finland, 20 September.

Bertaud, A. and B. Renaud (1995), "Cities without land markets: Location and land use in the socialist city", *Policy Research Working Paper*, The World Bank, Washington, DC.

Botero, J., J. Ponce and A. Shleifer (2012), "Education and the quality of government", *NBER Working Paper*, No. 18 119, National Bureau of Economic Research, Cambridge, MA.

Brandenburgisches Institut für Existenzgründung und Mittelstandsförderung e.V. (n.d.), www.biem-brandenburg.de (accessed 10 December 2013).

Calgary Economic Development (2012), *Energy Sector Profile, 2012*, Calgary, Alberta, Canada.

Charron, N., V. Lapuente and M. Nistotskaya (2012), "The wealth of regions: Government quality and entrepreneurship in Europe", *The Quality of Government Institute Working Paper Series*, No. 2012:12, University of Gothenburg, Sweden, October.

Chong, A. et al. (2012), "Letter grading government efficiency", *NBER Working Paper*, No. 18 628, August.

Closed Nuclear Cities Partnership, www.pe-international.ru (10 December 2010).

Crane, K. and A. Usanov (2010), "Role of high technology industries", in: *Russia After the Global Economic Crisis*, Peterson Institute for International Economics, Washington, DC.

Dahl, R. (1971), *Polyarchy: Participation and Opposition*, Yale University Press, New Haven, CT.

Desjardins, P.-M. (2010), "Infrastructure – Accessibility or connectivity?", OECD Workshop on Improving Productivity in Lagging Regions, Paris, 28 June.

Diamond, L. (1992), "Economic development and democracy reconsidered", in: G. Marks and L. Diamond (eds.), *Re-examining Democracy: Essays in Honor of Seymour Martin Lipset*, Sage Publications, Thousand Oaks, CA.

Dollar, D. and A. Kraay (2003), "Institutions, trade, and growth: Revisiting the evidence", *Policy Research Working Paper*, Series 3 004, The World Bank, Washington, DC, available at: http://ideas.repec.org/s/wbk/wbrwps.html.

Easterly, W. and R. Levine (2003), "Tropics, germs, and crops: How endowments influence economic development", *Journal of Monetary Economics*, Vol. 50, No. 1.

Enterprise Surveys (2009), "Enterprise Survey and Indicator Surveys: Sampling methodology", 29 August, available at: www.enterprisesurveys.org/~/media/FPDKM/EnterpriseSurveys/Documents/Methodology/Sampling_Note.pdf.

Ernst & Young (2012), *How to Make PPP Work in Russia: 2012 Overview*, Ernst & Young, available at: http://ey.com/Publication/vwLUAssets/Russian-PPP-Survey-2012-ENG/$FILE/Russian-PPP-Survey-2012-ENG.pdf.

European Bank for Reconstruction and Development (EBRD) (2012), *Diversifying Russia. Harnessing Regional Diversity*, EBRD, London.

European Bank for Reconstruction and Development (n.d.), "BEEPS: About", http://ebrd-beeps.com/about (accessed 12 December 2013).

EBRD/World Bank (2013), *Business Environment and Enterprise Survey 2013*, http://data.worldbank.org/data-catalog/BEEPS (accessed on 14 December 2013).

GEM (2013), *GEM 2012 Global Report*, Global Entrepreneurship Research Association, London School of Economics, London, 17 January, www.gemconsortium.org/docs/2645/gem-2012-global-report.

Gill, I. and A. Dar (2000), "Germany", in: I. Gill, F. Fluitman and A. Dar (eds.), *Vocational Education and Training Reform: Matching Skills to Markets and Budgets*, The World Bank, Washington DC.

Gill, I., F. Fluitman and A. Dar (eds.), *Vocational Education and Training Reform: Matching Skills to Markets and Budgets*, The World Bank, Washington DC.

Hadenius, A. (1992), *Democracy and Development*, Cambridge University Press, Cambridge, MA.

Hausmann, R. and D. Rodrik (2003), "Economic Development as Self Discovery", *Journal of Development Economics*, December.

Hausmann, R., D. Rodrik and A. Velasco (2005), "Growth diagnostics", John F. Kennedy School of Government, Harvard University, Cambridge, MA, April, available at: www.hks.harvard.edu/fs/rhausma/new/growthdiag.pdf.

Helliwell, J. (1994), "Empirical linkages between democracy and economic growth", *British Journal of Political Science*, Vol. 24, No. 2.

Imbs, J. and R. Wacziarg (2003), "Stages of diversification", *Journal of Development Economics*, Vol. 72, No. 4, December.

Institut Français des relations internationales (IFRI) (2012), *Les universités Russes sont-elles compétitives?*, IFRI, Paris.

Jefferson, G. and T. Rawski (1994), "Enterprise reform in Chinese industry", *Journal of Economic Perspectives*, Vol. 8, No. 2, Spring.

Kaufmann, D. and A. Kraay (2008), "Governance indicators: Where are we, where should we be going?", *The World Bank Research Observer*, Vol. 23.

Kiselev, V. (2010), *Comparative Innovation Analysis of Russian Federation Regions*, Centre for Science Research and Statistics, Ministry of Education and Science, Moscow.

Klinger, B. and D. Lederman (2004), "Discovery and development: An empirical exploration of 'new' products", *World Bank Policy Research Working Paper*, No. 3 450, The World Bank, Washington, DC, 5 November.

Kolesova, E. (2013), "Integral'nyi reiting krupneishikh gorodov Rossii", Institut territorial'nogo planirovaniya "Urbanika", Presentation to the XII All Russian Forum on Strategic Planning in the Regions and Cities of Russia, St. Petersburg, 21 October.

La Porta, R. et al. (1999), "The quality of government", *Journal of Law, Economics and Organisation*, Vol. 15, No. 1.

Lychagin, S. et al. (2010), "Spillovers in space: Does geography matter?", *CEPR Discussion Paper*, No. 7 928, July.

Ministry for Foreign Affairs and Investment Policy (2008), "Investment passport of Krasnoyarsk Krai", Ministry for Foreign Affairs and Investment Policy, available at: www.krskstate.ru/dat/File/invest/invt_pas_2008.pdf.

Mukand, S. and D. Rodrik (2002), "In search of the holy grail: Policy convergence, experimentation and economic performance", *NBER Working Papers*, No. 9 134, September.

Naughton, B. (1995), *Growing Out of the Plan: Chinese Economic Reform, 1978-1993*, Cambridge University Press, New York.

North, D. (1990), *Institutions, Institutional Change and Economic Performance*, Cambridge University Press, Cambridge, MA.

OECD (2014), *OECD Economic Surveys: Russian Federation 2013*, OECD Publishing, Paris, http://dx.doi.org/10.1787/eco_surveys-rus-2013-en.

OECD (2013a), *OECD Product Market Regulation Statistics* (database), http://dx.doi.org/10.1787/pmr-data-en.

OECD (2013b), *Investing Together: Working Effectively across Levels of Government*, OECD Publishing, Paris, http://dx.doi.org/10.1787/9789264197022-en.

OECD (2013c), *Interconnected Economies: Benefiting from Global Value Chains*, OECD Publishing, Paris, http://dx.doi.org/10.1787/9789264189560-en.

OECD (2013d), *Green Growth in Cities*, OECD Green Growth Studies, OECD Publishing, Paris, http://dx.doi.org/10.1787/9789264195325-en.

OECD (2012a), *OECD Territorial Reviews: The Chicago Tri-State Metropolitan Area, United States 2012*, OECD Publishing, Paris, http://dx.doi.org/10.1787/9789264170315-en.

OECD (2012b), *Compact City Policies: A Comparative Assessment*, OECD Green Growth Studies, OECD Publishing, Paris, http://dx.doi.org/10.1787/9789264167865-en.

OECD (2012c), *OECD Territorial Reviews: Skåne, Sweden 2012*, OECD Publishing, Paris, http://dx.doi.org/10.1787/9789264177741-en.

OECD (2012d), Linking Renewable Energy to Rural Development, OECD Publishing, Paris, http://dx.doi.org/10.1787/9789264180444-en.

OECD (2011a), *OECD Economic Surveys: Russian Federation 2011*, OECD Publishing, Paris, http://dx.doi.org/10./1787/eco_surveys-rus-2011-en.

OECD (2011b), *OECD Reviews of Innovation Policy, Russian Federation 2011*, OECD Publishing, Paris, http://dx.doi.org/10.1787/9789264113138-en.

OECD (2009a), *How Regions Grow: Trends and Analysis*, OECD Publishing, Paris, http://dx.doi.org/10.1787/9789264039469-en.

OECD (2009b), *The Impact of Culture on Tourism: Universities, Innovation and Entrepreneurship: Criteria and Examples of Good Practice*, OECD Publishing, Paris.

OECD (2008), *Public-Private Partnerships: In Pursuit of Risk Sharing and Value for Money*, OECD Publishing, Paris, http://dx.doi.org/10.1787/9789264046733-en.

OECD (2007), *Infrastructure to 2030 (Vol.2): Mapping Policy for Electricity, Water and Transport*, OECD Publishing, Paris, http://dx.doi.org/10.1787/9789264031326-en.

OECD/ITF (2008), *Transport Infrastructure Investment: Options for Efficiency*, OECD Publishing, Paris, http://dx.doi.org/10.1787/9789282101568-en.

Pack, H. and L. Westphal (1986), "Industrial strategy and technological change: Theory versus reality", *Journal of Development Economics*, Vol. 22, No. 1, June.

Popodko, G. and O. Nagaeva (2012), "A change in the structure of training of qualified specialists for providing sustainable development of the region", *Journal of Federal Siberian University*, Krasnoyarsk, Russian Federation.

Région Fértil (n.d.), www.Regionfertil.com (accessed 15 December 2013).

Rodríguez-Clare, A. (2005), "Clusters and comparative advantage: Implications for industrial policy", *Latin American Research Network Working Papers*, No. 523, Inter-American Development Bank, Washington, DC, December, available at: http://siteresources.worldbank.org/EXTEXPCOMNET/Resources/2463593-1213975515123/12_RodriguezClare.pdf.

Rodríguez-Pose, A. and R. Crescenzi (2006), "R&D, Spillovers, Innovation Systems and the Genesis of Regional Growth in Europe", ERSA Conference Papers ERSA06p371, European Regional Science Association.

Rodrik, D. (2004), "Industrial policy for the twenty-first century", *Faculty Research Working Papers Series*, John F. Kennedy School of Government, Harvard University, November.

Rodrik, D. (1996), "Coordination failures and government policy: A model with applications to East Asia and Eastern Europe", *Journal of International Economics* No. 40, Vol. 1-2, pp. 1-22, February.

Rodrik, D. et al. (2004), "Institutions rule: The primacy of institutions over geography and integration in economic development", *Journal of Economic Growth*, No. 9.

Rosatom, www.rosatom.ru/aboutcorporation/nuclearindustry/zato (accessed 10 December 2013).

SFU (2012), "Background report for the OECD Territorial Review of Krasnoyarsk", Siberian Federal University, Krasnoyarsk, Russian Federation, November.

SIR World Report (2012), "SCImago Institutions Rankings", data source: Scopus, www.scimagoir.com (accessed 10 December 2013).

US Congress, Office of Technology Assessment (1994), *Assessing the Potential of Civil-Military Integration: Technologies, Processes, and Practices, OTA-ISS-611*, US Government Printing Office, Washington, DC, September, available at: http://ota.fas.org/reports/9402.pdf.

US Department of Defense (2012), "Strategy and action plan for accelerating technology transfer and commercialisation of federal research in support of high growth business", US Department of Defense, Washington, DC, 4 October, available at: www.nist.gov/tpo/publications/upload/DOD-Tech-Transfer-Plan.pdf.

WEF (2012), *Global Competitiveness Report 2012-2013*, World Economic Forum, Geneva, available at www3.weforum.org/docs/WEF_GlobalCompetitivenessReport_2012-13.pdf.

Woolcock, M. (1998), "Social capital and economic development: Towards a theoretical synthesis of policy framework", *Theory and Society*, Vol. 27, No. 1.

World Bank (2013), "World Bank Governance Research Indicator Country Snapshots", The World Bank, Washington, DC, http://data.worldbank.org/data-catalog/worldwide-governance-indicators (accessed 14 December 2013).

Chapter 3

Knitting the Krasnoyarsk Agglomeration together

This chapter focuses on the spatial dimension of governing the Agglomeration. First, it situates the Agglomeration in the larger context of multi-level governance in the Russian Federation. It then explores the potential for deeper integration at the level of the Agglomeration to improve performance in a number of major areas linked in one way or another to spatial form: land use, housing and transport. Finally, it shifts the focus from local transport (internal connectivity) to the Agglomeration's links to the rest of the world (external connectivity) and explores its potential to develop as a transport and logistics hub.

This chapter focuses on two distinct areas: governance of the Agglomeration and the management of the built environment, encompassing transport as well as such issues as housing and land use, and governance. These two broad policy domains are central to efforts to turn the Krasnoyarsk Agglomeration into a close-knit and smoothly functioning metropolitan area. The consistent theme running through the discussion concerns the ways in which policy makers can overcome fragmentation in the Agglomeration to allow the development of policies and institutions capable of addressing its challenges at the scale of the Agglomeration as a whole. Transport, in turn, is critical to addressing a further ambition, also explored here – to develop Krasnoyarsk into one of the main transport and logistics hubs on the Eurasian land mass.

The Krasnoyarsk Agglomeration's institutional and policy context

Regional policy has fluctuated between de- and re-centralisation

Russian municipal authorities (often referred to as "organs of local self-management") are situated in a complex territorial governance structure that reflects the Russian Federation's vast expanse and ethnic diversity. The precise number of federal units has varied over time, owing to mergers and other developments. At the end of 2013, there were 83 constituent units, known as the subjects of the Federation: 46 *oblasti* (provinces), 9 *krai* (territories), the cities of Moscow and St. Petersburg (the only cities to enjoy the status of federal subject) and 26 autonomies with ethnic designations (including 21 republics, one autonomous *oblast'* and four autonomous districts). The chief executives of the federal subjects (governors in most cases but bearing the title of president in the ethnic republics) have since 2004 been nominated by the President of the Russian Federation and then elected by legislative bodies of the relevant subjects. A phased return to direct election of the heads of the subjects of the Federation is now under way, however. The administrative sub-units of the subjects of the Federation are self-governing cities, municipalities, districts and settlements (Figure 3.1).

Figure 3.1. **Governance framework in the Russian Federation**

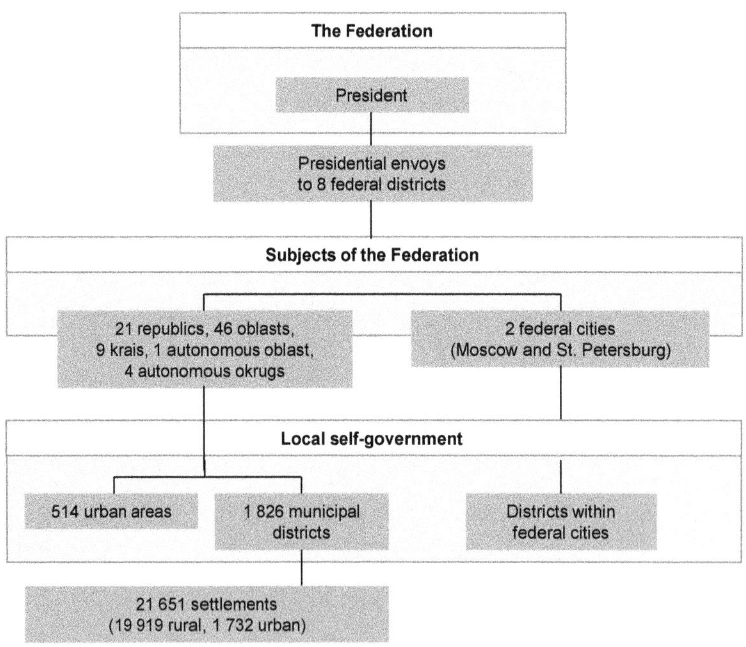

Source: Former Ministry of Regional Development of the Russian Federation, 2013.

The competencies of the Federation and its subjects and local authorities are defined by the Constitution and federal law. Article 71 of the Constitution defines issues of authority for different levels of government. Federal Law 131 "On the general principles of organising legislative (representative) and executive authorities of the Russian Federation subjects" determines the jurisdiction of the Russian Federation state authorities. Article 72 determines issues governed in joint competence by the Federation and its subjects. Additional joint competences can be defined by federal law or regulation. Article 73 defines all other competencies (no list of issues) of the subject of the Federation. An exhaustive list of issues to be managed by local self-governments in rural communities, municipal and urban territories is given in the Federal Law "On the general principles of local self-management in the Russian Federation".

Regional policy is designed and implemented at the level of the Federation and its subjects, the regions. At the federal level, the main directions for regional policy are given by the President. Sector-specific regional programmes and policies are developed and financed by sectoral ministries, and the annual budget for regional policy measures is approved by the Federal Assembly. Until September 2014, the Ministry of Regional Development was responsible for the implementation of policy measures, monitoring the effective use of budgetary funds, and inter-regional co-operation. However, the ministry was abolished, and its functions dispersed among a number of other federal ministries, including the Ministry of Economic Development, the Ministry of Construction and Utilities, the Ministry of Finance, the Ministry of Culture and the Ministry of Justice. There are, moreover, dedicated ministries focusing on the problems of specific territories, such as the North Caucasus and the Far East.

Achievement of regional policy objectives is monitored and evaluated by the President and controlled by sectoral ministries. A similar structure of responsibility is replicated at the regional level, including in Krasnoyarsk Krai, where the governor gives the main policy directions and monitors the achievement of policy objectives. The Krai government and its sectoral ministries develop state-supported mechanisms for regional development, finance and implement regional policy measures, and control the effective use of funds. The budget is also overseen by the Krai Ministry of Economics and Regional Development, which is responsible for implementing regional policy measures that imply inter-regional co-operation.

The objectives of regional policy in Russia have changed over the past 20 years. During the 1990s, it was opaque, largely *ad hoc* and focused on: *i)* supporting the poorest regions; and *ii)* responding to political pressure from stronger regions for fiscal privileges and greater autonomy. This changed in the early 2000s as bilateral agreements between the centre and the regions were scrapped and the system of fiscal federalism was reformed. Nonetheless, the transition to a modern, growth-oriented regional policy is incomplete. There is still a tension between the need for sustained federal support to very poor regions and the desire to foster the emergence of growth poles that might aid economic diversification but might also reinforce inter-regional disparities. In reality, most regions (and most citizens) fall between these two groups. The problem of devising appropriate regional development strategies is most acute in the large number of cities and towns organised around a single branch or enterprise – the so-called mono-cities. Attempts to restructure them have met with little success.

Today, the three most important objectives are to: *i)* reduce inter-regional disparities in per capita income; *ii)* promote inter-regional co-operation; and *iii)* ensure the provision of quality of public service in sparsely populated areas (Table 3.1). As seen in Chapter 1,

Russia's enormous size and diversity make these challenges particularly difficult, especially the first and third. Inter-regional disparities are high by OECD standards and have risen significantly over the last 20 years or so (Figure 3.2).

Table 3.1. **Evolution of the objectives of regional policy**

	Early 1990s	Late 1990s	Early 2000s	Present
Reduce inter-regional disparities in per capita income				
Solve specific regional challenges (e.g. problems of remote or rural areas)				
Promote regional economic competitiveness				
Promote decentralisation				
A polycentric territorial structure of economic development				
Promote inter-regional co-operation				
Avoid de-population of regions				
Ensure quality of public service in sparsely populated areas				

Legend:

	Very important		Somewhat important		Not very important

Source: SFU (2012), "OECD background report on the Krasnoyarsk Agglomeration", Siberian Federal University, Krasnoyarsk, Russian Federation, November.

Figure 3.2. **Inter-regional disparities in GDP per capita**

Inter-regional Gini coefficient, 1995 and 2010

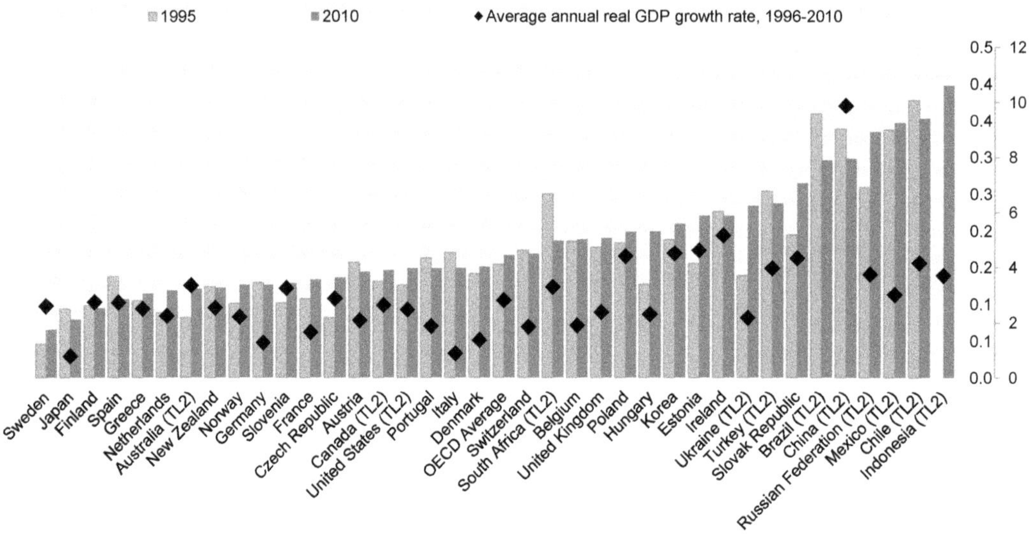

Notes: The Gini coefficient is shown on the inside axis, the GDP growth rate on the outside. Data for China do not include the special administrative regions of Hong Kong, China; Macao, China; and Chinese Taipei.

Source: OECD (2013a), *OECD Regional Statistics* (database), http://dx.doi.org/10.1787/region-data-en.

Large inter-regional disparities are in part linked to settlement patterns that leave an enormous part of Russia's territory very sparsely populated, which creates particular challenges for the provision of public services and economic development. The country's overall population density was just 8.4 persons per square kilometre in 2010, as compared with an OECD average of 34, and less than half that of any OECD country except

Australia, Canada and Iceland. Moreover, this low density is despite the concentration of a large share of the population in the urban regions of European Russia. Much of the rest of the country is even more sparsely settled: altogether, some 39 federal subjects, which are home to around 47.5 million people, have population densities lower than 20 persons/km². As noted in Chapter 1, Krasnoyarsk Krai is no exception, with a density of just 1.2. While the population is often concentrated in the main cities of such federal subjects, in 2010, the Russian Federation had roughly 37 million people living in settlements of fewer than 5 000 inhabitants, including 16 million in places with fewer than 1 000 residents.

Given such a settlement pattern, it is not surprising that economic activity is highly concentrated: eight regions, with 30% of the population, generated just over half of Russia's GDP. Indeed, the city of Moscow and the oil-rich province of Tyumen', which are together home to just over 10% of the country's population, accounted for just under one-third of GDP. Krasnoyarsk Krai accounts for almost 3%. These disparities in levels of development, though large, are comparable to those found in some other large, catching-up economies, and the exceptionally high inter-regional Gini in part reflects the very fragmented structure of Russian federalism and the presence, in particular, of a belt of very poor, politically unstable regions in the North Caucasus. It is also influenced by the larger-than-average role of informal activities in some of the Federation's poorer regions, which tends to increase the inter-regional Gini.

It is important to note that large inter-regional disparities are largely the product of extreme outliers at both ends of the distribution. Even when adjusting for differences in regional price levels, only 15 of the Russian Federation's 83 federal subjects recorded GDP per capita above the national average in 2010; four of these were above twice the national average. For the most part, these were the country's largest agglomerations, resource-rich (mostly low-density) regions and some of the major ports. By contrast, 18 mostly small regions fell below 50% of the national average, with four below 40%. Yet two-thirds of Russian's population inhabits the 50 regions in between. The real challenges stem not from the disparities themselves but from the barriers to convergence confronting this great mass of "middling" Russian regions. The large gap between the handful of leading regions and the rest is difficult to close, as low density, poor accessibility, barriers to factor (particularly labour) mobility and poor infrastructure handicap the great majority of regions: neither agglomeration processes nor first-nature (natural resource or location) endowments favour them. Indeed, geography and infrastructure limitations mean that many lagging regions, particularly in the far north and east of the country, have substantially above-average price levels.

While there is a growing focus in regional policy on more growth-oriented approaches, they have yet to take shape very clearly. Cluster policies are much discussed, but there is a tendency to mistake Soviet-era territorial production complexes for clusters. Regional authorities often seek federal support for local "clusters" as a way of helping to sustain incumbent firms. Similarly, concepts like "smart specialisation" and "strategic planning" are often misunderstood to imply planning regions' specialisations decades in advance, chiefly on the basis of what already exists (i.e. there is a pronounced bias in favour of support to incumbent firms). Instead of acting as a mechanism to reveal potential new opportunities, smart specialisation can then become an exercise in picking winners among incumbent firms and sectors. In general, regional authorities often see regional development chiefly in terms of extracting additional support from the centre. This means that rather than seeking to identify new niches and specialisms of their own, regions often try to align themselves with what they see as key federal priorities of the moment. Top-down thinking continues to prevail.

The fiscal system is highly centralised

The fiscal system is fairly centralised by OECD standards, in contrast to the extreme decentralisation that prevailed (*de facto* even more than *de jure*) in the 1990s (Box 3.1). Reforms at the end of the 1990s and in the early 2000s streamlined and clarified revenue and expenditure assignments, scrapped unfunded mandates (at least in principle) and allocated most federal transfers on the basis of clear equalisation formulae. This greatly enhanced the predictability and transparency of the system. However, the reforms left the vast majority of regions heavily dependent on transfers, as the federal share of general government revenues rose. At the same time, expenditure autonomy at regional level remains weak. Moreover, since the reform, there has been a sustained decline in the share of formula-driven transfers, owing to the multiplication of earmarked grants of various kinds, which have in recent years accounted for over half of all transfers. These are allocated by more than a score of central ministries and other federal bodies, often with little co-ordination or assessment of regions' own fiscal capacities. As a result, earmarked subsidies and subventions frequently serve to counteract the effects of equalisation. They are also more likely to be allocated annually and often with little transparency. The co-financing requirements attached to some (but not all) earmarked grants also reduce regions' expenditure autonomy. Finally, because they are often allocated in the course of the year, the window of opportunity for regions to use them can be as little as a few months. This "use it or lose it" situation is not conducive to good financial management.

Box 3.1. **Political decentralisation and re-centralisation in the Russian Federation**

During the period of political decentralisation in the 1990s, federal subjects were headed by popularly elected regional governors. Fiscal and political weakness at the centre made it possible for them to extract tremendous concessions from the federal authorities, in terms of both fiscal privileges and policy-making powers. This resulted in fiscal and political confusion, poor accountability and a situation in which many federal-regional arrangements were at odds with the Constitution and/or federal laws. From 2000 onwards, a number of legislative changes reversed this process and recentralised significant powers while putting an end to the kind of *ad hoc* power-sharing agreements that had previously existed. The innovations of the early 2000s included changes in the formation of the Federation Council (the upper house of parliament), which reduced the influence of regional governors on the federal level, the introduction of presidential envoys for eight large federal districts, each encompassing a number of subjects of the Federation, to control the implementation of federal legislation in the regions, and, after 2004, the abolition of direct election of regional executives (Zhuravskaya, 2010). Fiscal reforms also concentrated more revenue-raising power in Moscow and reduced the spending freedom of subordinate governments. The Russian Federation is now in the midst of a phased reintroduction of gubernatorial elections, but most of the other changes adopted after 2000 remain in place.

Sources: Ross, C. (2011), "Introduction: Russian regional politics under Putin and Medvedev", *Europe-Asia Studies*, Vol. 63, No. 3, pp. 361-366; Slider, D. (2009), "Putin and the election of regional governors", in: Ross, C. and A. Campbell (2009), *Federalism and Local Politics in Russia*, Routledge, Oxford; Zhuravskaya, E. (2010), "Federalism in Russia", Centre for Economic and Financial Research at New Economic School, Working Paper Series, *Working Paper No. 141*, April.

Reversing the erosion of the transfer reforms of a decade ago is particularly important because huge and persistent disparities in tax potential across regions mean that federal transfers will continue to play a large role in limiting disparities in access to key public services. For example, primary and secondary educational institutions are now exclusively financed from regional and municipal budgets. This results in considerable regional heterogeneity in public funding. To make the most of youth potential and reduce large spatial variation in educational outcomes, the authorities should consider implementing even stronger federal transfers, especially in the poorest regions, which suffer from lower spending per student. A critical challenge will be to ensure that such transfers are predictable, transparent and allocated according to appropriate criteria.

Krasnoyarsk Krai depends less on intergovernmental transfers than most other subjects of the Federation and has been able to consolidate its fiscal situation over the past years. Only 13% of its revenues are transfers, compared to an average of 23% for all Federation subjects. The share of tax revenues in the Krai remained stable from 2005 to 2011, while over the same period the average share across all subjects of the Federation fell from 74.4% to 69%. A similar trend can be observed over this period for non-tax revenues, which decreased from 9% to 7.2% on average across all federal subjects, while remaining stable at around 10% in Krasnoyarsk Krai (SFU, 2012).

While fiscal resources and decision-making power are now far more concentrated in Moscow than they were 10-15 years ago, regions play an important role in the implementation of policy. Large investment programmes are mostly implemented in co-operation with federal and regional institutions. The government of Krasnoyarsk Krai thus designs its own territorial development policies, strategies, programmes, governance partnerships, public-private partnerships (PPPs) and special economic zones (SEZ) within the framework established by federal legislation and policy. It can amend tax regimes in limited ways, e.g. by granting tax credits for business, including via favourable property tax rates, or subsidising interest and lease payments for private investments. For large investment projects the Krai partners with federal institutions, such as the Investment Fund of the Russian Federation, which acts as a regional development fund, supporting regional investment projects of national importance under the condition that they be implemented as PPPs (with at least 50% private investments).

Local governments have struggled to adapt to changes in the system of fiscal federalism

Initially a central element of decentralisation, the organs of local self-management (which will hereafter be referred to simply as "local governments") are responsible for tasks defined at higher levels of government. Soviet law reformed local governments in 1990, endowing them with tasks of "local importance". Since then, the rules and responsibilities of local governments were redefined in subsequent laws and reforms. In 1991, the Russian law consolidated the concept of local self-management as a self-standing local level of responsibility, including detailed regulation of elected local councils, which contributed to the decentralisation of governance in Russia. In 1993, the federal constitution gave shared legislative powers over local governments to the federal and regional levels, adding that "organs of local self-management can be endowed, by law, with specific state tasks" (Box 3.2). A list of "issues of local significance" for cities, municipal districts (*raiony*) and municipal settlements (urban and rural) was issued in the 1995 Law on "General Principles of the Organisation of Local Self-Government" (Federal Law 154); and a list of taxes to be levied by different types of local governments was defined in the Budget Code (Vetrov and Zaitseva, 2005; World Bank, 2009). The state's ability to assign "issues of local significance" to municipal districts and urban areas was reinforced through a 2003 reform that refines the list of specific tasks assigned to each level of local government (e.g. settlements and municipal districts). Since 2003, all settlements and districts of more than 1 000 inhabitants have to establish a local authority to carry out delegated tasks.

Box 3.2. Dual function of local self-governments

Local government serves a dual function, being accountable to local voters at the same time as having to implement federal government functions and expenditures. The main actors in local government are the mayor or head of municipality, the city manager or head of the municipal administration, and the local council. In most cases, mayors and local councils are elected directly, and city managers are appointed by the local council. Local councils are assigned to exercise "control over the discharge, by organs of local self-government and its position-holders, of their local level responsibilities", thus monitoring the implementation of delegated tasks from the state. Delegated state tasks are executed by the head of the local administration, the directly elected mayor. He acts as "chief executive", directing administrative functions assigned to the local administration, while alongside him the elected local council acts as a supreme local representative, rule-setting and scrutinising body (a quasi-division of power and checks and balances).

Federal law allows for exceptions in which municipal district councils are not elected directly but are elected by the councils of "member" municipalities (settlements). According to the Ministry of Regional Development, such a process of forming representative organs via delegation has become increasingly popular: use of this method rose by 66% during 2007-10. The number of municipalities in which municipal administrations rely on an appointed "city manager" also rose, by almost 24%, between 2007 and 2010. Local councils have the right to remove mayors from office by a two-thirds majority for general reasons such as "an unsatisfactory performance of duties over two years"; and recent changes in the charters of many Russian cities have introduced the possibility to elect mayors indirectly via the city council. In the case of violating federal or regional legislation, regional or central government authorities can remove both administrative and municipal heads, which can also happen by means of a local referendum.

The introduction in 2003 of indirect election mechanisms and of a separation between the roles of mayor and "head of administration" (city manager) has been widely seen as weakening the role of the mayor. The heads of administration (appointed by and accountable to the city council) act in many respects as city's chief executives, overseeing municipal budgets and daily operations of municipal departments and agencies. Yet mayors remain accountable to citizens and thus politically more vulnerable. The stated aims of these changes were to counter the unchecked power of local bosses heading often undemocratic, corrupt and inefficient city governments. However, critics argue that they will erode transparency and accountability, ultimately undermining the effectiveness of local government.

Sources: Wollmann, H. and E. Gritsenko (2009), "Local self-government in Russia: Between decentralisation and recentralisation", in: Ross, C. and A. Campbell (2009), *Federalism and Local Politics in Russia*, Routledge, Oxford; Moses, J.C. (2010), "Russian local politics in the Putin-Medvedev era", *Europe-Asia Studies*, Vol. 62, No. 9, pp. 1 427-1 452.

It is unclear whether the objective of local governments to increase local level autonomy for better local governance, growth and economic development can be reached effectively in the current setting. Excessive fragmentation is one problem: in 2012, the Russian Federation had some 23 650 municipalities, including 19 919 rural settlements, 1 732 urban settlements, 1 826 municipal districts (which brought together a number of smaller population centres) and 514 urban areas.

Local governments struggled with the challenge of financing unfunded mandates from superior governments from the very beginning of Russia's political and economic transition. Neither the right to raise additional local revenues introduced in 1994 nor subsequently introduced subventions and subsidies changed this much. Additional intergovernmental transfers, to be negotiated on an individual basis, relieved some of the financial pressure on sub-national governments, but they also increased their reliance on higher governments, especially the federal centre. The financial, political and social instability resulting from this unbalanced decentralisation were the grounds on which the federal authorities (re-)introduced a more uniform vision of the Russian state in the early 2000s. For regional and local governments, this meant tighter federal control, both via political as well as fiscal mechanisms (Gel'man and Ryzhenkov, 2011). The previous trend of growing sub-national shares of revenue and expenditure was reversed. Local revenues were reduced while local expenditure items largely remained unchanged, further increasing the challenge of unfunded federal mandates (Zhuravskaya, 2010). Then, in 2004 and 2005, changes in federal law transferring expenditure items from local to regional and federal levels, as well as the introduction of additional subventions and subsidies, eliminated most unfunded mandates.

While local budgets are more balanced today, revenues still do not cover all expenditure commitments and local budgets increasingly depend on intergovernmental transfers. In 2011, tax revenues represented less than one-third of the revenues of Russia's organs of municipal self-management, while inter-governmental transfers accounted for over 60% (SFU, 2012). In the Krasnoyarsk Agglomeration, local governments' tax revenues are slightly higher, but their reliance on transfers has grown. The 76.5% share of tax revenues in local budgets in 2000 fell to 40.5% in 2011. Conversely, inter-governmental transfers increased from 18% of local budget revenues in 2000 to 45.7% in 2011 (SFU, 2012). Subventions and subsidies have increased the most (Figure 3.3). This is not, however, simply a sign of weakening local autonomy. On the contrary, this shift is largely connected to the financing by superior governments of previously unfunded mandates. Overall, only 7.8% of taxes raised locally are collected by local budgets. Corporate taxes, in particular, are channelled to the federal budget. Such centralisation of revenues is probably inevitable given the very uneven distribution of activity and population in the Russian Federation, as well as the importance of subsoil resource sectors in its development – the subsoil belongs to the Federation and resource rents should, to a great extent, be centralised. However, very low levels of fiscal autonomy may also reduce the incentives for local governments to think about economic development and work to expand their tax bases.

Figure 3.3. **Revenue share in budgets of the Krasnoyarsk Agglomeration's municipal local governments**

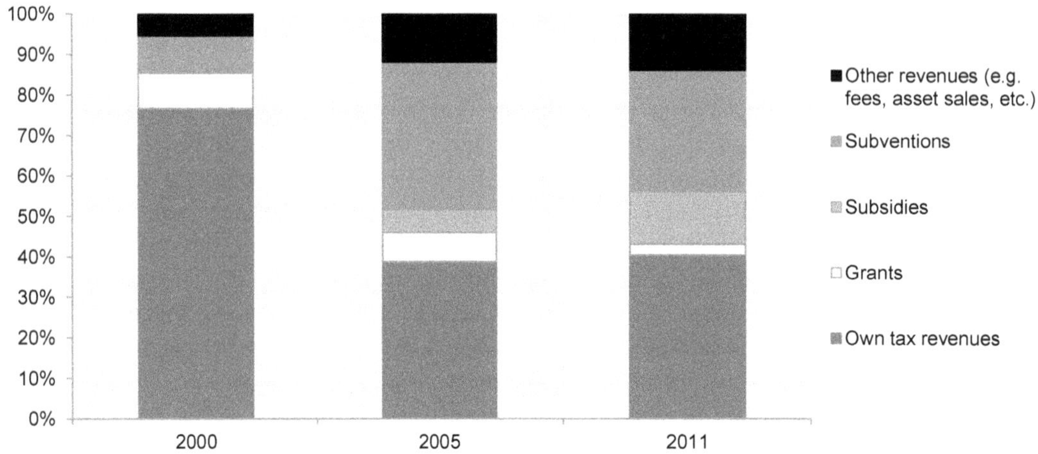

Source: SFU (2012), "OECD background report on the Krasnoyarsk Agglomeration", Siberian Federal University, Krasnoyarsk, Russian Federation, November.

Fiscal equalisation takes place within the subjects of the Federation, as well as across them. In Krasnoyarsk Krai, regional funds help municipal entities and settlements to cover their expenditure needs. The Krai Law No. 2-317 (2007) "On inter-budgetary relations in Krasnoyarsk Krai" regulates grant distribution to municipal level for the purposes of budgetary equalisation. Two regional funds, one for financial support to municipal entities and a second for financial support to settlements, make grants to municipal budgets based on a formula taking into account tax potential and expenditure needs: the formulae employed include an expenditure index that considers differences in demographic, socio-economic, climatic, geographic and other objective factors, as well as other conditions that may influence the cost of providing municipal services.

The challenge of metropolitan governance

OECD members are increasingly focused on metropolitan areas

There has been increasing attention in recent years to the benefits of governing cities as *functional economies* rather than administrative units. Across much of the world, cities have "grown into each other", so that the administrative boundaries of individual municipalities correspond poorly to socio-economic realities on the ground. Commuting flows, trade in goods and services and various positive and negative externalities associated with urban development all transcend urban administrative boundaries. Many problems, including the provision of essential infrastructure and the supply of many basic public services, are more efficiently organised at the level of the functional urban area (OECD, 2014a) – that is, at the level of the city as defined by human settlement and activity rather than administrative jurisdictions. In many countries, such complex, multi-jurisdictional conurbations are known as "metropolitan areas"; in Russia, they tend to be called "urban agglomerations".[1] Many large functional urban areas are extremely fragmented. The greater Chicago tri-state area in the United States, for example, is home to no fewer than 1 700 governmental authorities of various kinds, including municipalities, counties, states and numerous "special purpose" public authorities, like school districts, water districts, transport authorities and so on. In France, Greater Paris counts 1 400. Even relatively modest-sized urban agglomerations are often quite fragmented (Figure 3.4).

Figure 3.4. **Twenty most fragmented OECD metropolitan areas, 2012**

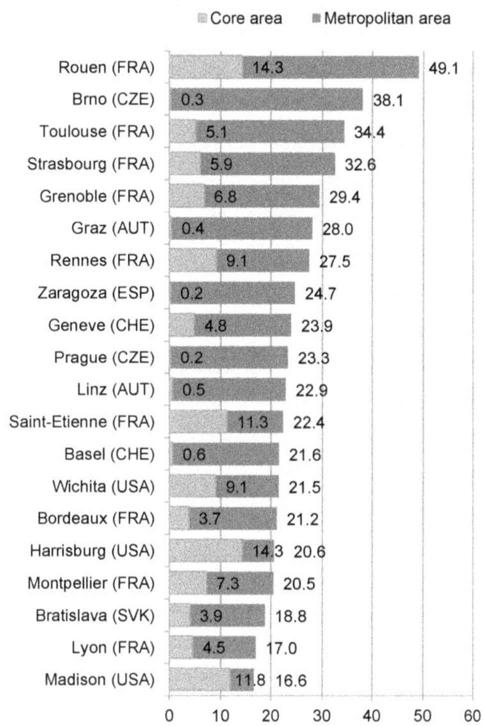

Source: OECD (2013b), *Regions at a Glance*, OECD Publishing, Paris, http://dx.doi.org/10.1787/reg_glance-2013-en.

Recent OECD research, moreover, underscores the degree to which the prosperity of the smaller towns and rural districts surrounding the city of Krasnoyarsk is likely to be linked to the city's development. This gives them a direct interest in metropolitan co-operation. While there is often a tendency to see large cities as an economic threat to their neighbours, attracting talent and resources from their hinterlands, an analysis of OECD regional growth performance over the period 1995-2010 found regions with metropolitan areas of more than 500 000 grew faster than other places. More generally, population density of the most densely populated parts of a region is a very good predictor of *per capita* GDP growth. The influence of cities goes beyond their boundaries: places close to large cities are more prosperous and have experienced higher economic and population growth than more remote places. While these positive spill-overs decline with distance, they can benefit the economic performance of rural areas as far as 200-300 km away (OECD, 2014a; Veneri and Ruiz, 2013). Finally, regions surrounding large cities tend to restructure more rapidly (Ahrend and Schumann, 2014).

Cities in the former Soviet Union tend, on the whole to be less fragmented in administrative terms than many of their western peers, but they are often *more* fragmented physically, owing to the way that Soviet planners built cities. The administrative allocation of land uses in the absence of markets resulted in a number of striking spatial anomalies (Bertaud and Renaud, 1995; Finogenov, 2012). The tendency to organise cities around major enterprises resulted in many cases in the development of cities that were, in important respects, collections of "company towns". Workers typically did not often change places of work or residence very often, and housing, employment, social infrastructure, etc., were typically organised around the main enterprise or enterprises in a district, within which fairly strict functional zoning was applied. This model corresponded well to a simplified model of life in an industrial city but its defects had become apparent long before the end of the Soviet period. Cities were often segmented by large transport arteries, which were often land-intensive and constituted significant barriers to movement among (as opposed to within) parts of the city, while also reducing the potential uses of adjacent land. Mobility was far better provided at a very local level than at a city-wide scale. The socialist land use process also created sizable tracts of "dead land" areas, which combined low levels of economic activity with negative environmental qualities; as will be seen, the latter constitute a particular barrier to any kind of in-fill redevelopment.

As a result, there was a great deal to be done after 1991 to integrate existing cities better, so as to create larger, deeper functional labour markets and more efficient flows of goods and services. In Krasnoyarsk, the legacies of the Soviet era are compounded by the fact that the city stretches for a considerable distance along the banks of one of Eurasia's largest rivers. Its form, like those of some other riverside cities is thus far less compact than might otherwise be the case.

Fragmentation has implications for urban performance. If left to pursue policies in isolation, the municipalities of a complex functional urban area are likely to *collectively* fail to address the metropolitan challenges of developing its economic potential and the well-being of its citizens – even if they *individually* achieve their short-term political objectives. In this respect it is also important that policies are not only coherent across an urban agglomeration, but also that they exploit spatial complementarities, i.e. policies undertaken by some entities can yield greater benefits if complementary policies are undertaken by others. Municipal fragmentation may therefore affect the economic growth of metropolitan cities. This could, for example, arise if municipal fragmentation, together with insufficient cooperation, led to sub-optimal provision of transport infrastructure. This is not just a theoretical possibility: there are many cities across the OECD area and beyond where certain public transport systems stop at administrative borders even in defiance of economic rationality. Yet the evidence suggests that transport services are one of the areas in which co-operation across municipal boundaries tends to be easiest: where indivisible assets like schools and hospitals are concerned, collaboration can be harder. For example, in low-density places like Slovenia or south-eastern Sweden, municipalities readily see the scale economies to be realised by collaborating infields like education and health care, but may fear that their own long-term viability and attractiveness depend in part on ensuring that the key facilities (and related employment) are located within their own jurisdiction.

Recent OECD work, based on the Metropolitan Governance Survey[2] has found a number of empirical regularities that merit attention. Metropolitan areas without some form of central governance body have experienced greater urban sprawl (Figure 3.5), even though they seem to be less attractive (as indicated by lower population growth) than in metropolitan areas with central governance bodies; this points to the dangers of uncoordinated spatial planning. Metropolitan areas without a central governance body also have, on average, higher levels of CO_2 emissions, possibly resulting from less efficient land use and transport planning: greater sprawl and poor co-ordination of transport result in longer commutes and less efficient public transport, with, as a consequence, greater reliance on private cars and thus greater congestion. Similarly, in metropolitan areas without a coordination body for transport, such as a sectoral transport authority, citizens express much less satisfaction with the public transport system; these metropolitan areas have also significantly higher levels of air pollution (Ahrend and Schuman, 2014).[3]

Figure 3.5. **Governance institutions and selected outcomes**

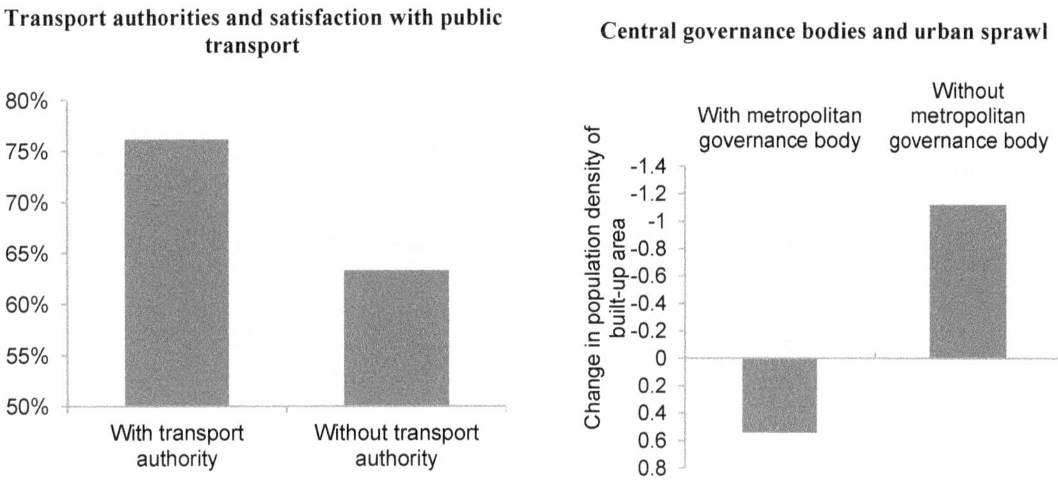

Note: Controlling for country fixed effects.

Source: Ahrend, R., C. Gamper and A. Schumann (2014), "The OECD Metropolitan Governance Survey: A Quantitative Description of Governance Structures in large Urban Agglomerations", *OECD Regional Development Working Papers*, 2014/04, OECD Publishing, http://dx.doi.org/10.1787/5jz43zldh08p-en.

Municipal fragmentation also affects economic growth. OECD estimates indicate that doubling the number of municipalities per 100 000 inhabitants in a given metropolitan area is associated with a 6-8% decrease in productivity (Figure 3.6). Growth, too, appears to be lower in more fragmented jurisdictions. This effect, however, can at least be substantially mitigated through adequate governance arrangements: formal municipal mergers are not required. More precisely, the existence of a central metropolitan governance body is estimated to reduce the negative effect of municipal fragmentation roughly by half (Ahrend et al., 2014).

The need for co-ordination is particularly acute in fields where there are considerable (positive and negative) spill-overs across jurisdictions resulting from local decisions: these areas include public investment, land-use planning, environmental management and transport. With respect to growth-enhancing public investments, the problem is that fragmentation at the local level can affect the type of investments that are prioritised: local leaders tend to focus on smaller-scale projects with a lower – but more localised – return on investment. Investments that generate a payback across a much larger area (i.e. where there are positive externalities to be realised) may be under-developed, as municipal leaders may have little incentive to focus on benefits to neighbouring jurisdictions (OECD, 2014a).

Figure 3.6. **Less fragmented metropolitan areas have experienced higher growth**

Annual average GDP per capita growth, 2000-2010

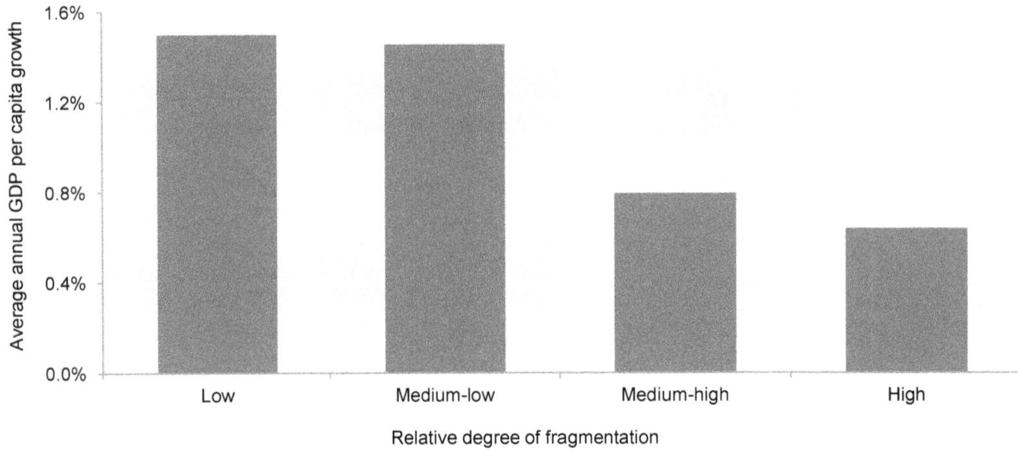

Source: Ahrend, R. and A.C. Lembcke (2015), "Economic and demographic trends in cities", *OECD Regional Development Working Papers*, OECD Publishing, Paris, forthcoming.

While some governments have chosen to re-draw administrative boundaries to better match functional urban areas (e.g. via municipal mergers), this remains a relatively unusual solution across the OECD. More common are efforts to build inter-municipal partnerships, within more or less institutionalised frameworks. Metropolitan governance bodies – broadly defined as bodies organising responsibilities among public authorities in metropolitan areas (including voluntary associations of municipalities, with few or no legal powers) – are now extremely common in OECD countries. OECD research covering more than 200 metropolitan areas with populations above 500 000 finds that more than two-thirds of large metropolitan areas in the OECD have a metropolitan governance body. There has been renewed momentum in the creation of such bodies (or in the reform of existing ones) since the 1990s. There is great diversity in the structure of such bodies, not only across countries but within them: rarely are all metropolitan areas in a single country served by the same sort of structure. The typology in Table 3.2 shows how municipalities – often the administrative level closest to citizens and the most comparable unit in cross country analysis – organise themselves (or are sometimes organised by upper levels of government). The categories of the typology are not mutually exclusive: two or more metropolitan arrangements sometimes coexist in the same country, and occasionally within the same region. Some instances can also encompass rural urban partnerships within metropolitan areas.

The choice of a specific type of metropolitan governance needs to be considered in the context of three challenges that any governance arrangement meets: (1) *the capacity to act*, (2) *trust*, and (3) *co-ordination*. A governance arrangement's capacity to act crucially depends on both financial and human resources as well as on legislative power, the power to impose laws and regulation. Informal/soft arrangements and inter-municipal authorities tend to have less of these capacities, compared to supra-municipal authorities and metropolitan cities. In the OECD, less than 20% of metropolitan governance bodies have legislative power. Trust in metropolitan governance depends much on political accountability and popular legitimacy of the respective arrangement or body. Direct elections are most common for supra-municipal authorities, but they only represent 10% of OECD metropolitan governance bodies. Indirect representation can take different forms, e.g. through local government officials, and is found in about 65% of OECD metropolitan governance arrangements. For the Krasnoyarsk Agglomeration, capacity to act and trust are essential elements that need to be further addressed, as the experience with the first strategy for the Agglomeration shows, which failed to get the support of all concerned actors. Insufficient representation, legitimacy and accountability may have impeded integrating the interests and needs of all stakeholders, and compromised trust. Reviewing the fiscal basis on which all municipalities can provide the necessary financial and human resources to construct the Agglomeration should also be considered.

Table 3.2. **Typology of metropolitan governance arrangements in OECD countries**

a) Informal/soft co-ordination. Often found in instances of polycentric urban development, lightly institutionalised platforms for information sharing and consultation are relatively easy both to implement and to undo. They typically lack enforcement tools and their relationship with citizens and other levels of government tends to remain minimal.	
b) Inter-municipal authorities. When established for a *single purpose*, such authorities aim at sharing costs and responsibilities across member municipalities – sometimes with the participation of other levels of government and sectoral organisations. *Multi-purpose* authorities embrace a defined range of key policies for urban development such as land use, transport, and infrastructure.	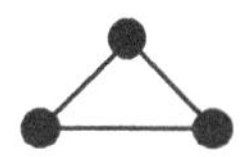
c) Supra-municipal authorities. An additional layer above municipalities can be introduced either by creating a directly elected metropolitan government, or with the upper governments setting down a non-elected metropolitan structure. The extent of municipal involvement and financial capacity often determine the effectiveness of a supra-municipal authority.	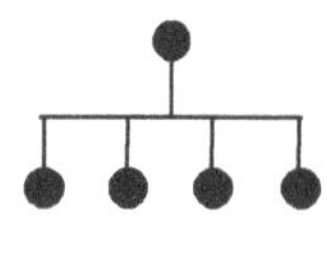
d) Special status of "metropolitan cities". Cities that exceed a legally defined population threshold can be upgraded into a special status as "metropolitan cities", which puts them on the same footing as the next upper level of government and gives them broader competencies.	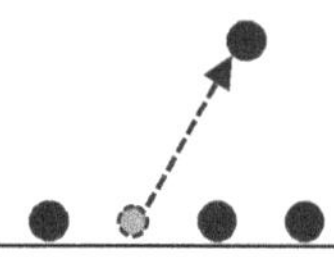

Source: OECD (2014a), *OECD Regional Outlook 2014: Regions and Cities: Where Policies and People Meet*, OECD Publishing, Paris, http://dx.doi.org/10.1787/9789264201415-en.

The evidence thus suggests that leadership from higher levels of government is often required to bring about the cross-jurisdictional co-operation among municipalities that is needed in complex metropolitan areas. Horizontal collaboration across jurisdictions is difficult, even in situations where the actors involved clearly recognise the need for it. Transaction costs, competitive pressures, resource constraints, differing priorities and fears that the distribution of costs or benefits from co-operation will be one-sided, can all impede efforts to bring regional or local governments together, even in the face of common problems. Recent research in Russia suggests that Russian municipalities face similar challenges (Box 3.3).Thus, leadership from above is often critical in resolving the collective-action problems that such co-operation poses: the Krai's role in fostering the development of the Krasnoyarsk Agglomeration is thus typical of similar efforts to develop metropolitan-scale co-operation in complex urban areas.

The multi-association survey described in Box 3.3 explores four models of metro-level co-ordination: (1) unitary cities (mergers), (2) two-level solutions (with an agglomeration-wide authority as a supra-municipal body), (3) regional models (placing metro-level governance more or less in the hands of the relevant federal subject), and (4) agreement-based solutions (voluntary co-operation). These categories map reasonably well onto Table 3.2 above, which reflects OECD experience. Not surprisingly, many Russian experts see the unitary model as flexible, simple and able to resolve a wide range of tasks. The down side is seen in terms of distance between leaders and people, centralisation of resources, bureaucratisation of management and an overall reduction in local control over local affairs. The two-level model is seen as risking the replication of the conflicts and confusions that now exist between the governors of many federal subjects and the mayors of their major cities. The third model is seen largely as an example of the imposition of model 2 from above. And the agreement-based model is seen as weak and complex but also less threatening. It takes longer to establish well – building partnership relations, achieving a balance of interests, etc., takes time. Overall, though, it was the model viewed most favourably by the mayors surveyed, even if most thought that federal legislation was not very favourable to it.

Box 3.3. Barriers to inter-municipal co-operation in Russia

In April-May 2012, a collection of city associations (the Association of Siberian and Far Eastern Cities, the Association of Cities of the Volga, "Cities of the Urals" and the Union of Cities of Central and North-western Russia) conducted a survey of 78 leaders of municipalities of various sizes and 39 leaders of subjects of the Russian Federation. The key findings of the survey included the following:

- Some 36.5% of city leaders spoke of existing inter-municipal links and a further 31.1% were inclined to develop such links. However, 60% regarded inter-municipal ties as "average" and 37.1% as "weak". Almost none spoke of strong ties among municipalities. Most existing co-operation efforts focused on water supply, transport, wastewater and waste processing. Only one in eight saw co-operation among adjacent municipalities as a way to improve economic performance.
- Most inter-municipal ties are linked to commuting flows, trade and services. Least developed were co-operation on real-estate markets and co-operation in the management of municipal property or services (one in three indicated that they were engaged in no such co-operation).
- The main barriers to developing inter-municipal co-operation were seen to be the lack of a basis for such co-operation (40%), the lack of need for such co-operation (29%) and the absence of any possibility of co-operation owing to remote location (21%).
- Nevertheless, the positive side of co-operation was acknowledged – particularly increased efficiency from combined efforts. But conflicts of interest were seen as common and the normative-legal basis for co-operation was felt to be weak. Five-sixth of the mayors saw "substantial barriers to the development of horizontal ties". Only 3.2% saw no big barrier to the development of metro-level governance.

The main barrier identified was municipalities' fear of losing independence (63.5%), gaps in federal legislation, which recognises no such concept as an urban agglomeration (52.4%), the weakness of legislative basis for inter-municipal co-operation (50.8%), and differences in the quality of life between the centre and periphery of large conurbations (49.2%). Lack of agreed strategies for the development of municipal formations was cited by 39.7%, insufficient or poor quality transport links by 22.2% and insufficient support for such projects from the administration of the subject of the federation (the oblast or republic): 12.7%.

Source: ASDG (2013), "Gorodskie aglomeratsii: vzglyad rukovoditelei munitsipal'nykh obrazovanii Rossii", Association of Siberian and Far Eastern Cities, April.

Governing the Krasnoyarsk Agglomeration

The institutional architecture of the Agglomeration has evolved

It is against this backdrop that the efforts to develop the Krasnoyarsk Agglomeration should be seen. By international standards, the Agglomeration is not particularly fragmented in administrative terms, and there is a strong regional authority in a position to help provide co-ordination among its constituent municipalities. Nevertheless, regional and local authorities have identified a number of areas in which greater co-ordination could lead to better outcomes with respect to both economic performance and quality of life. Under the leadership of the Krai and with the support of the federal authorities, the city of Krasnoyarsk has joined forces with surrounding municipalities and towns to form the Krasnoyarsk Agglomeration (hereafter, simply "the Agglomeration"). Their ambition is to establish the Agglomeration as the leading city in Siberia.

Early on, there was even some consideration of merging the municipalities and districts into a "Greater Krasnoyarsk". Instead, however, the participants opted for a softer form of collaboration, at least for the foreseeable future. On 17 April 2008, a memorandum "On the Organisation and Execution of the Inter-municipal Project 'Complex Development of the Krasnoyarsk Agglomeration during the Period to 2020'" was signed by three cities (Krasnoyarsk, Sosnovoborsk, Divnogorsk) and four municipal districts (Mana, Emelyanovo, Sukhobuzim and Berezovsk). Rosatom, the state nuclear energy corporation, refused to let the closed city of Zheleznogorsk participate. The main aim was to create the conditions for advancing socio-economic, infrastructural, industrial and cultural development of Krai territories located around the financial and business centre, the city of Krasnoyarsk.

The original memorandum envisaged the preparation of a scheme of territorial planning for the Agglomeration by 2011, as well as a strategy for the socio-economic development of the Agglomeration to 2020 and a complex investment programme for the period to 2020. These three documents were then to be implemented in 2012-20. The chosen mechanism of co-operation was the inter-municipal investment project – no mergers were envisaged, nor was the creation of another tier of authority. The Krai plays a co-ordinating role – which, OECD experience suggests, does indeed to be taken on by a higher level of government in most serious inter-municipal collaborations. The corporation "Krasnoyarsk-2020" was established to organise the preparation of the above-listed documents on behalf of the Krai. Drafts were prepared, roundtables were conducted, etc., but the global crisis led to a basic reappraisal of plans. Sluggish growth in the Agglomeration in 2009-10 and meagre local budgets impaired the investment potential of municipalities. In early 2011, the Committee on the Complex Development of the Krasnoyarsk Agglomeration was formed (Box 3.4). Headed by a deputy governor, the committee serves as a permanent collegial cross-sectoral consultative body, charged with issues of planning, civil construction and forecasting socio-economic development in the Krai. It makes proposals for economic and social policy, spatial planning, and regulations, strategies and socio-economic development programmes.

Box 3.4. The Committee on the Complex Development of the Krasnoyarsk Agglomeration

In accordance with Decree № 238-r of 26 April 2011, a committee on the complex development of the Krasnoyarsk Agglomeration was established as a permanent, collegial cross-sectoral consultative body of the Krai administration. Its remit includes issues of planning and forecasting socio-economic development of municipalities of Krasnoyarsk Krai included into the Krasnoyarsk Agglomeration and civil construction. The committee's objectives are as follows:

- assistance in the formation of a consistent approach to the Agglomeration's development; and
- ensuring the co-operation of Krai executive authorities and municipalities in developing the Agglomeration.

The committee's jurisdiction includes:

1. Formulation of proposals in the main fields of economic and social policy for the efficient development of the Agglomeration.
2. Formulation of proposals for the strategy of socio-economic development and consideration of forecasts of socio-economic development of the Agglomeration.
3. Formulation of proposals for the strategy of socio-economic development and consideration of forecasts of socio-economic development of the constituent municipalities of the Agglomeration.
4. Formulation of proposals and consideration of issues regarding changes to the scheme of spatial planning of the Agglomeration.
5. Consideration of draft schemes of spatial planning of municipal areas comprising the Krasnoyarsk Agglomeration and formulation of proposals for such draft schemes, as well as formulation of proposals for changes to the schemes.
6. Consideration of draft general plans of urban areas and communities comprising the Agglomeration and formulation of proposals for draft general plans and/or amendments to existing plans.
7. Consideration of the spatial planning proposals, including placement of regional capital construction facilities, and the formulation of proposals for changes to such plans.
8. Consideration of a complex programme of socio-economic development of the Agglomeration and the formulation of proposals for this programme.
9. Consideration of complex programmes of socio-economic development of municipal areas and city districts comprising the Krasnoyarsk Agglomeration, formulation of proposals for these complex programmes.
10. Consideration of draft departmental targeted programmes, formulation of proposals for these programmes and proposals about their approval, formulation of proposals for changes to these targeted programmes, as well as consideration of reports about the realisation of departmental targeted programmes in the field of socio-economic development of the municipalities comprising the Agglomeration.
11. Consideration of draft regulations of the Krai and of the municipalities comprising the Agglomeration aimed at complex development of the Agglomeration and the formulation of proposals for these regulations.
12. Formulation of proposals for the reservation of land plots for state and municipal needs of the municipalities comprising the Agglomeration.
13. Formulation of proposals for exercising the right of eminent domain by the Krai in respect of agricultural lands within the territory of the Agglomeration.

Box 3.4. The Committee on the Complex Development of the Krasnoyarsk Agglomeration *(cont.)*

14. Consideration of issues concerning the complex development of the Agglomeration until 2020.
15. Analysis of problems arising among executive authorities of the Krai and local municipal authorities regarding the establishment and development of the Agglomeration until 2020.
16. Consideration of proposals of the Krai executive authorities and local municipal authorities regarding the challenges facing the Agglomeration until 2020.
17. Elaboration of proposals for the Krai Government regarding basic measures and mechanisms, as well as enhancement of regulations of the Krai necessary for ensuring the complex development of the Agglomeration until 2020.

Source: SFU (2012), "OECD background report on the Krasnoyarsk Agglomeration", Siberian Federal University, Krasnoyarsk, Russian Federation, November.

The goals remain constant in an uncertain institutional environment

Perhaps paradoxically, this initiative has been undertaken with the support of the federal authorities but in the absence of federal legislation concerning the management of urban agglomerations (complex metropolitan areas). The federal government promotes the concept of "urban agglomerations", comprising clusters of interlinked municipalities around urban cores, as centres of economic growth (as noted above, in western parlance, "urban agglomerations" would be designated "metropolitan areas"). There is particular emphasis on optimising transport infrastructure, settlement patterns and engineering infrastructure, as well as the management of natural resources and ecological problems. There has also been much discussion of the potential of urban agglomerations to act as "growth locomotives". The Ministry of Economic Development's "Concept for Long-term Socio-economic Development of the Russian Federation to 2020" identifies large industrial, export-oriented cities, notably those with mineral deposits such as in Siberia, as potential centres of growth and economic development (Kinossian, 2013).

At present, however, no federal legislative framework exists to structure the governance of such areas. The federal Ministry of Regional Development concluded in 2013 that real movement towards effective governance of urban agglomerations would require amendments to a large number of federal laws. Financing rules may also have to change – at present, financing from a municipal budget that leaves the municipality risks being challenged on legal grounds as unauthorised use (*нецелевое использование*). At present, the law envisages the conduct of spatial planning, zoning and civil construction only within specific municipal entities. That said, federal law does allow the formation of associations of municipalities for the resolution of common problems, as well as contracts and other agreements among municipalities. Inter-municipal bodies may not, however, be endowed with the powers of municipal authorities (i.e. no delegation of municipal competences to them is permitted).

Thus, while the recognition of cities as drivers for economic growth and regional development provides an important indicator of federal support for agglomerations, the absence of an official definition and a legislative framework for governing them make such a project likely to be one of trial and error. This is precisely what the Krasnoyarsk

Agglomeration has been going through since the initiation of the Agglomeration project in 2008. The overall goal of the vision for the Agglomeration is to make it the Eastern Siberia's "growth locomotive". Yet while the modalities have, as noted above, changed over time, the main objectives of the Agglomeration project have been consistent:

- to develop infrastructure, including energy, transport and logistics, to reach economies of scale through a better integrated regional market;
- to improve the business environment for existing companies and to attract new business into the region; and
- to deepen the local labour market and make it more fluid to the benefit of both employers and employees.

Wide-ranging research on the economic effects of urban agglomeration shows that these objectives can contribute to the overall goal of the Agglomeration (Ahrend et al., 2014). An important element of implementing the strategies was to review spatial planning of the Agglomeration. In 2010, a planning scheme, including for the Agglomeration, was developed by "Urbanistika", a St. Petersburg-based enterprise. However, no specific overarching plan exists yet for the territory of the Agglomeration.

The implementation of the Agglomeration strategies and programmes is co-ordinated by the Krai government, chiefly the Krai Ministry of Economics and Regional Development. Responsibility for different urban sectors, services and development, including spatial economic development, transport, water and waste management, public safety, culture, education, health, housing and environmental protection are the responsibility of the cities and districts of the Agglomeration, in accordance with Federal Law No 131-F (2003), which defines the jurisdiction and governance of the Federation's subjects. Local management issues in rural communities, municipal and urban territories listed in the Federal Law "On the general principles of local self-management in the Russian Federation".

Getting governance right in the Agglomeration will be crucial for attaining the objectives and achieving the goal of the Agglomeration's strategies and vision. In the absence of any legislative framework for metropolitan governance, this will require innovation and experimentation. This is true in particular for those areas that have structural impact and long-term effects on the Agglomeration's development potential and economic performance. The priority areas for governance are: land-use planning, housing and services, and transport. These are addressed in the following sections. Another key area for governance is investment, which will be looked at below in the context of multi-level governance and vertical co-ordination in particular.

Governing land use in the Agglomeration

Land-use planning needs to be reformed and more transport-oriented

While one might suppose that centralised planning during the Soviet era enabled co-ordination between transport and land-use planners, the reverse was true. Location decisions for industries and residential areas were made in rival ministries and the permanent shortage of housing regularly resulted in *ad hoc* decisions. These were mostly taken to the detriment of housing, which ended up on low-value land at the urban periphery, while industries occupied central urban areas. This had negative consequences for urban transport. For example, it contributed to excessive commuting times for workers (Pucher, 1990). While much has changed over the past 20 years, the form and functioning of many former Soviet cities still need fundamental spatial reorganisation in order to benefit from the advantages of market forces (World Bank, 2012).

The relocation of industries in the Agglomeration and transport planning need to be closely co-ordinated and integrated to optimise the use of land and transport infrastructure. Among the strategic priorities for the Agglomeration is the "economically efficient and environmentally sustainable use of land". One measure currently taken in the Agglomeration for achieving better land use is the relocation of industries from the urban centre to the periphery, notably to the north-eastern fringe of the city of Krasnoyarsk. Industrial areas that this process will free up are intended to be used for multi-story residential or commercial buildings and are supposed to stimulate new urban activities. While this approach promises to make central urban areas more attractive and lively places, it should also strike an appropriate balance of residential and commercial development in view of making optimal use of existing transport infrastructure in these areas. On the other hand, the choice of new industrial locations should be co-ordinated with Agglomeration-wide transport planning in order to minimise the need for new infrastructure and to optimise commuting flows related to new industrial locations. In order to achieve the strategic priority of economically efficient and environmentally sustainable land use, transport and land-use planning will need to be closely co-ordinated and integrated at the level of the Agglomeration.

Current legislation limits inter-municipal co-ordination of land-use and transport planning, but federal law does allow voluntary contractual agreements among municipalities. In accordance with current legislation, spatial planning, zoning and civil construction are dealt with in each municipal entity separately. Each community or metropolitan area in the Krasnoyarsk agglomeration approves its own general plan, including regulations for land use, territorial development and civil construction. This is prescribed in the federal Urban Development Code, which also defines the hierarchies, documents and procedures that municipalities are required to adapt. General plans include "functional territorial zoning", but do not provide legally binding rules for the private sector, which in turn are part of land-use and development rules (Hirt, 2012). The Krai Ministry of Economics and Regional Development has defined its own guidelines for inter-municipal co-ordination, but it does not provide an explicit framework for co-ordinating transport or land-use planning across municipalities. The legal basis on which co-ordinated planning can take place is given by Federal Law No. 131-FZ (points 3 and 4 in Article 8), which permits the establishment of a "contractual model of agglomeration governance" that enables municipalities to conclude voluntary contractual agreements. Such agreements could be the basis for:

- voluntary networks of municipal units, taking into account their territorial and organisational foundations; or
- representative bodies of inter-municipal networks, economic entities and other inter-municipal organisations, with the aim of pooling financial, material and other resources.

Such contractual agreements, though authorised, are not extensively codified in federal legislation. This leaves flexibility for defining different forms of inter-municipal co-operation, but it could also result in unclear situations – both for the actors taking part in inter-municipal relations as well as for supervising (enforcement) agencies.

Better integration of land-use and transport planning might necessitate the creation of a separate inter-municipal advisory body. Land-use and transport planning ultimately shapes urban form and is governed by the Russian Urban Planning Code. As soon as the plan of one municipality affects the interests of another municipality or a regional planning document, the Urban Planning Code regulates all spatial planning procedures. Spatial plans that have implications for more than one municipality must thus follow the rules, criteria and procedures for inter-municipal approval of plans as prescribed by the Urban Planning Code. While the latter provides a regulative framework for conflicting spatial plans among municipalities, it does not provide guidance or a framework for pro-active inter-municipal planning, and it often hampers rather than facilitates inter-municipal co-ordination. In order to improve the co-ordination of land-use and transport planning, municipalities could form an inter-municipal association, which could act as a representative and co-ordinating body for associated municipalities. Such a body would need to be open to representatives of the Krai and the Federation but could act upon relevant inter-municipal planning issues in the Krasnoyarsk Agglomeration. Experiences with inter-municipal planning organisations may offer guidance (Box 3.5).

An effective instrument for integrating land-use and transport planning is transit-oriented development (TOD). TOD can be defined as an urban development strategy designed to maximise access to mass-transit systems by promoting relatively dense, mixed-use development around existing or new public transport infrastructure (OECD, 2012a). TOD shows how complementarities between transport and land-use policies can lead to economically and environmentally efficient urban development. The essence of TOD is to develop first in areas close to existing or new public transport infrastructure, as opposed to developing greenfields and serving them with new road transport infrastructure. By optimising the synergies between land use and existing transport infrastructure, TOD helps minimise congestion. Cities such as Toyama (Japan) or Portland (United States) are examples of successful TOD. Beyond co-ordinating land-use and transport plans to increase TOD, Toyama introduced incentives to encourage development adjacent to transit stations and in central urban areas. This led to an increased use of public transport and gradual migration of citizens from suburbs into targeted central urban areas (OECD, 2012b).

Box 3.5. Chicago Metropolitan Planning Agency

The Chicago Metropolitan Planning Agency (CMAP) was created in 2005 as a merger between the Chicago Area Transportation Study and the Northeastern Illinois Planning Commission. It is responsible for transport, land-use planning, housing and economic development. The CMAP, the Southeastern Wisconsin Planning Commission and the Northwestern Indiana Regional Planning Commission already co-ordinate transport and economic development, as well as land use, in their particular metropolitan jurisdictions. Although their legal mandates are geographically limited, there is no barrier to their discussing and collaborating with each other to ensure coherence at the regional level. Some steps have already been taken and more should be encouraged.

Source: OECD (2012b), *Compact City Policies: A Comparative Assessment*, OECD Green Growth Studies, OECD Publishing, Paris, http://dx.doi.org/10.1787/9789264167865-en.

Spatial planning would gain from co-ordination across the Agglomeration…

Spatial planning priorities for Krasnoyarsk Krai are defined in the spatial planning scheme of the Krai, implemented as of 2008. Within the Agglomeration, each municipality develops, in accordance with the Russian Urban Planning Code, its own general plan, spatial planning schemes, land-use zoning and development rules. The Krai Ministry of Construction and Architecture defines the requirements for spatial planning schemes and general plans. The current general plans of the Agglomeration's municipalities (Krasnoyarsk, Divnogorsk and Sosnovoborsk) and the spatial planning schemes of municipal districts (Berezovsk, Emelyanovo, Mana and Sukhobuzim) were developed between 2008 and 2011 with a time horizon to 2018 or longer. The schemes and plans were developed by municipalities' Departments of Urban Development and Architecture, including public hearings, and adopted by the representative organs of local self-management. The fact that private land in the Agglomeration was privatised before the development of general plans and spatial planning schemes creates a structural challenge, however, for implementing them, in particular because plans and schemes have no legal power over the use of private land.

The effectiveness of general plans and spatial planning schemes in the Agglomeration has yet to be evaluated, but a strong focus on economic objectives and large investment projects may come to the detriment of larger goals, such as socially inclusive and environmentally sustainable development. The way the plans are designed in the Agglomeration is much influenced by the history of planning in the Russian Federation and the requirements of federal law defining crucial parameters of local planning (Box 3.6).

Box 3.6. Spatial planning and land-use zoning in the Russian Federation

An influential heritage of the Soviet planning system is the institution of general plans. General plans exist for each city, are usually renewed every 10-15 years, and used to be developed by the state. The Urban Planning Code of 2004 (first introduced in 1998 and last revised in 2011) passes the responsibility for developing general plans down to the municipal level. This was a logical step following the transition of land ownership to the local level, where land is either owned by municipalities or privately. The code also prescribes the hierarchies and documents that govern spatial planning, including the procedures for urban development control and the issuance of permits. General plans are still the main planning documents for urban development in Russian cities.

The actual rules that govern local development are legally binding "development rules" that define land use according to the federal code within zones and land-use classes: agricultural, industrial, residential, public and business, infrastructure. In contrast to strictly mono-functional zoning during the Soviet era, land use in these different classes and zones is more flexible and allows for mixed-use development to some extent. For example, residential zones (*zhilye zony*) can have social, cultural and communal constructions, including schools, hospitals or retail business. In practice, the size of zones is usually fairly small, which fosters mixed uses, if looked at on a bigger scale. On the base of general plans and development rules, planning design and land surveying projects are obligatory documents to be provided for receiving a construction permit (Beregovskih, et al. 2010).

The Urban Development Code and the current legal framework for planning more generally have been criticised for several shortcomings. A central critique is that the overall approach to urban planning did not fundamentally touch on basic Soviet principles, notably spatial planning, which continues to be defined in general plans (Glubchikov, 2006). Another issue is the legal uncertainty of strategic and detailed urban plans, which leaves them in a weak position, while the legally more forceful zoning practice – being derived informed by general plans – cannot always deliver the necessary detail and, in particular, does not allow for integrated strategic planning. With zoning being the main "regulative" tool, both more strategic and more individualist approaches to land use and economic development are difficult; detailed planning instead is replaced by development control, e.g. through requirements for technical approvals necessary before applying for a building permit (Glubchikov, 2006).

Sources: Hirt, S. (2012), "Mixed use by default: How the Europeans (don't) zone", *Journal of Planning Literature*, Vol. 4, No. 27, pp. 375-393; Glubchikov, O. (2006), "Urban planning in Russia: Towards the market", *European Planning Studies*, Vol. 12, No. 2, pp. 229-247, http://dx.doi.org/10.1080/0965431042000183950.

More specifically, many spatial planning decisions in the Agglomeration cater to large investment projects, which promise positive effects on growth and revenues (SFU, 2012). The current design of plans is seen in direct relationship with the way local leaders are evaluated, that is being pushed to compete on economic indicators. This is seen as counteracting comprehensive and integrated planning that could factor in social and environmental goals and concerns (SFU, 2012). It should be mentioned that the regulations for spatial and general plans, as well as for socio-economic development programmes in Russia, include environmental requirements and standards for social facilities (SFU, 2012). Furthermore, experience in OECD countries shows that integrated planning that favours socially inclusive and environmentally sustainable territorial development can significantly contribute to economic growth (OECD, 2013c).

There is much to be said for inter-jurisdictional competition – cities often grow and develop by competing to offer better services, better conditions for business and better quality of life. However, some forms of competition simply distort markets and focus local leaders' attention on persuading people and firms to shift places, rather than on the development of new activities. Yet in a functional economy such as the Krasnoyarsk Agglomeration, such small-scale competition can undermine competitiveness on a larger – national or international – scale. Complex metropolitan areas must learn to overcome such tendencies and recognise that, in the larger picture, they constitute a single functional economy whose prosperity often depends on their ability to co-ordinate. Among the many causes of the city of Detroit's decline was persistent conflict between Detroit and the surrounding municipalities which formed part of the larger agglomeration (Hildebrandt, 2013). This is more than anecdotal: as described above, recent OECD work confirms that metropolitan economies characterised by co-operation at metropolitan scale tend to be more successful. And not only economically: integrated planning can also favour better social and environmental (as well as economic) outcomes (OECD, 2014a). Many such problems need to be dealt with at a larger scale than the municipality.

...And the upgrading of local capacities

Inter-sectoral co-ordination problems in Russia, as in many countries, are often aggravated by fragmentation and capacity bottlenecks at lower levels of government. Most regions and cities still lack the resources and know-how for truly effective strategic urban planning, including the tools and systems needed for implementation, monitoring and evaluation and audit. To a great extent, urban planning is still understood as a highly specialised, largely technocratic and top-down exercise, the aim of which is to produce periodic plans that are to guide development, although recent legislation has tried to build in mechanisms for public consultation that were previously lacking. This approach, with its focus on period updates of cities' general plans (*genplany*) is too static, since in a fast-changing economy such plans are often out of date by the time they are completed, and they are rarely linked to implementation mechanisms anyway. Arguably, the *process* of planning is more important than any actual "plan" that results, in the sense that a truly dynamic, participatory planning process serves as both an on-going analytical exercise and a co-ordination device that can strengthen communication among public and private-sector stakeholders, reveal information and promote economic "self-discovery". Any actual "plans" produced in the course of such procedures tend to be provisional and/or evolving documents (OECD, 2001). Given high levels of uncertainty about the future, such an approach is vital, since strongly prescriptive economic and spatial planning tends not to reduce uncertainty but create – at best – the illusion of having done so.[4]

In addition, development planning in Russia often suggests a lack of faith in markets. In large part, this stems from the tendency to hold governors, in particular, responsible for all kinds of outcomes in their regions, from growth and investment to health and mortality indicators. Such pressures tend to lead to "manual management" – the tendency of policy makers to rely on direct, *ad hoc* interventions rather than stable regulatory and policy frameworks – and also to weaken incentives to take a longer-term view. In many countries, spatial planning is gradually moving from land-use regulation frameworks towards long-term strategic documents, focusing on the co-ordination of diverse issues and interests across sectors as well as between levels of government and often incorporates monitoring, feedback and revision mechanisms. Examples include the National Strategic Reference Framework in EU countries, the National Spatial Strategy in Japan, and the Comprehensive National Territorial Plan in Korea.

Co-ordination of spatial planning and socio-economic development programmes in the Agglomeration could improve integrated planning. General plans and spatial planning schemes of all municipalities and districts that signed the agreement about the "establishment of the Agglomeration in the field of programmes of socio-economic development of municipal entities until 2020" are co-ordinated by the Krai government. Socio-economic development programmes are co-ordinated locally, among municipalities, and include specific sections on inter-municipal co-ordination. All city or district councils of municipalities and districts in the Agglomeration, apart from Emelyanovo, have recently adopted "programmes for socio-economic development" which include more or less detailed sections on inter-municipal co-ordination. In addition, the Krai Ministry of Economics and Regional Development has developed guidelines for inter-municipal co-operation and planning documentation. If well implemented, these approaches and instruments to co-ordinate planning and socio-economic development programmes should help to further integrate spatial plans and align economic, social and environmental policy goals.

An Agglomeration-wide spatial and development plan is in the making, but the roles of the various actors involved need to be clarified in order for it to become an effective tool for territorial development. In 2009, an overarching draft spatial planning scheme for the Agglomeration was developed in agreement with all municipalities, for the period until 2020. This scheme has not yet been approved and is thus only an advisory document for the time being. It includes corrections of individual general plans at municipal level. The plan was developed by different ministries of the Krai government. At the same time, spatial planning at the Agglomeration level is overseen by the "Committee on the Complex Development of the Krasnoyarsk Agglomeration", including the development of municipalities' individual general plans. While such oversight should be beneficial, it is not clear how the committee's work relates to the Krai government's role in co-ordinating local spatial and general plans and in developing an overarching plan for the Agglomeration. Rules and powers for different bodies currently involved in planning, oversight and co-ordination should be better defined, delineated and clearly established. This is a condition for an effective multi-level planning and governance system in the Agglomeration, including for territorial planning, zoning and inter-municipal projects, which could help overcome current fragmentation.

These represent steps in the right direction but there is more that the Krai and participating municipalities can do, not least within the framework of the Committee on the Complex Development of the Krasnoyarsk Agglomeration. Co-ordination of planning falls squarely within its remit. Bearing in mind the opportunities and constraints arising from federal legislation on urban and land-use planning, the commission could pursue a number of objectives in its planning co-ordination function, including:

- the promotion of multi-functional zoning (urban *genplany* in Russia have traditionally been based on functional zoning, sometimes to an extreme degree);
- integrating, to the extent possible, the various planning processes, especially transport, land-use, economic development and environmental planning, as well as urban planning *stricto sensu*;
- defining a hierarchy of planning objectives within the Agglomeration, distinguishing those that are purely local from those that need to be addressed at an Agglomeration-wide scale;
- planning to facilitate both in-fill re-development and better planning of greenfield developments; and
- applying the methods of urban strategic planning (UCLG, 2010) to achieve greater flexibility, wider participation and more emphasis on continuous planning as a tool, as opposed to periodic updates of fixed plans.

Planning practices and the lack of land markets impede redevelopment

Most of residential development in the Agglomeration is currently implemented in greenfields, as low-rise housing, resembling general trends in the Russian Federation. Novoland, currently the largest development project in the Agglomeration, builds new individual detached houses in greenfields of Emelyanovo. Much smaller quantities of multi-story family housing are developed on the Solontsi territory. Novoland is no exception to other development projects in Russia, responding for demand of low-rise individual housing in suburban areas, which has strongly grown in recent years. In most cases, this tendency is supported by the local administration, generating poorly planned and controlled suburbanisation and *ad hoc* conversion of agricultural to urban land (Beregovskih et al., 2010). Research and evidence shows that urban sprawl negatively impacts economic and environmental efficiency of territorial development (OECD, 2012b). Externalities of excessive urban sprawl and low-density development include higher costs for infrastructure and service provision and higher resource consumption, notably due to more energy consumed in lone-standing buildings in longer commutes.

Freeing up centrally located industrial land for other uses can benefit the Agglomeration economically and increase the efficiency of urban land use. Industries placed in central urban areas and residential development around the urban core by Soviet urban planners still characterise many Russian cities, including Krasnoyarsk. The absence of a land price in the Soviet era made it affordable for companies to be located downtown. Even then, however, fully-serviced central urban land would have yielded higher benefits if not used for industrial use (World Bank, 2012). As soon as land markets started to evolve, the opportunity cost of under-utilised industrial urban land increases. Where this happened in Russia, companies started relocating to the urban periphery (Bertaud and Renaud, 1995). In other places, land under privatised companies stayed in public hands, which kept prices artificially low and hindered market forces to take effect on redistributing urban land more efficiently. In the places where industrial land was freed and redeveloped, positive spillover effects can be noticed on more dynamic urban real estate markets in general (World Bank, 2012). These arguments call for improving the foundations of land markets, which in turn can help to reallocate land uses in urban territories in economically more efficient ways than is the case today.

Brownfield redevelopment in central urban areas has significant potential to improve urban form and functions and to make urban living more attractive. Centrally located former industrial land plots not only have the advantage of being connected to urban infrastructures and services, they are also attractive for developers due to their size that offers opportunities for centrally located residential, commercial or mixed-use development at scale. Attracting people and commercial activities into central urban areas increases proximity to jobs, commerce and services, and improves the conditions for work and life in cities. Mixed-use and dense urban areas prove to reduce car dependency and resource consumption; and therewith reduce unwanted externalities in urban areas, such as pollution (OECD, 2012b). Increasing the quality, convenience and efficiency of urban living through redeveloping former industrial sites in central urban areas can strongly contribute to making these areas more attractive. Finally, this might be a key to reversing the current preference for individual detached houses in suburban areas.

Several conditions need to be in place in order to make brownfield redevelopment an economically viable alternative to greenfield development. Non-existing land prices in Soviet Russia removed all incentives for redevelopment of built up areas. Allocated land was hardly ever recycled and greenfield development at the urban periphery was easier than redevelopment of central urban land plots with obsolete use. This meant that cities spread out, while central urban land stayed underused (Bertaud and Renaud, 1995). For brownfield redevelopment to become attractive to developers a functioning land market based on market prices and additional incentives for developers to favour brownfield over greenfield development are needed. The underdeveloped land market in the Agglomeration is the biggest challenge to overcome. Land prices at market value would exert a strong influence on redeveloping urban land in central areas. That said, market prices for urban land would allow new financing mechanisms to be used for brownfield redevelopment, as successfully implemented in numerous OECD cities. One mechanism, tax increment financing (TIF), has particular potential for contaminated industrial sites, although western experience suggests that it must be approached with care (Box 3.7).

Box 3.7. Financing brownfield redevelopment via tax-increment financing (TIF)

Tax increment financing (TIF) is a method used to subsidise redevelopment, infrastructure, and other community-improvement projects in many countries. TIF is a method to use future increases in tax revenues generated by new development to subsidise the current improvements that will yield those increases. Cities typically rely on property taxes, and contaminated sites have low property values. When they are cleaned up, property values rise, and they rise still more when new developments take place on the cleaned-up sites. The tax increase resulting from the clean-up and redevelopment is the tax increment. This increment is typically refunded annually to the new owners who have cleaned up and redeveloped the site, until the costs of remediation are fully compensated; such refunds usually finance the debt issued to pay for the project. In short, TIF creates funding for public or private projects by borrowing against the future increase in these property-tax revenues. The Canadian city of Kitchener, for example, has in recent years attracted 1.5 billion dollars into the redevelopment of old chemical factories. There are technical solutions to virtually all of the contaminants: the challenge, as in Krasnoyarsk, was to finance the clean-up and ensure that the new owners were not subsequently held liable for damage done by previous owners. Kitchener has used TIF to achieve this. Distressed sites within a TIF district are typically offered for tender by the municipality, with a view to addressing economic challenges, environmental hazards and land-use conflicts.

That said, TIF should be approached with caution, as it is open to abuse:

- Additionality is hard to assure. TIF districts may be drawn up where development would occur even without TIF, particularly where TIF districts are drawn too large.

Box 3.7. Financing brownfield redevelopment via tax-increment financing (TIF) (*cont.*)

The result will be public subsidy for activities which would have occurred anyway ("deadweight losses") and which yield little additional public benefit. Moreover, increases in property values that would have occurred in any case (e.g., as a result of overall price inflation) can be captured by private developers under poorly prepared TIF arrangements.

- The designation of urban areas in need of clean-up or redevelopment can be politically manipulated and has in some countries led to court battles over the exercise of the authorities' right of eminent domain to redevelop areas where no environmental clean-up was required.
- The TIF process can also be manipulated to favour politically connected developers and others involved in the process.
- Capturing the full tax increment and directing it to repay the development bonds is arguably excessive compensation, since the incremental increase in property value is also likely to be associated with an increase in the provision of public services to the TIF district.
- TIF works best in jurisdictions with a relatively sophisticated and well-administered property tax, linked to market values.

Empirical analysis of TIFs in the US state of Illinois suggests that the non-TIF areas of municipalities that use TIF do not grow faster (and may even growth more slowly) than similar municipalities that do not use TIF (Dye and Merriman, 2006). This runs counter to the claim that stimulating development in TIF districts generates benefits for the surrounding areas as well; in some cases, it may simply lead to displacement of activity from other places to the TIF district. TIF also appears to have different impacts when land use is considered. For example, commercial TIF districts tend to reduce commercial development in the non-TIF portion of the municipality. This makes intuitive sense: most retail trade needs to be located close to its customers. Subsidising a store in one location is thus likely to reduce demand for a store in a nearby location. Industrial land use, though, is different. Since industrial goods are mostly exported and sold outside the local area, a local offset is not expected, and the evidence presented in Dye and Merriman (2006) is consistent with this prediction.

Source: Dye, R. and D. Merriman (2006), "Tax Increment Financing: A Tool for Local Development", *Land Lines*, Vol. 18, No. 1, January, available at: https://www.lincolninst.edu/pubs/dl/1076_Jan2006-Final.pdf.

Other challenges need to be overcome to make redevelopment a viable option for obsolete residential buildings. Some of the current housing built in the later Soviet period is of such bad quality and in such a bad state that redevelopment would in many cases be economically more efficient than renovation and deep retrofits. Again, a functioning land market is a key condition for this to become economically viable. Another important challenge needs to be addressed, however: the scattered and complicated ownership structure and user rights of large apartment buildings (World Bank, 2012). Incentives may be put in place for owners that are reluctant to move out of their building, a common problem currently met by developers in the Agglomeration.

The housing sector

The housing sector also needs action at an Agglomeration-wide scale

Housing in the Agglomeration faces several challenges: an underdeveloped real estate market, an immature rental market, a dispersed settlement pattern and a housing stock in poor condition. Many of the roots of these challenges are to be found in the historic context of Soviet-era housing supply, rules for land use and real estate ownership structures. Privatisation, a new Urban Planning Code and the gradual development of the property market in Russia have changed the housing sector dramatically since 1991, but there are several important impediments to further progress, such as largely publically owned land, inadequate institutions for a property and rental market, an inflexible and inefficient zoning system, and a large number of poor property owners who lack the resources to maintain or renew the building stock.

During the housing privatisation in the post-Soviet years, many Russians became homeowners overnight but never had the means to maintain their properties. Some 88% of housing across the Agglomeration is privately owned; 11% is public and 1% is held in other ways (Figure 3.7). Much of the housing stock dates from Soviet times and is of poor quality (Bertaud and Renaud, 1995). In particular, the prefabricated buildings of the later years were poorly insulated and in most cases built for a lifetime of about 30 years. Many low-quality buildings are still in use and in very poor condition. Extensive resource consumption of these buildings was not a problem in Soviet times, when energy and water were heavily subsidised (World Bank, 2012). Today, however, this poses a problem, particularly for poor owners who lack the means to retrofit their homes. Many of them are in multi-family buildings in which scattered ownership structures and municipal responsibility for building management further complicate comprehensive overhauls. While the federal Fund for the Promotion of the Housing and Utility Sector Reform allocates funds for building refurbishment, even the 5% co-financing required to receive such funds is too much for most homeowners in Russia (Puzanov, 2009).

Figure 3.7. **Housing ownership in the Krasnoyarsk Agglomeration**

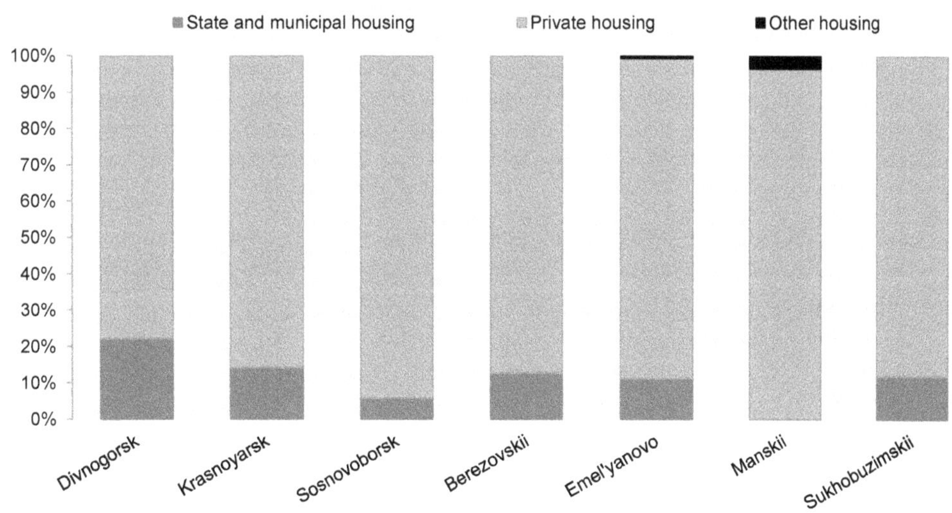

Source: SFU (2012), "OECD background report on the Krasnoyarsk Agglomeration", Siberian Federal University, Krasnoyarsk, Russian Federation, November.

Improvements of the building stock come less and less from public investments. The main expenditure responsibility for housing and utilities lies with municipalities, which explains why expenditure on housing and utilities as a share of total budgetary expenditures is relatively high compared to regional expenditures. At all levels of government, expenditures on housing and utilities fell over the last decade, and the drop was particularly pronounced in the Agglomeration (Figure 3.8). This tendency is partly the result of a budget reform in 2006, which aimed at shifting expenditures for housing and utilities to households. Maintaining and improving the building stock is still too expensive, however, for many households.

Figure 3.8. **Expenditures on housing and utilities, 2000-11**

% of total budget expenditures

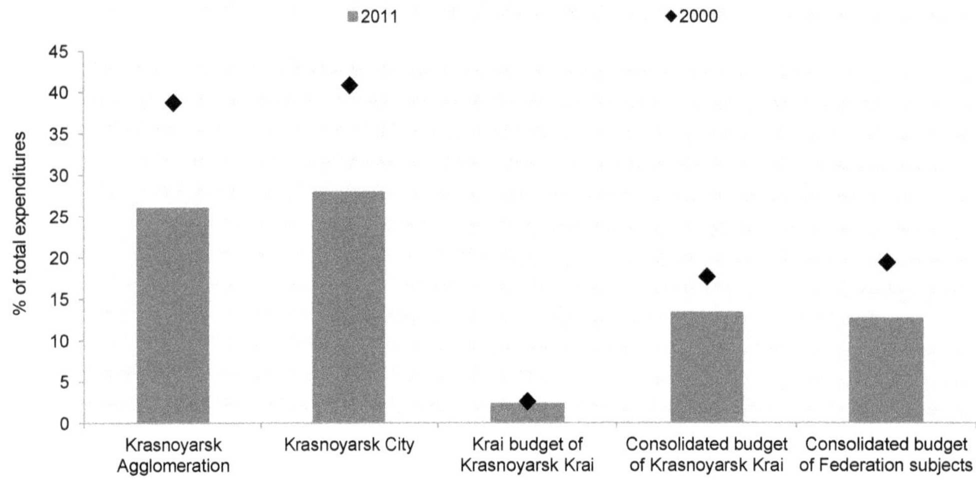

Source: SFU (2012), "OECD background report on the Krasnoyarsk Agglomeration", Siberian Federal University, Krasnoyarsk, Russian Federation, November.

Box 3.8. Financing building retrofits for energy efficiency

Buildings tend to be the most energy-intensive sector in cities; however, little has been done so far to improve the energy efficiency of the building stock in Russian cities. Experience from OECD countries shows that under certain conditions, energy efficiency measures can be implemented successfully through a market-based approach. Key elements for such an approach are:

- political commitment and a legal framework that provide incentives to implement energy efficiency measures and that enable or support their effective financing;
- sufficiently high energy prices that allow refinancing energy efficiency investments through energy savings over a maximum of 10-15 years;
- financial institutions with specialised competences and financial products or mechanisms tailored to financing energy efficiency measures for buildings;
- energy service companies and energy performance contracting to facilitate the organisation of implementing energy efficiency measures and to guarantee their effectiveness; and
- public support to address potential market failures, e.g. through tax deductions, public banks, grants, loans, credit default guarantees or interest rate subsidies.

Box 3.8. **Financing building retrofits for energy efficiency** *(cont.)*

Most of these elements are not in place in Russia. For example, Russian law (the Russian Housing Code and the Federal Law "On making amendments to the Housing Code" adopted in the end of 2012) lacks specific targets for energy efficiency. While in general no restrictions are imposed on public or private financing of building retrofits, current regulations do not facilitate risk sharing between the public and the private sectors.

Source: OECD (2013c), *Green Growth in Cities*, OECD Publishing, Paris, http://dx.doi.org/10.1787/9789264195325-en; UNECE (2013), *Good Practices for Energy-Efficient Housing in the UNECE Region*, United Nations, Geneva.

Maintaining and improving the building stock could become more affordable if coupled with energy-efficiency measures. Energy-efficiency retrofits can lower utility bills to a point at which it becomes possible to refinance the retrofit through the energy savings it yields. Several conditions must be in place to achieve such a result, however (Box 3.8). For example, if energy prices are too low (often because they are subsidised), then the savings from reduced energy consumption will be insufficient. Also, flat-rate fees that do not reflect the amount of energy consumed are counterproductive. Instead, gradually increasing rates for increased consumption create an incentive for energy savings. The same is true for water consumption, combined with water savings from resource-efficient appliances. Furthermore, governments can consider incentives to finance energy efficiency measures, such as credit guarantees.

Municipalities could play a more important role in improving the building stock if their tax base were more substantial. Two types of property tax exist in Russia, on land and on built structures, the latter distinguishing between the property of persons and that of organisations. Property taxes are based on a property inventory, with specific criteria such as age, structure, size of building and a unified cadastre value of the land. These values are usually well below market prices. Municipalities have the right to adjust the tax within a maximum threshold for land tax that is set at federal level. Today, property tax revenues for municipalities are very low. To reform this system, a comprehensive evaluation of market values is needed, as well as legislative changes, which have been discussed at the federal level for a number of years and might come into effect in 2014. When property taxes will be paid for the market value of land and buildings, municipalities are likely to enjoy a significant increase in tax revenues, parts of which could be reallocated to improving the building stock.

In the Krai and the Agglomeration, several laws and public programmes provide housing finance or financial help for maintenance.

- Social housing programmes: *i)* the federal and regional "Dwelling" programme and regional sub-programmes and laws to provide targeted support for specific social groups, including former military, citizens exposed to radiation and young families; *ii)* the programme "The House" provides housing for inhabitants living in uninhabitable municipal housing stock; and *iii)* there is a Krai programme on housing provision for young families in the region.
- Improvement of the building stock: "Improvement of Stability of Residential Buildings, Basic Objects and Life-support Systems in Seismic Areas of

Krasnoyarsk Krai" aims at improving the structure of buildings in targeted areas in the Krai. Krai law and the "Dwelling" programme also ensure the provision of housing or support for housing improvements to in-migrating persons who have suffered from radiation exposure, emergency services personnel or veterans.

- New housing construction: under the regional investment project "Novoland" a total floor area of 22 000 m^2 will be constructed, distributed among 596 apartments in 329 low-rise residential houses (135.9 m^2 on average per apartment) and 1 620 apartments in 46 multi-story apartment blocks (61.1 m^2 on average per apartment); as well as utility, energy and transport infrastructures.
- Resettlement programmes: *i)* "The North to the South" aims at resettling citizens from the far northern to southern Krai territory; *ii)* there is also a programme for "Resettlement of Citizens Residing in the Urban Okrug Norilsk City and the Urban Settlement Dudinka to the City of Krasnoyarsk Krai and into Regions with Favourable Environmental Conditions on the Territory of the Russian Federation". As noted in Chapter 1, the shift in population to the warmer and more densely inhabited part of the Krai is likely to have economic, social and health benefits.
- Mortgage support programmes: Krai law guarantees public workers the repayment of interest rates incurred from improving housing conditions, as well as the repayment of the loan principal for housing conditions improvements when public sector workers have four or more children.

Most of these laws and programmes have social objectives; however, they seem insufficient to address the large housing demand and poor state of the building stock in large parts of the Agglomeration. In particular, they focus on short-term repairs rather than on long-term improvements of the conditions for affordable and higher quality housing. For this, the roots of the problem, a dysfunctional land, construction and housing market, would need to be addressed. Furthermore, there does not seem to be any explicit co-ordination between the different levels – federal, regional and municipal – involved in housing policy, measures and programmes.

A cumbersome framework for land and real estate ownership hampers transactions

Land ownership structures and the institutions governing them (Box 3.9) complicate the development of a functioning land market. Land and real estate are legally distinguished in Russian law and the majority of land is publically owned. Today, 92% of Russian land is publically owned, either at federal, regional or municipal level, while 0.6% is held by legal entities and the rest by individuals. Owners of individual houses usually own the land under their house. The main form of private use of public land is organised via "leaseholds" (Bartholomy and Krutik, 2013). The large public ownership, insufficiently inventoried land and a lack of transparency on ownership hinder the development of a functioning and dynamic land market, which does not pick up despite low land prices. Prices are fixed by the federal law "On the enactment of the Land Code of the Russian Federation" (Article 2), which defines a minimum and maximum floor repurchase price of land plots under privatised enterprises and buildings. Since 2008, the land price is set at the maximum of 2.5% of the land plots' cadastre value (up to 20% in Moscow and St. Petersburg). Experts estimate that this has reduced the repurchase price by five times on the average. Even this drop in prices has not significantly spurred the market, however, which apart from a market of land plots under detached houses continues to be virtually non-existent (Puzanov, 2009). To develop a dynamic land market, a functional and reliable framework is needed, including clearly enforced property rights (complete land and ownership inventory), transparency, fight against corruption and clear urban planning regulations for land use (World Bank, 2012).

Given the persisting dominance of public land ownership, public authorities have a lot of power over the allotment of land plots to private persons and for construction purposes. Public land is owned at different levels of government. Every government level decides separately over the use of the land. In some areas, land-use decisions are co-ordinated across levels of government; however, in many cases, decisions are taken without co-ordination. Municipalities are the least independent in making land-use decisions, linked to their dependency on regional and federal transfers. Generally, public authorities actively participate in allotting land to private actors (Puzanov, 2009). The lack of transparency in this process raises the price of land and the cost for developers. Furthermore, public authorities have the right to reserve land plots, which leads to economically inefficient spatial planning, often driven by rent seeking. In the Agglomeration, the "Committee on the Complex Development" is meant to formulate proposals for reserving land plots for state or municipal needs as well as for acquiring agricultural land. An important step to establishing the conditions for a functioning land market in the Agglomeration would be to make information and access to land as well as allotment fully transparent.

Box 3.9. Legal framework for land and real estate transactions

The 2001 Land Code of the Russian Federation creates a legal framework for urban land plot transaction, but the separation in ownership of land and buildings or building structures hampers the real estate market to develop. The Land Code gives building owners exclusive rights to purchase or rent the underlying publically owned land. The code prescribes that the privatisation of buildings must be done jointly with privatising the land plot under the building (Puzanov, 2009). Today, many private buildings are standing on land plots held on different titles and by different parties. In the absence of a unified real estate cadastre, which unifies the registration of land and buildings, the situation is unlikely to improve. Furthermore, privatisation is slowed down in many places due to missing or absent land titles, claims by previous owners or the reluctance of some cities to release public land.

A federal cadastre, unifying the databases for land and real estate is in the making, but not yet implemented. In 2007, a Federal Law "On the State Real Estate Cadastre" was approved, aiming at developing a unified system for state-owned real estate within the framework of a single real estate cadastre. Following this, a presidential decree from late 2008, "On the federal service of state registration, cadastre and cartography" initiated a dedicated service to implement the unified system of a state cadastre inventory of real estate, including state registration of real estate rights and transactions. This service should also handle all spatial data infrastructure of the Russian Federation. The service is not yet operational, however. To date, before any real estate transactions, property must be registered in the State Real Estate Cadastre and real estate rights need to be registered with the Unified Register of Rights to Transactions with Real Property. These separate databases are envisaged to merge subject to the current reform process.

Sources: Bartholomy, M. and A. Krutik (2013), "Russian real estate", Law Business Research, http://whoswholegal.com/practiceareas/13/real-estate (accessed 30 November 2013); World Bank (2012), *Eurasian Cities. New Realities Along the Silk Road*, The World Bank, Washington, DC.

The management of commercial and private property is often complicated by unclear rules about common property and complicated ownership structures. The status of common property in high-rise office buildings lacks clear regulation. The rights of common property usually stay with the managing company and/or the developer, which creates risks for businesses or organisations interested in purchasing commercial buildings. Furthermore, owners of private premises in commercial buildings have very limited rights to influence decisions on property management (Puzanov, 2009). This might also hamper commercial real estate development and discourage developers to pursue mixed-use development. Given the greater obstacles for the commercial real estate market, it is not surprising that the more mature real estate market in the Russian Federation so far is the residential market (Puzanov, 2009).

Imperfect conditions to finance construction thwart development

The residential real estate market is not yet supported by a well-functioning mortgage market. After several laws, legislation and presidential decrees from the early 1990s onwards had prepared the grounds for private construction and real estate financing, in 1998, the Federal Law "On mortgage" created a legal basis on which in 2006 the federal government Resolution "On the Agency for House Mortgage Lending" initiated an Agency for Housing Mortgage Lending. Since then, the development of housing mortgage loans in the Russian Federation was largely positive. The number of housing transactions with mortgage-lending funds involved grew from 1 in 11 in 2006 to every 6th in 2008. The immediate aftermath of the financial crisis saw a downturn in lending; however, since 2009 the market for housing mortgage loans grew again. Outstanding loans on the balance sheet of the Russian Central Bank amounted to RUB 690 billion in the third quarter of 2012 (Zadonsky, 2012). In early 2013, growth was stifled, however, by record high interest rates (Zadonsky, 2013). In the Agglomeration, in addition to high interest rates, restrictive requirements for down payments are weakening the mortgage market.

Conditions for other financing options are also imperfect. Given that the mortgage market is still in its early stages of development, a large part of construction and housing finance still comes from private savings, bank loans and cost-sharing (as defined in Federal Law 214). Bank loaning for the construction industry lacks transparency, however, and is generally underdeveloped or not being demanded much yet, given that developers for a long time were used to cheap money from co-investors or pre-construction sales to private individuals (Puzanov, 2009). Cost-sharing schemes are found to be disadvantageous for investors since they weaken their rights and increase the risk of ownership denial (Puzanov, 2009). Commercial developers are facing the additional challenge that most land plots in Russia are still owned publically and are rented out to developers. This means land cannot be used as collateral.

Figure 3.9. **Projected housing demand in the Krasnoyarsk Agglomeration, 2013-15**

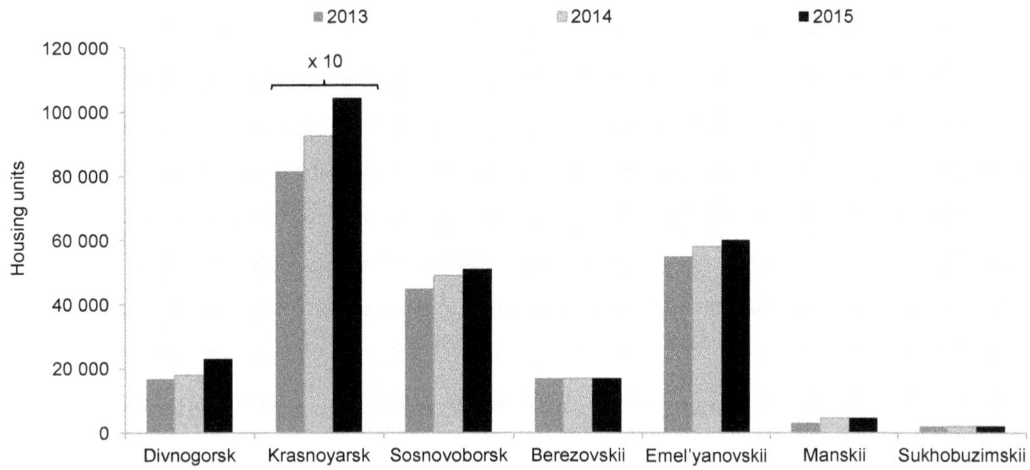

Source: SFU (2012), "OECD background report on the Krasnoyarsk Agglomeration", Siberian Federal University, Krasnoyarsk, Russian Federation, November.

Projections of housing demand in the Agglomeration show that significant new housing will need to be constructed over the next years. By 2015, a total of 1.2 million new housing units will be required for the Krasnoyarsk Agglomeration, with the largest part in Krasnoyarsk (Figure 3.9). In Krasnoyarsk, the bulk of new housing is planned to be constructed outside the city centre, such as in the Vzlyotka District, a former airport. Plans for new constructions are developed at the federal level by the Ministry of Construction and Utilities, based on high growth projections. Each municipality has its own housing programme and the construction is organised locally, with the exception of the federal construction projects. Furthermore, private companies get permission to construct in suitable locations, which are often approved rather *ad hoc* by municipal governments and are often not integrated in larger and long-term strategic planning.

A weak and informal rental market calls for reform

The absence of a rental market in the Soviet era and the high rate of home ownership in Russia today hamper the emergence of a dynamic rental market. Owning a place in the post-Soviet Russian Federation made economic sense, since real estate values increased significantly in many places, while property taxes were still fairly low. Statistics on the Russian rental market are unreliable. The real numbers are likely to be higher than official figures, given the existence of a significant grey rental market linked to tax avoidance and (legal) sub-letting of social housing, which is registered as state- or municipal-owned housing. In 2010, experts estimated the private rental sector to account for 8% of the country's total housing stock, including unofficial rentals (Puzanov, 2009). Data on the tenure structure of the Agglomeration are unavailable – the overwhelming bulk of housing is now privately owned but it is not clear what proportion is owner-occupied and what proportion is rented. Currently low rental rates in Russia are discouraging developers from investing in multi-family housing for rental buildings. Furthermore, terms for private developers in land-use agreements with public authorities using "model rent agreements" are often not attractive enough to stimulate investment (Puzanov, 2009).

The underdeveloped rental market reduces the flexibility of the Agglomeration's labour market. This calls for reforms. When most people own their home, mortgages are difficult or expensive to obtain, and the rental market is underdeveloped and uncompetitive, people are less flexible to follow their job. In particular, young people have difficulties finding a job in places they would need to move to, since first salaries are insufficient to cover rent plus living costs. Consequently, young people often live with their parents until they can afford to buy a home. Unsurprisingly in a homeowner society, renting is also less popular than owning a place. This creates a burden for firms that consequently have greater difficulties to attract the talent they need or in turn need to prop up pay. Large companies may be able to do this, but medium-sized and smaller companies are left with few options. This situation calls for reforms to unlock rental markets. Some of the public land in urban areas could, for example, be dedicated to constructing affordable rental housing; or developers may be encouraged to include a minimum share of rental space in new buildings. Also, tenancy laws in favour of better renter protection could stimulate investment in rental housing (World Bank, 2012).

Distorted tariff regimes and governance weaken utilities and infrastructure

Concerns about the deteriorating quality of utilities in the Agglomeration, notably electricity, merit attention. Chronic under-investment in utilities, infrastructure and networks, and unbalanced tariff structures are major problems. The main networks are owned federally, but the state does not contribute much to the maintenance or improvement of local infrastructures. At the same time, municipalities' investments are declining and tariffs are rising. However, higher tariffs are not used to cover maintenance costs or to generate funds for investment in infrastructures and networks. The most pressing example is electricity. Residential tariffs are cross-subsidised with revenues from electricity sold to (mostly small) private companies, since the big industrial customers have direct access to the wholesale market. While household tariffs have been rising in recent years, shifting some of the investment costs to consumers, most of the burden still lies on small companies, which find themselves confronted with both high electricity prices and deteriorating infrastructures and networks.

Unbalanced prices and a lack of investment in networks bear witness to an opaque and poorly governed electricity system. Power distribution suffers from a number of structural shortcomings: outdated infrastructure, partly inefficient power generation, a large number of network companies and system operators, and arbitrary pricing for final consumers, all of which are poorly co-ordinated. The main effects are tariffs for many firms that are too high compared to the cost of power production in Krasnoyarsk, and losses in the network of up to 20%. A lack of competition and a complicated network structure push up prices, while underinvestment leads to continuous deterioration of the distribution system. Other Russian regions have introduced a separate investment fund for renovating the electricity network. This might also be a possibility for the Agglomeration to tackle the challenge of lacking funds. However, it will not help in addressing the fundamental shortcomings of the system. Streamlining the system and creating incentives for private investments should be complementary measures. For this, it would be necessary to simplify ownership structures, ensure transparency in the distribution system, clearly attribute responsibilities for maintenance, and create a level playing field for private investors beyond concessions.

The Agglomeration's transport system

Transport and infrastructure are central to the Agglomeration's future

Governance of the Agglomeration's transport system will determine its potential as a backbone for socio-economic development in and around Krasnoyarsk. The current transport system is based on poorly developed road and public transport infrastructure and is plagued by heavy congestion, providing limited conditions for mobility and commuting in the Agglomeration: indeed, the Institute for Territorial Planning "Urbanika" consistently finds the city of Krasnoyarsk to be one of the most congested of the Russian Federation's top 100 cities, though there has been some improvement over the last 3 years.[5] Much of this is due to the neglect of road transport and notably road infrastructure in the Soviet era. Since 1991, there has been a strong focus on developing road infrastructure; this period has also witnessed the break-up and partial privatisation of the previously monolithic public transport system. Together with the reduction of subsidies for public transport, this has resulted in deteriorating service quality and a dysfunctional, fragmented transport market and system. Today, the city of Krasnoyarsk alone counts almost 100 private transport businesses, in addition to several municipal public transport companies, operating buses on various routes in the city (Krasnoyarsk, 2013b). Such factors are not unique to Krasnoyarsk, but they have a particular impact on congestion there because it is a regional transport hub in its own right and it straddles a major river. This makes the severity of the congestion challenge greater than it would otherwise be, particularly around the bridges.

While competition has led to lower prices for public transport, excessive fragmentation impedes efficient operations, notably for inter-modal operations. Prices for public transport are generally low in Russia, which is partly linked to the tradition of highly subsidised public transport in Soviet times, but also due to competition introduced in the market over the past decades. Privatisation of transport services has led to great fragmentation of the market however. Routes, transfer stations, schedules and ticketing are poorly co-ordinated and integrated in the Agglomeration. Changing this and developing a long-term perspective for system improvements will necessitate political, economic and organisational measures (Solodkij and Gorev, 2013). An integrated and efficient transport system will need to be built on clear rules and close co-ordination among different stakeholders of the system. Incentives are needed for the different operators in the Agglomeration to collaborate, create synergies and eliminate current frictions and inefficiencies.

A number of other transport challenges remain to be tackled at an agglomeration-wide scale:

- Rail transport better serves the right-bank portion of the city of Krasnoyarsk, half the city of Divnogorsk and a number of smaller settlements. Rail lines run through the city, connecting up different portions of it, so most rail traffic is intra-city or inter-city local (75%+ altogether). More could be done to connect up the left bank. This would increase alternatives to road traffic.
- Some 22 settlements in the Agglomeration are not accessible via roads with hard surfaces. Also, only 8% of the roads in the region have more than one lane in each direction. There are few main roads linking urban centres and few streets with non-stop traffic flows. The city of Krasnoyarsk itself has no ring road, adding to congestion through the centre and reducing the connectivity of other parts of the Agglomeration.
- The Krai Ministry of Transport estimates that road congestion in the city of Krasnoyarsk costs RUB 4.1-5.3 trillion (around 7 to 9% of GDP), owing to slower transport times, higher transport costs, accidents and emissions. Around one-third of federal roads in the area suffer from over-use. Rush-hour congestion in the city is mainly south to north in the morning and north to south in the

evening, with the river bridges as bottlenecks. This should be eased with the completion of the fourth bridge over the Yenisei, which is now under construction.

Improving external and internal connectivity necessitates the participation and co-ordination of all stakeholders and levels of government. Transport policies designed at different levels of government and implemented at different territorial scales cannot be considered in isolation. Regulatory, financial and administrative powers are clearly attributed to the different levels of government (Table 3.3), but policies are not always well co-ordinated and integrated. For example, key transport infrastructures influencing external connectivity, and thus exports, such as rail infrastructure, are under the jurisdiction of the federal Ministry of Transport, while other transport infrastructures that contribute to the same objective, such as regional roads, are under the responsibility of the Krai. Logistics infrastructure, also affecting the conditions for exports and cargo transit, is governed at the local level and financed partly by federal or private funds. Improving the conditions for exporting firms in the Agglomeration thus depends on aligning all levels of government and involved actors and stakeholders around this common goal, and on co-ordinating policies in an integrated framework that allows transport to be governed at the relevant territorial scale.

Table 3.3. **Transport infrastructure expenditures by different levels of government**

Transport modes and infrastructures	Powers		
	Normative legal regulation	Provision of finance	Administering of expenditures
Federal road facilities	F	F	F
Regional road facilities	F+R	F+R	F+R
Local road facilities	F+R+M	R+M	R+M
Air and maritime transport	F	F	F
Motor and river transport	F+R+M	F+R+M	F+R+M
Intercity motor passenger transport	F+R	R	R
Local (intra-urban) public transport	F+R+M	R+M	R+M

Notes: F = federal, R = regional, M = municipalities.

Source: SFU (2012), "OECD background report on the Krasnoyarsk Agglomeration", Siberian Federal University, Krasnoyarsk, Russian Federation, November.

Since the 1990s, transport in Russian urban areas has been characterised by two major trends: a rising number of private cars and a decreasing share of trips on public transport. This represents a sharp break with past patterns of transport use. In the late 1980s, at least every second US citizen owned a car, whereas there were only 45 private automobiles per 1 000 citizens in Russia; in US urban areas, 82% of trips were by car and 3% by public transport, whereas 88% of journeys in urban Russia were on public transport and 11% by car in Russia (Pucher, 1990). Since the beginning of the market transition, the Russian Federation has shifted investment priorities from public to private transport as car ownership has expanded. This initially improved people's mobility but increasingly leads to congestion, particularly in cities with over 250 000 inhabitants (Donchenko, 2013). A strong mismatch in Russia between needed investments in road infrastructure and growing car ownership results in congestion, overused roads in poor conditions and deteriorating public transport systems. The share of car trips in Russia (68%) is still lower than in such OECD countries as France (84%), Sweden (83%) and Belgium (75%), and it is likely to increase further, to similar levels (Donchenko, 2013). While in some OECD countries, car ownership and use seem to have hit a high and public transport use increases, trips on public transport in the Russian Federation, notably of buses, tramways and trolley-buses, is continuously declining (Figure 3.10).

Figure 3.10. **Use of public transport in the Russian Federation, 1992-2011**

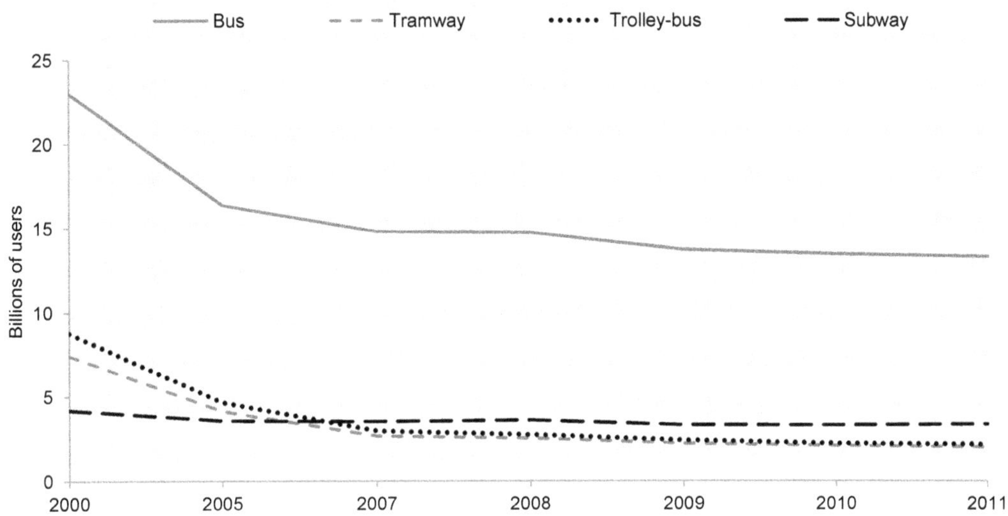

Note: For bus transport since 2000 – data is presented by legal entities (including small businesses, excluding micro businesses) and individuals.

Source: Federal State Statistics Service (FSSS) (2013), "Main indicators – Transport and communication", FSSS website, www.gks.ru/wps/wcm/connect/rosstat_main/rosstat/en/figures/transport (accessed 15 February 2014).

The situation is particularly challenging in the largest Russian cities, where traffic jams have become the norm (Figure 3.11). Investments in transport, particularly urban public transport infrastructure, are insufficient to accommodate growing urban mobility needs and to compensate for chronic under-investment during the late Soviet period. Sub-national investment capacity for urban transport infrastructure is low and federal investment programmes are too sparse to have a sustainable impact on municipal transport systems (Box 3.10).

Figure 3.11. **Average traffic speed during peak hours in selected cities**

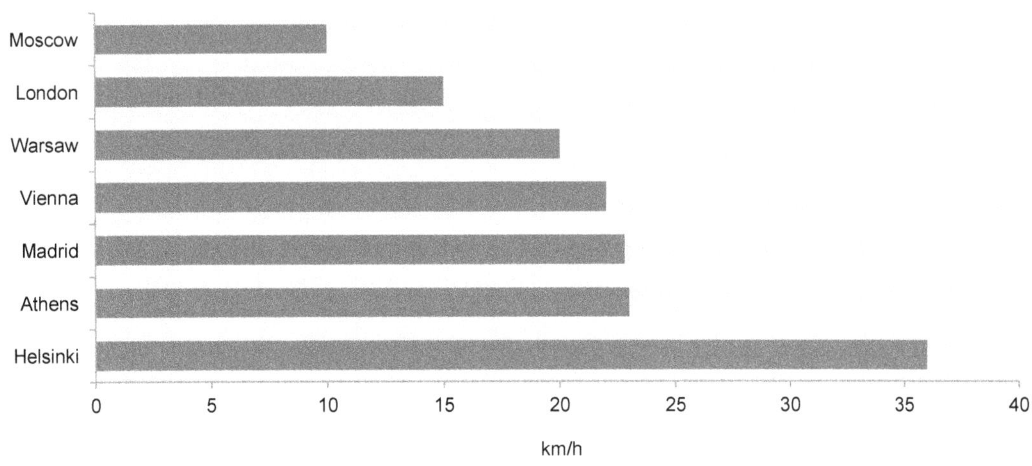

Source: Donchenko, V. (2013), "Towards the sustainable mobility in Russian cities: Problems, challenges and risks", paper presented at the International symposium OPTOSOZ, Moscow, 14 March.

Box 3.10. Federal urban transport infrastructure programmes

Individual federal programmes provide targeted support for regional and urban transport systems. However, in the absence of a more systematic approach, the tangible long-term effects of such programmes are difficult to assess. In 2005-06, a federal programme supported regions and cities in compensating the costs of providing free access to public transport for certain groups of the population (e.g. pensioners). Most regions handed out "social tickets" to privileged users, reimbursed by the central government, which helped monetise the public transport system and inventory "privileged" passengers. While the effects of the programme were felt temporarily, it did not lead to structural change. Fees for public transport are still very low in most places and far from covering operations and maintenance cost. In 2009-10, in response to the global financial crisis, a federal programme distributed funds to selected regions in order to renovate or replace passenger buses. This helped improve bus fleets in some cities. Still, over 45% of buses in Russian cities are more than ten years old and only 15% meet Euro-3 standard (the European emission norm which was in place between 2000 and 2005; today, Europe has passed to stricter norms, Euro-4 and Euro-5). In 2012, a one-off support scheme injected RUB 3.5 billion into regional budgets to renovate rolling stock, such as trams and trolley-buses (Larionova, 2013). Federal funding can reach the local level through different kinds of co-financing mechanisms, for example through joint investments with federal financial institutions or in the framework of targeted federal development programmes. In the Krasnoyarsk Agglomeration, RUB 3.4 billion in federal funds has been invested into the modernisation of commuter rail infrastructure (SFU, 2012).

Sources: Larionova, T. (2013), "Sozdat' Pravovoe Pole" (To create the legal base), *Transport of Russia*, No. 25 (780), Moscow; SFU (2012), "OECD background report on the Krasnoyarsk Agglomeration", Siberian Federal University, Krasnoyarsk, Russian Federation, November.

Governance matters not only for infrastructure provision but also for the management of public transport. While competition has led to lower prices for public transport, excessive fragmentation impedes efficient operations, notably for inter-modal operations. Prices for public transport are generally low in Russia, which is partly linked to the tradition of highly subsidised public transport in Soviet times, but also due to competition introduced in the market over the past decades. Privatisation of transport services has led to great fragmentation of the market, however. Routes, transfer stations, schedules and ticketing are poorly co-ordinated and integrated in the Agglomeration. Changing this and developing a long-term perspective for system improvements will necessitate political, economic and organisational measures (Solodkij and Gorev, 2013). An integrated and efficient transport system will need to be built on clear rules and close co-ordination among different stakeholders of the system. Incentives are needed for the different operators in the Agglomeration to collaborate, create synergies and eliminate current frictions and inefficiencies.

Transport infrastructure in Krasnoyarsk was shaped under centralised Soviet urban planning, which is still influencing its development today (Bertaud and Renaud, 1995). Industrial facilities were placed on prime central urban land while residential areas tended to be situated at the urban periphery. The result was often low-density industrial development in central urban areas surrounded by higher density mono-functional residential belts. Basic urban services were provided according to a norm of minimum individual needs; in particular, urban transport infrastructure was in a weak position to compete with industries for capital investment. Transport was seen as a means to the end of industrial urban growth, rather than as a good in itself (Hunter, 1965; Glubchikov, 2006). Public transport served the urban worker and had to be affordable rather than efficient. Workers in bigger cities often spent one to two hours commuting every day.

Connectivity between different modes of public transport was extremely weak (Crouch, 1979; Pucher, 1990). Today, most Russian cities have improved their transport systems, but many, including Krasnoyarsk, are still struggling with the legacy of land-use and transport infrastructure decisions made in Soviet times.

The Agglomeration's road network is ill-equipped to accommodate growing traffic

Road infrastructure in the Agglomeration is insufficient for the increasing number of cars and the intensive use of roads. In 1984, only 4% of Krasnoyarsk's inhabitants owned a car. This number reached 38.4% in 2012. Car ownership in the Agglomeration as a whole reached 38.6% in 2010. Annual person-kilometres travelled in the Krai increased from 2 064 kilometres in 2006 to 3 937 kilometres in 2010 (SFU, 2012). In the Krai, one-third of federal roads are over-used. The majority of regional roads (92%) only have a single lane in each direction (SFU, 2012). Over-use of these roads slows traffic and accelerates infrastructure deterioration. A significant share (38%) of regional roads in the Agglomeration has only temporary road cover, which is neither suited to withstand the extreme Siberian climate nor made for the heavy trucks and agricultural machinery that frequent the roads. Sprawling urban development, coupled with insufficient infrastructure provision in the Agglomeration, further leads to a growing deficit of its mainline network, currently estimated at almost 140 kilometres (SFU, 2012).

The Agglomeration's current transport system is not able to accommodate the increasing flow of commuters to and through Krasnoyarsk. Roughly 70 000-80 000 commuters enter and leave Krasnoyarsk every day. The city's roads were not built to accommodate such traffic and consequently heavy congestion forms almost every day on the radial highways leading into the city. Traffic is particularly intense on the narrow incoming roads from Divnogorsk (south-west), Zheleznogorsk and Sosnovoborsk (north-east), which are well beyond capacity (Table 3.4). Already before arriving at the edge of Krasnoyarsk, poor road quality slows down traveling speed on many routes. In addition to infrastructure challenges, inefficient traffic management, frequent violation of traffic rules and under-performing public transport services worsen mobility in the Agglomeration.

Table 3.4. **Traffic overload on Krasnoyarsk's main radial highways**

Radial highway/connection	Vehicles per day	Carrying capacity
Krasnoyarsk–Zheleznogorsk	20 000	7 000
Krasnoyarsk–Saline	25 000	7 500
Krasnoyarsk–Divnogorsk	20 000	7 000
Krasnoyarsk–Enisejsk Siberian section on the site – Minderla	15 000	7 000

Source: SFU (2012), "OECD background report on the Krasnoyarsk Agglomeration", Siberian Federal University, Krasnoyarsk, Russian Federation, November.

The large amount of traffic going through the centre of Krasnoyarsk every day leads to heavy congestion around several bottlenecks. Krasnoyarsk is stretched along the banks of the Yenisei River. Three bridges currently connect the right and left banks of the city. Serving as the main arteries, they accommodate a large part of rush-hour traffic, which mainly goes south-north in the morning and north-south in the evening. Only a handful of main roads lead into and out of the city centre, and few of these allow non-stop traffic flow. A ring road, currently in planning, could lead parts of the traffic around the city. Additional bridges, also in planning, could relieve pressure in central areas. Whether new road capacity will be sufficient to address the congestion challenge depends on whether it is combined with other measures that improve the public transport system and traffic management.

Box 3.11. Causes, impacts and costs of urban traffic congestion

Numerous causes can generate congestion. They can be distinguished in micro-level and macro-level factors. Micro-level factors relate to traffic "on the road", whereas macro-level factors relate to overall demand for road use. Macro-level factors include indirect factors such as land-use and employment patterns, income levels, car ownership trends, infrastructure investments and regional economic dynamics. Micro-level factors include the number of vehicles on the road, the design and capacity of intersections, driving behaviour, traffic management systems, etc. While micro-level factors "trigger" congestion incidents, macro-level factors "drive" congestion trends. Policy design addressing congestion must consider both how it influences micro- and macro-level factors causing congestion (ITF, 2007).

Direct impacts of congestion include queuing, slower travel speed, increased travel time, accidents, stress, increased pollution, noise. These effects have a more indirect impact on mobility, commuting times, delivery times, economic efficiency, productivity and growth, people's health, accessibility to urban facilities and services, safety and quality of life. Given that congestion can occur irregularly and thus reduces the reliability of road transport, it impairs predictability and thus the ability of people and firms to plan just-in-time. The environmental impacts of emissions and the health impacts of pollution further impact environmental quality and health costs, adversely affecting the local economy. By concretely compromising economic growth and productivity, environmental quality and people's health and quality of life, congestion reduces the overall attractiveness of an urban region to people, firms and investors (OECD/ECMT, 2008).

The impacts of congestion have direct and indirect costs for people, firms and the urban economy as a whole. Time spent on roads is not or little productive. Spending more time than expected due to congestion reduces productivity further. While people tend to take the extra congestion time from their personal time, for firms delivering products or having employees traveling to town during their working hours, time spent in congestion is always a loss. As a whole, the urban economy suffers from congestion in that it directly cancels some of the agglomeration benefits it profits from. Research on firm-to-firm access finds that congestion lowers agglomeration benefits of proximity and with respect to firm-to-employee access, congestion tends to increase jobs-housing imbalances. Indirect costs also incur through the impact of congestion on accessibility premiums and changes in land-use patterns (Sweet, 2011).

Sources: ITF (2007), "Transport infrastructure inside and across urban regions: Models and assessment methods", in: OECD and ITF, *The Wider Economic Benefits of Transport: Macro-, Meso-, and Micro-Economic Transport Planning and Investment Tools*, OECD Publishing, Paris, http://dx.doi.org/10.1787/9789282101834-en; OECD/ECMT (2008), *Managing Urban Traffic Congestion*, OECD Publishing, Paris, http://dx.doi.org/10.1787/9789282101506-en.

The Agglomeration faces increasing congestion-related costs, which need to be taken into account in cost-benefit-analyses for infrastructure investments. The Krai Ministry of Transport estimates that Krasnoyarsk's annual cost of congestion amounts to RUB 4.1-5.3 trillion (7-9% of GDP). This calculation is based on slower transport times, higher transport costs, accidents and emissions (SFU, 2012). Policies to reduce this costly drag on the Agglomeration's economy need to be based on a thorough analysis of the causes, impacts and costs of congestion (Box 3.11). Based on a good understanding of congestion in the Agglomeration, cost-benefit analyses (CBA) should help strategic planning and efficient allocation of investments into transport infrastructure. Standard CBA approaches take into consideration the: *i)* time gains of different user categories of the transport system; *ii)* reduced accident risks, reduced vehicle costs, other cost effects, including monetary value of environmental and health effects. In addition, dynamic changes in the use of the transport network and the spatial organisation associated with traffic system changes should be taken into consideration (OECD/ECMT, 2008). A robust CBA should help answer the question of whether the price of mitigating congestion is lower than the cost that congestion impedes on people, firms and the urban agglomeration at large (ITF, 2007).

Investments in the Agglomeration's transport infrastructures, fragmented over different levels of government, seem insufficient to meet needs. The Krai is responsible for regional roads, Krasnoyarsk is responsible for urban roads and urban public transport, and municipalities take care of local infrastructure. The Krai allocates 57.6% of its capital expenditures to transport, but this represents less than 1% of its total expenditure. At the level of the Agglomeration, transport and machinery account for 32% of capital expenditures. Municipalities spend, on average, less than 2% of their budgets on transport, half of which is capital expenditure (SFU, 2012). Experts point out that local budgets are largely insufficient to cover the investments needs in the Agglomeration in order to expand and maintain transport infrastructure and services.

Public transport infrastructure and services are underdeveloped

Decades of under-investment mean that, even given current congestion problems, public transport in the Agglomeration cannot present an attractive alternative to most car users. The most important modes of public transport in the Agglomeration are buses, trolley-buses and light rail tram, which primarily operate in Krasnoyarsk. The share of trips on trolley-buses and trams decreased from 28% in 1999 to 11.2% in 2011 (DOTK, 2011). Most trips (88% in 2010) are by bus. In 1994, Krasnoyarsk started removing tramway tracks and in 2004 it had removed them entirely from the left bank. Remaining tracks are worn out and tramway cars are in bad condition. Public transport services are operated partly by municipal companies, partly by private carriers. Since 2007, the rolling stock of buses increased significantly. Municipal companies acquired 280 new buses, private carriers 177 (Krasnoyarsk, 2013b). Connectivity across different modes of public and private transport is weak. Less central municipalities are poorly connected with Krasnoyarsk. One train connects Krasnoyarsk with Divnogorsk and a commuter shuttle bus runs between Krasnoyarsk, Sosnovoborsk and Zheleznogorsk, which is planned to be complemented or replaced by a passenger railway (SFU, 2012).

Dormant potential might lie in Krasnoyarsk's unfinished metro system,[6] but bus rapid-transit (BRT) could hold greater potential to improve public transport in the Agglomeration. An operational metro system would be beneficial for Krasnoyarsk, but is likely to absorb large sums of public investment and subsidies and to cover a limited part of the area. Any plan to continue constructing the metro should be compared with alternative solutions such as BRT, which is by an order of magnitude cheaper to implement than a metro. Another advantage of BRT is its flexibility. It would create less spatial and infrastructure path dependence. BRT could better be adapted to changes in commuting patterns and land-use arising from, for example, the relocation of industries currently situated in the centre of Krasnoyarsk and the development of new residential settlements. Furthermore, synergies could be achieved between extending and improving road infrastructure for both BRT and car use.

Transport infrastructure projects focus on road network improvements

The majority of current transport infrastructure projects in the Agglomeration aim to improve road infrastructure. The most important transport infrastructure projects are road repair (15 km), a new bridge (7.4 km), a highway overhaul (6.75 km), road interchanges and a railway overpass (1.57 km) for a total cost of cost of RUB 16.6 billion. Over the period through 2018, further projects for RUB 1.6 billion are planned, mainly for 26.6 kilometres of road repairs (SFU, 2012). These projects only address a fraction of the necessary repairs of the Agglomeration's road network; Krasnoyarsk alone has over 1 000 kilometres of roads. A fourth bridge is being constructed over the Yenisei in the city to relieve some of the pressure on central urban roads and to provide a direct link between north-western parts of the city and the south-west highway to Divnogorsk. A fifth road bridge over the Yenisei is also planned. Around Krasnoyarsk, a ring road is planned to further reduce traffic that currently passes through the city centre (Figure 3.12). Furthermore, road and multi-level interchanges and a new west entrance to the city are in planning. As for rail and logistics infrastructure, Krasnoyarsk's rail bridge 777 is currently being retrofitted in order to allow for more than one train to pass at a time and to open the bridge to car use. A passenger railway is planned to connect Krasnoyarsk with Sosnovoborsk and Zheleznogorsk. Finally, a transport logistics centre is planned to be implemented in the area of the fourth Yenisei bridge, including a link of road and railway cargo systems.

In contrast to the ambitious plans for new and better roads, urban public transport receives comparatively little attention. Current efforts to improve the system are concentrated on buses and on retrofitting remaining rail infrastructure in central urban areas with new light rail trains. In several areas, dedicated lanes are to be reserved for public transport, for example on Prospekt Mira and on the Kopylovsky bridge. Several new tram and light-rail projects are being studied, including high-speed tram lines and new stations covering both the left and right bank of Krasnoyarsk (Figure 3.13).

Transfer points are being planned at the edge of Krasnoyarsk, which should encourage commuters and shoppers from surrounding municipalities to leave their cars outside the city and take public transport to the centre. Theoretically such transfer points could present a promising option to reduce inner urban traffic, but their success depends on a number of factors and complementary measures. For example, the points need to offer people a seamless connection to a well-functioning public transport system. Furthermore, the trip via transport points needs to be cheaper and ideally faster compared to doing the whole trip by car. This requires cheap or free parking at the transfer point and the introduction of parking fees or other road pricing in central urban areas, which need to be accompanied by decisive enforcement of traffic rules. The implementation of such transfer points can thus only be successful if it is one component of a number of more systemic measures.

Financing challenges

Public-private partnerships could help address transport bottlenecks…

Both at regional and at municipal level funds for infrastructure investments are insufficient to respond to the Agglomeration's needs. The establishment of regional or municipal road funds could improve this situation. Such funds existed in the Russian Federation at the federal level until 2000 and in the regions until 2004. In 2011, road funds were revived at all levels, including at municipal level. At the regional level, road funds are financed mostly by fuel excise (73%), by annual transport tax paid by vehicle owners, as well as by other charges such as for heavy vehicles or violations of weight limitations. Additional revenues for regional road funds could come from toll roads, which can be established in the Russian Federation since 2010, as defined by the Law "On roads and road activities" that also authorises federal and regional road authorities to collect fees. These funds could be used to guarantee financing for multi-annual road construction and maintenance contracts. This would help overcome current challenges and mitigate risks linked to the annual revision of budgets in the course of public budget cycles. However, experience shows that, while creating a dedicated road fund can signal the authorities' understanding of the importance of road maintenance and construction, it may not improve financing. Much more important is the use of such a fund as the basis for vertical co-ordination of transport infrastructure investments across national, regional and local levels. All levels need to work together when identifying needs and bottlenecks, as well as designing the best measures to address road capacity constraints. This would be in line with federal recommendations, which encourage co-ordination and co-operation between regional and federal road authorities in key areas such as fund utilisation, road network, systematic upgrading and improvement of road quality (Rosavtodor, 2011).

Transport infrastructure investment could also be enhanced through better use of public-private partnerships (PPPs). PPPs are still not well defined in Russian law and the only type of PPP recognised by federal law is the concession. However, PPPs have increasingly been used in Russia since the 2008 financial crisis, and a recent study finds the transport sector to hold the largest potential for PPPs in the country (Ernst & Young, 2012). The Krai is currently preparing the implementation of a number of concession agreements, including for road infrastructure. Large transport infrastructure projects currently developed as PPPs in the Krai include the railway line from Kyzyl to Kuragino and new infrastructures developed in the Novoland area within the Agglomeration. In both projects, the Russian Federation's investment fund plays a significant role. Of all capital-forming investments in the Agglomeration, 87% are done within some form of PPP, although the modalities vary, including co-financing agreements, partial subsidies for specific expenditures or loan interest payments. Public securities on private loans have not been used much yet. PPPs could be used more, including for urban public transport solutions. Experience from OECD cities, such as Mexico City, shows the potential of PPPs for public transport (Box 3.12).

Box 3.12. The Metrobus bus rapid transit in Mexico City and public-private partnerships

The bus rapid transit (BRT) system Metrobus was launched as part of the 2002-10 "Programme to Improve Air Quality in the Mexico City Metropolitan Area (MCMA)", led by the Ministry of Environment of Mexico's Federal District. The project's objective was to support a long-term modal shift towards climate-friendly, more efficient and less polluting, less carbon-intensive transport in Mexico City. In the absence of a public-private partnership (PPP) law at the time of the implementation of Metrobus, the project was not implemented explicitly as a PPP. It nevertheless discloses important elements of a PPP, and may have contributed to passing a PPP law in Mexico in 2012.

Metrobus was financed publically and privately through a number of financial mechanisms tailored to the different Metrobus lines (1-5), and implemented consecutively. The financing mechanisms included a "payment for service" scheme, private concessions, public bids, a federal mass transit programme and international financing. The project received, for example, USD 4.8 million from the Global Environment Facility (GEF), implemented by the World Bank,

Box 3.12. The Metrobus bus rapid transit in Mexico City and public-private partnerships (*cont.*)

and line 1 "Insurgentes" registered under the Clean Development Mechanism. Furthermore, Metrobus' first phase generated USD 1.1 million from the sale of carbon credits.

Realising the project as a quasi PPP in the absence of a PPP law in Mexico made it more complicated, but not impossible. For example, the public sector negotiated and designed specific contracts with numerous private bus companies, previously operating on the lines chosen for Metrobus. These negotiations had to be led in many cases on an *ad hoc* basis, creating delays in the implementation. However, the project was successful and contributed to showing the necessity for a PPP law in Mexico.

On 16 January 2012, a Public Private Societies Law was introduced in Mexico. The law aims at increasing investment, provides legislative certainty for private actors, improves public fund efficiency, speeds up project development and increases transparency in infrastructure investments. The law also aims at increasing transparency, including anti-corruption mechanisms, and available resources due to legal certainty.

Principles for transparent and competitive PPPs should include:

- An estimation of the project's affordability. PPPs, considered as an alternative to traditional public sector procurement, should be used whenever they provide a higher benefit-cost ratio than conventional public procurement. This is defined as the "value for money", or as the "efficiency" of infrastructure provision (OECD, 2008).
- A competitive bidding process in tendering procedures and project allocation.
- Full disclosure of conditions in the bidding stage to facilitate negotiations and limit future conflicts.
- Clear responsibility sharing, through detailed agreements between public authorities and private investors on the allocation of responsibilities and risk.
- Flexibility in sub-contracting to encourage innovation and future adjustments.
- Clear rules on project cancelation and compensation.
- Pricing regulations to secure revenue flows and incentivise new entrants.
- The independence of PPP operators, through a clear separation of operating and regulatory functions.
- Competitive markets with a level playing field whenever feasible (e.g. the appropriate competition level for bus services supply varies, from liberalised entry in small cities to franchises in large ones).
- The creation of PPP units (e.g. in Australia, the Netherlands and the United Kingdom) to create effective institutional capacity to plan, implement, manage and evaluate PPP projects.

Sources: Ang, G. and V. Marchal (2013), "Mobilising private investment in sustainable transport: The case of land-based passenger transport infrastructure", *OECD Environment Working Papers*, No. 56, OECD Publishing, Paris, http://dx.doi.org/10.1787/5k46hjm8jpmv-en; Francke, E., J. Macías and G. Schmid (2012), "The mobilisation of private investment for low-carbon, climate-resilient infrastructure: The case of Metrobus Bus Rapid Transit System in Mexico City", draft case study prepared by CTS EMBARQ Mexico for the OECD; GEF (2002), Results from the GEF Climate Change Program: Evaluation Report No. 1-02, Global Environment Facility, Washington, DC; World Bank (2002), *Cities on the Move. A World Bank Urban Transport Strategy Review*, The International Bank for Reconstruction and Development/The World Bank, Washington, DC.

... But they are also fraught with risks, especially in the Russian Federation

PPPs are one way for private actors to contribute to local and regional economic development. A broad definition of PPP involves different types of co-operation and tenders between public and private actors to deliver public or semi-public services. They are often implemented via a consortium of public and private entities (universities, research centres and companies). A narrower definition of PPPs concerns a way of delivering and funding public services using a capital asset where project risks are shared between the public and private sector. A PPP is here defined as a long-term agreement between the government and a private partner where the service delivery objectives of the government are aligned with the profit objectives of the private partner. The effectiveness of the alignment depends on a sufficient and appropriate transfer of risk to the private partners. In a PPP, the government specifies the quality and quantity of the service it requires from the private partner. The private partner may be tasked with the design, construction, financing, operation and management of a capital asset and the delivery of a service to the government or to the public using that asset. A key element is the bundling of the construction and operation of the asset. The private partner will receive either a stream of payments from the government, user charges levied directly on the end users or a combination of the two. This definition excludes a wider array of arrangements where non-governmental organisations such as non-profit civil society groups, trusts, church groups, etc. are involved in the development and delivery of public or semi-public services.

If the government is responsible for a stream of payments to the private partner for services delivered, their actual payment will likely depend on the private partner's delivery of service and compliance with the contractually set quality and quantity specifications. Public-private partnerships are often undertaken by a special purpose vehicle acting as the government's private sector counterparty. A special purpose vehicle is typically (but not always) a consortium of companies responsible for the main activities of the public-private partnership. A key argument for PPPs is that through harnessing the private sector's expertise in combining the design and operation of an asset – applying a whole-of-life view – the service can be provided in a more efficient manner than under traditional forms of procurement and production. There are, however, a number of conditions that need to be in place for a PPP to be successful. The ability to write and negotiate PPP contracts are an important public sector capacity requirement, especially given the long-term nature and the large transaction costs associated with PPPs. There are a number of particular challenges that need to be addressed when contemplating the use of PPPs to provide services or infrastructure (Box 3.13).

Box 3.13. **Key challenges in the use of PPPs**

PPPs are complex instruments which require a number of capacities to be present in government. These involve setting up a robust system of assessing value for money using a prudent public sector comparator and transparent and consistent guidelines regarding non-quantifiable elements in the value for money judgement. The public authorities must also be able to classify, measure and allocate risk to the party best able to manage it and to adhere to sound accounting and budgeting practises.

The starting point for assessing the desirability of a PPP is the public-sector comparator, a comparison of the net present cost of bids for the PPP project against the most efficient form of delivery according to a traditionally procured public-sector reference project. The comparator takes into account the risks that are transferable to a probable private party, and those risks that will be retained by the government. Thus, the public-sector comparator serves as a hypothetical risk-adjusted

Box 3.13. Key challenges in the use of PPPs (*cont.*)

cost of public delivery of the project. The risk here is of manipulation in favour of PPPs, not least because much depends on the discount rate chosen or on the value attributed to a risk transferred. The evaluation, moreover, encompasses qualitative aspects that involve an element of judgement on the part of government. The question is what the government judges to be an optimal combination of quantity, quality, features and price (i.e. cost), expected (sometimes, but not always, calculated) over the whole of the project's lifetime. It ultimately depends, then, on a combination of factors working together, such as risk transfer, output-based specifications, performance measurement and incentives, competition in and for the market, private sector management expertise and the benefits for end users and society as a whole.

The second challenge is risk management. To ensure that the private partner operates efficiently and in the public interest, a sufficient, but also appropriate, amount of risk needs to be transferred. In principle, risk should be carried by the party best able to manage it. In this context, "best" means the party able to manage the risk at least cost. This may mean the party best able to prevent a risk from materialising (*ex ante* risk management) or the party best able to deal with the results of realised risk (*ex post* risk management). However, not all risks can be managed and cases may exist where one or more parties to a contract are unable to manage a risk. To those parties, such unmanageable risks are exogenous risks (an example is uninsurable *force majeure* risk that affects all parties, while political and taxation risk is exogenous to the private party and endogenous to government).

The third key issue is affordability. A project is affordable if government expenditure associated with a project (whether or not it is a PPP) can be accommodated within the inter-temporal budget constraint of the government. A PPP can make a project affordable if it results in increased efficiency that causes a project that did not fit into an inter-temporal budget constraint of the government under traditional public procurement to do so with a PPP. It can be tempting to ignore the affordability issue where PPPs are off budget, but this is very unwise. Using PPPs also reduces spending flexibility, and thus potentially allocative efficiency, as spending is locked in for a number of years. Given that capital spending in national budgets are often accounted for as expenditure only when the investment outlay actually occurs, taking the PPP route allows a government to initiate the same amount of investments in one year while recording less expenditure for that same year. However, the obligation to pay over time will increase expenditures in the future, reducing the scope for new investment in coming years. Government spending might also be affected if the government provides implicit or explicit guarantees to the PPP project and thus incurs contingent liabilities. The system of government budgeting and accounting should provide a clear, transparent and true record of all PPP activities in such a way that there is no incentive take the PPP route based on its accounting treatment.

In some cases, PPPs may be used to circumvent spending ceilings and fiscal rules. There are those that argue that this need not be a problem and that PPPs should be used to invest in times of fiscal restraint. The fiscal constraint argument for public-private partnerships is driven by pressures for governments to reduce public spending to meet political, legislated and/or treaty-mandated fiscal targets. In parallel with this, many governments face an infrastructure deficit stemming from a variety of factors, including a perceived bias against budgeting for capital expenditures in cash-based budgetary systems. However, when responding to fiscal constraints, governments should not ignore efficiency and affordability considerations. PPPs may also create future fiscal consequences if they violate the budgetary principle of unity, i.e. that all revenues and expenditures should be included in the budget at the same time. Potential projects should be compared against other competing projects and not considered in isolation to avoid giving priority to the consideration and approval of lower value projects.

Source: OECD (2011), "From lessons to principles for the use of public-private partnerships", 32nd meeting of the Network of Senior Budget Officials, Luxembourg, 6-7 June, OECD, Paris, www.oecd.org/gov/budgeting/48144872.pdf.

As noted above, the use of PPPs is at an early stage in the Russian Federation, and the concession agreement is the only form for which a fully developed legislative framework exists. There is much discussion in Russia concerning the technical legal aspects of PPPs and there are numerous proposals for amending federal legislation in order to clarify matters and make PPPs easier to pursue. However, there are a number of much more fundamental issues that the Russian Federation must address if it is to develop PPP investments, particularly at sub-national level.

- Much depends on the government's success in improving the overall business climate. PPPs are long-term undertakings and are unlikely to be attractive to investors in an environment characterised by high levels of legal, institutional and policy uncertainty. As noted in Box 3.13, one of the crucial affordability issues concerns the discount rate – the higher the investor's discount rate, the more expensive the PPP is to the public authorities. This is directly influenced by the degree of uncertainty confronting investors. Prospects for developing PPPs simply cannot be divorced from the broader institutional reform agenda.
- PPPs present particular risks in the context of high levels of corruption, such as are observed in Russia. Corruption in public procurement is already a major problem (OECD, 2014a). The adoption of a new Law on Public Procurement in April 2013 was widely seen as an important step forward; it offers more transparency throughout the entire project cycle, and implementation should be carefully monitored to allow for corrections as necessary. Yet a hasty move to widespread use of PPPs could make things worse, given their greater complexity and longer time-scales.
- The use of PPPs in specific sectors will also depend on the progress of economy-wide reforms in those sectors. For example, PPPs in the local utilities sector will require much greater assurance about the direction of state policies – particularly tariff policies – in the housing and utilities sphere. In all likelihood, the state will have to take on some kind of guarantor's role, even in PPPs concluded with *oblasts* or cities.
- Successful PPPs involving sub-national governments will require considerable capacity-building in many places. Regional or local officials must be capable of identifying strategic opportunities, planning technical projects that co-ordinate many actors over long periods, building local support, identifying and managing financing streams, monitoring and evaluating on-going efforts, etc. PPPs require a fairly high level of financial sophistication on the part of officialdom, as well as a structure of incentives that prompts them to seek the best outcomes for the public and audit, reporting and control mechanisms that ensure that opportunities for abuse are minimal.

Despite these risks, it is difficult to see how Russia as a whole, and the Krasnoyarsk Agglomeration in particular, can address infrastructure investment needs without developing effective forms of public-private co-operation. Ultimately, PPPs are likely to be a part of this picture. With that in mind, there are a number of specific steps the authorities can take to maximise the likelihood of success. Ultimately, they should aim for consistent adherence to the OECD Principles for the Governance of Public-Private Partnerships (Box 3.14). Even bearing the principles in mind, the authorities in Krasnoyarsk will want to proceed with caution in rolling out PPPs. Pilot projects should be undertaken, monitored and evaluated carefully and only then scaled up. In addition, it will probably make sense to focus first on projects where the technical and other risks are relatively well understood – basic infrastructure, for example.

Box 3.14. OECD Principles on Public Governance of Public-Private Partnerships

Establish a clear, predictable and legitimate institutional framework supported by competent and well-resourced authorities

1. The political leadership should ensure public awareness of the relative costs, benefits and risks of PPPs and conventional procurement. Popular understanding of PPPs requires active consultation and engagement with stakeholders as well as involving end users in defining the project and subsequently in monitoring service quality.
2. Key institutional roles and responsibilities should be maintained. This requires that procuring authorities, public-private partnerships units, the central budget authority, the supreme audit institution and sector regulators are entrusted with clear mandates and sufficient resources to ensure a prudent procurement process and clear lines of accountability.
3. Ensure that all significant regulation affecting the operation of PPPs is clear, transparent and enforced. Red tape should be minimised and new and existing regulations should be carefully evaluated.

Ground the selection of public-private partnerships in value for money

4. All investment projects should be prioritised at senior political level. As there are many competing investment priorities, it is the responsibility of government to define and pursue strategic goals. The decision to invest should be based on a whole-of-government perspective and be separate from how to procure and finance the project. There should be no institutional, procedural or accounting bias either in favour of or against PPPs.
5. Carefully investigate which investment method is likely to yield the most value for money. Key risk factors and characteristics of specific projects should be evaluated by conducting a procurement option pre-test. A procurement option pre-test should enable the government to decide whether it is prudent to investigate a PPP option further.
6. Transfer the risks to those that manage them best. Risk should be defined, identified and measured and carried by the party for whom it costs the least to prevent the risk from realising or for whom realised risk costs the least.
7. The procuring authorities should be prepared for the operational phase of the PPPs. Securing value for money requires vigilance and effort of the same intensity as that necessary during the pre-operational phase. Particular care should be taken when switching to the operational phase of the PPP, as the actors on the public side are liable to change.
8. Value for money should be maintained when renegotiating. Only if conditions change due to discretionary public policy actions should the government consider compensating the private sector. Any re-negotiation should be made transparently and subject to the ordinary procedures of PPP approval. Clear, predictable and transparent rules for dispute resolution should be in place.
9. Government should ensure there is sufficient competition in the market by a competitive tender process and by possibly structuring the PPP programme so that there is an on-going functional market. Where market operators are few, governments should ensure a level playing field in the tendering process so that non-incumbent operators can enter the market.

Box 3.14. **OECD Principles on Public Governance of Public-Private Partnerships** *(cont.)*

Use the budgetary process transparently to minimise fiscal risks and ensure the integrity of the procurement process

10. In line with the government's fiscal policy, the central budget authority should ensure that the project is affordable and the overall investment envelope is sustainable.
11. The project should be treated transparently in the budget process. The budget documentation should disclose all costs and contingent liabilities. Special care should be taken to ensure that budget transparency of PPPs covers the whole public sector.
12. Government should guard against waste and corruption by ensuring the integrity of the procurement process. The necessary procurement skills and powers should be made available to the relevant authorities.

Source: OECD (2012c), *Recommendation of the Council on Principles for Public Governance of Public-Private Partnerships*, OECD, Paris, May, available at: www.oecd.org/gov/budgeting/PPP-Recommendation.pdf.

The Agglomeration's potential as a transport and logistics hub

The Russian Federation is far from realising its potential in international transport networks

Exports are an important pillar of the Agglomeration's economy and external connectivity directly influences the conditions for exports. External connectivity depends much on the Russia's transport system as a whole and is directly affected by the performance and trends in Russian railways, roads, air cargo and maritime routes, which affect both the Agglomeration's distance to external markets as well as its potential to thrive as a logistics and transport hub. As seen in Chapter 1, these areas are not without considerable problems. On the whole, transport logistics infrastructure in the Russian Federation is characterised by a lack of advanced logistics, low containerisation and weak intermodal transport. Russia particularly lacks logistics infrastructure and services for high value-added supply chains. While non-transport services represent 47% of the logistics market worldwide, in Russia they only account for 11.4%.

Containerisation in Russia is very low. In 2010, only 22% of goods suitable for transport by container were so shipped (RBK-Research, 2011). Many inland container terminals are out-of-date, and most container depots of leading international operators are located in sea-ports, which limits container shipping into deeper hinterlands. Container block-train services are hardly developed. Most Russian logistic centres are large-scale warehouses without intermodal transport terminals or logistic facilities. Intermodal transport development has great potential but would need to be driven by Russian Railways (RZhD), which seems to have little interest in investing substantially in intermodal projects that would result in public benefits but be costly for it. Container business only represents 1.5% of RZhD's transport volumes and 4.5% of its revenues; it is therefore likely to keep its focus on bulk freight in the coming decade (RZhD, 2011). Intermodal contrailers (semitrailers transported on railway platforms) are not used at all; in Europe, one in ten loaded semitrailers is transported intermodally by rail (International Union of Railways, 2012).

Inland waterways traditionally played an important role for freight transport in Russia, but have lost much of their share. After the collapse of the USSR, Russia had lost free access to many important newly-built ports in the Baltic and Black Sea basins. Today, shipping is mostly domestic (91%), exports account for only 8% and imports for 1% (Ministry of Transport, 2013). Between 2000 and 2012, inland water freight turnover decreased by 35%, whereas the transport of goods by inland water increased by 5% (FSSS, 2013). The increase of goods transported on waterways in recent years is likely a result of deteriorating conditions in the railway system and might slow down again, not least given the fact that Russian waterway capacity is not far from its limits (Voevodin, 2012). A large part of inland water freight is construction materials (80%); the rest is oil, oil products, metals, grain, fertilisers and timber. The major Siberian rivers – the Ob, the Yenisei and the Lena – offer good conditions for freight transport. However, while they are northbound, most long-distance freight transport in Russia is latitudinal, which means they mostly serve local and intra-regional freight transport.

Among all freight transport modes in the Russian Federation, air cargo grew strongest over 2000-12. Freight turnover grew by 104% and goods transport by 50% (FSSS, 2013). The total volume of air cargo in Russia increased from 779 kt in 2008 to 988 kt in 2012 (Okulov, 2013). However, its share in freight turnover among all transport modes is only 0.1% and for goods transport only 0.01% (FSSS, 2013).

Despite its geographically advantageous position between Europe and Asia, Russia attracts less air cargo traffic than some of its neighbours. This largely reflects inefficient customs procedures, high fuel prices and high air navigation charges.

- In order to avoid inefficient custom procedures, some companies fly to airports close to the Russian border and provide the final leg into the Russian Federation by truck. Customs procedures are currently being addressed through the introduction of an e-Freight system.
- Russian jet kerosene prices tend to be 10-25% higher than the world average. For example, in 2011, average air kerosene prices in Russia were at USD 1 100 per tonne, compared to USD 1 050 per tonne in North America, and USD 980 per tonne in Europe and Asia (Okulov, 2011). This is particularly important given that fuel has become one of the largest components of airlines' cost structures (Boeing, 2013).
- High kerosene prices are linked to a lack of competition in the Russian aviation fuel market. Most jet fuel is sold at the airport's fuel terminal by a sole supplier, at fixed prices (Argus, 2011). The Ministry of Transport's "Concept of air cargo transport development in Russia until 2020" addresses these issues, and the current implementation of a more integrated system of air traffic management is expected to increase Russian air route capacity (Okulov, 2011; 2012). Time will be needed, however, until these changes take effect, in particular given the meagre investments in airports so far.

The Russian airport system is going through significant restructuring and air traffic concentrates increasingly in large international airports. The number of Russian airports decreased from 1 302 in 1992 to 533 in 2000 and further to 315 in 2012. This shrinkage reflects a transfer of responsibility over many small airports from the national to regional governments, which often did not have the means to protect small airports from bankruptcy. While regional and domestic airports closed, the number of international airports increased from 19 in 1992 to 69 in 2000 to 70 in 2011 (Ministry of Transport,

2011). Current federal plans envisage the formation of a unified multi-level national airport network consisting of international hubs, domestic hubs, regional and local airports. The Emelyanovo airport in the Krasnoyarsk Agglomeration is 1 of 11 international hubs.

Emelyanovo could be further developed as an asset for the Agglomeration

As seen in Chapter 1, the Krasnoyarsk Agglomeration sits at the crossroads of rail, road, river, air and pipeline connections and is a transfer point for cargo and passengers. Krasnoyarsk is one of the largest connecting stations of the Trans-Siberian railway and lies at the intersection of two important highways, the east-west M53 from Irkutsk to Novosibirsk and the southbound M54 going until the Mongolian border. During the warmer months of the year, the Yenisei serves as a waterway to the Northern Sea, connecting to the transcontinental transport corridor and to North America and Southeast Asia via the Arctic. Domestic and international air cargo and passenger flights are handled at Emelyanovo Airport. These infrastructures are crucial assets for exports from Krasnoyarsk as well as for serving goods and passenger transit through the Agglomeration.

Though in many respects a challenge, Krasnoyarsk's remote location also gives it the potential to become a transport and logistics hub. By boosting the capacity and performance of its international airport at Emelyanovo as well as transport logistics, including intermodal facilities, Krasnoyarsk could become an important stopover destination for goods and people transiting over or through Russia between Europe and Asia. Long-distance cargo flights can stopover for refuelling, over-haul, storage or other services. And Krasnoyarsk can function as a reloading and intermodal connection point for freight and goods transiting by air, road, rail and waterways, internationally as well as to other economic centres in the Krai.

The international airport in Emelyanovo is the central element of the Agglomeration's potential to develop into an international transport hub. Located 27 kilometres north-west of Krasnoyarsk, Emelyanovo serves both international and domestic air travel and cargo in the Krasnoyarsk Agglomeration. It operates regular flights all year round served by more than 30 Russian and overseas carriers which connect Krasnoyarsk with 44 domestic and 28 international destinations in Europe and the Asia Pacific region (LH Consulting, 2012; Emelyanovo Airport, 2014). Among the 11 Russian international airport hubs identified by the Ministry of Transport, Emelyanovo airport ranks third in terms of domestic air passengers, after Moscow and St. Petersburg, and third for the amount of regional airports it serves (22), after Yakutsk and Arkhangelsk (Ministry of Transport, 2011). Furthermore, the Agglomeration is home to an important local airport, "Cheremshanka" (SFU, 2012).

Both passenger and cargo throughput at Emelyanovo airport is growing. From 2011 to 2012, the total number of passengers grew by 16% and again by 9% from 2012 to a historic high of over 2 million passengers serviced in 2013 (Emelyanovo Airport, 2014; 2013). This growth corresponds to passenger growth on Russian airlines (in the Russian Federation), which rose by 15.5% from 2011 to a total of 74 million in 2012 (MOT in Boeing, 2013). In 2012, Emelyanovo airport processed almost 20 000 tonnes of cargo, around 13 000 of which were delivered via passenger planes. While cargo in passenger planes decreased by 5% in 2012, goods delivered by cargo airlines grew by 48% from 2011 to 2012 (Interros, 2013). While these growth figures indicate a current dynamic, they should be taken with caution, since they also reflect the strong setback in air cargo and passenger transport before 2011 in relation to the world financial and economic crisis since 2008. Lufthansa Consulting is currently undertaking an in-depth study of the airport's potential to develop its route network and to attract new carriers in the passenger and cargo segments (LH Consulting, 2012).

Emelyanovo airport has significant potential to serve international air cargo stopovers. Freight turnover by air transport in the Russian Federation more than doubled from 2.5 billion tonnes-km in 2000 to 5.1 billion tonnes-km in 2012. The increase of air transport of goods increased by 50% from 0.8 million tonnes in 2000 to 1.2 million tonnes in 2012 (FSSS, 2013). Most of Russian air cargo is export or import related, however, cargo transit is not yet living up to its potential. So far, only 8 200 of the annual 18 000 cargo flights that go over the country and need landing for fuelling or technical services are stopping there. The main share of stopovers is attracted by neighbouring countries, despite the advantageous geographic position of several Russian airports, notably of Emelyanovo in the Agglomeration. According to the Ministry of Transport, the revenues from air transit and technical landings in Russia could amount to RUB 90 billion until 2020 (Ministry of Transport, 2012). Lufthansa Cargo estimated that it can optimise its routing and shorten flying times to the Far East by 12 minutes per flight, using Krasnoyarsk as a stopover instead of Astana in Kazakhstan (Aircargonews, 2009).

Nevertheless, the Emelyanovo airport is not yet realising its potential. As mentioned above, several factors are slowing progress at Russian international airports. The most important ones are inefficient customs procedures, high kerosene prices and expensive air navigation fees for air cargo, discussed above (Okulov, 2011). In addition, it should be noted that Krasnoyarsk has particularly high technical landing charges (Figure 3.12).

Taken together, these factors curb the attractiveness of Emelyanovo for international air cargo companies to stop over for refills or technical services in Krasnoyarsk. With respect to airport customs procedures, Emelyanovo is engaged in one of two Russian pilot projects implementing the IATA's (International Air Transport Association) e-Freight handling standards in advance of worldwide implementation in 2015. This new standard allows paperless and cheaper cargo handling and increases the efficiency of service delivery, reliability and transparency (Emelyanovo Airport, 2012). The initiative is an important step towards accelerating customs clearance, especially for carriers with many small articles, which currently face the largest repelling effects both on transit flights landing in Russia and import-bound air traffic. However, more effort is needed to tackle the different challenges currently holding back Krasnoyarsk's potential to develop an international air transport hub.

Figure 3.12. **Technical landing charge in selected airports, 2010**

USD thousands

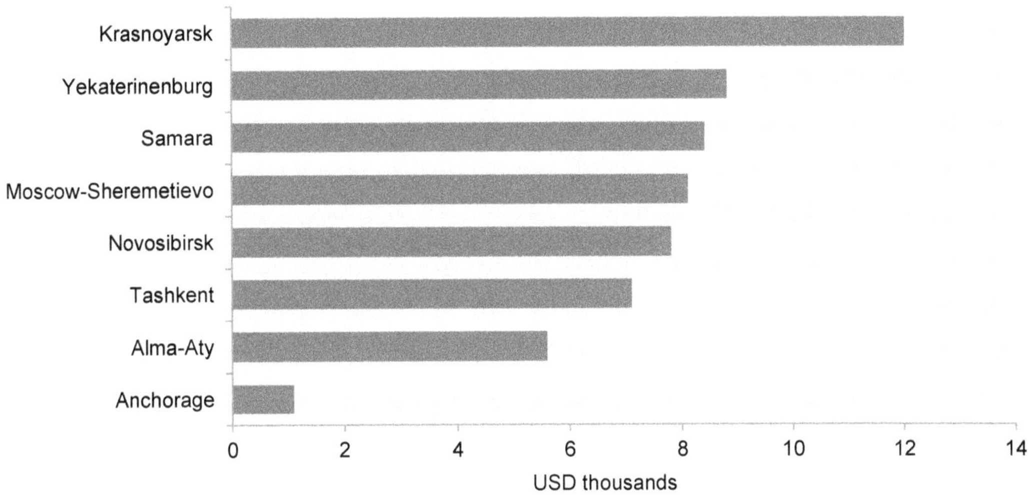

Source: Okulov, V. (2011), "The Russian Ministry of Transport initiatives in air cargo transport development on domestic and international markets", presentation at the 2nd AirCargoForum, Moscow, available at: http://c-ca.ru/assets/files/AirCargoForum_24_11_11_V_Okulov_Presentation.pdf.

Transport logistics and intermodal transport facilities merit more attention

Intermodal transport logistics and container transport are important elements of the role Krasnoyarsk can potentially play for cargo transit between Asia and Europe. The volume of container cargo transit between Asia and Europe over the Trans-Siberian railway is expected to increase over the next years. The Russian Federation's share international container cargo (5% in 2008) could be much higher. Russia uses only 8-10% of its total transit potential and could, in the view of some analysts, attract up to 10-15% of the European-Asian container flow via its networks (Filina, 2012). Whether or not this will be achieved depends on the competitiveness of container transport via international sea routes versus the competitiveness of Russian rail container transport. The sea route from the People's Republic of China to EU countries is almost four times longer than the Russian rail track and costs are over USD 250 more per container. Russian container transport needs to become more reliable and more flexible. The Ministry of Transport's "Transport Strategy of the Russian Federation until 2030" therefore addresses several key bottlenecks in the rail system and has identified 35 large transport and multi-modal logistics centres with storage facilities and intermodal connection and transhipment facilities, including in Krasnoyarsk, where such a logistics centre is under construction in the area of the fourth bridge (SFU, 2012).

Krasnoyarsk's position at the crossroads of important rail and road links underpins its potential for developing intermodal transport services. The Krasnoyarsk-Taishet line was identified as one of three most important Russian clusters for container transport via the Trans-Siberian railway (Filina, 2012). Complementing the east-west connection, the federal government is considering developing the north-south corridor that crosses Krasnoyarsk, partly by resuming navigation on the Yenisei river, but notably through constructing a new railway connection to the Republic of Tyva (south) and a link with the North Siberian railway line (north). The southern track will relax the situation on the currently overloaded southbound highway M54 and will connect Krasnoyarsk with the planned exploitation of the Elegest coking-coal deposit in Tyva (Alklychev and Zoidov, 2012; mission interviews). The northern track would stimulate the meridian connection area between Krasnoyarsk and Lesosibirsk, establish a link between the Trans-Siberian and the North Siberian railways, and would improve the connection to the lower Angara region, where the development of a metallurgical complex is in planning in connection with a hydropower station in Boguchan (Alklychev and Zoidov, 2012). These projects will increase Krasnoyarsk's position and its importance at the crossroads of road and rail cargo, including for intermodal transport.

For this potential to materialise, a number of challenges need to be addressed. The main barriers include: aged infrastructure in a large part of the region; bottlenecks e.g. through low carrying capacity of infrastructure; constraints for long container trains in suburban areas, including in the approach of Krasnoyarsk; inefficient container terminals and low routing speed of container trains (Krasnoyarsk, 2012). In particular, decreasing carrying capacity in eastern railroad networks needs to be addressed. Furthermore, the development of better highways and railway infrastructure is challenged by climatic conditions as well as a lack of labour and capital.

Improved connectivity could support productivity growth

Internal and external connectivity improvements are a means to boost productivity, growth and economic development in the Agglomeration. The impacts of access to local versus distant markets play out on different levels (Table 3.5). Amongst the most important endogenous drivers of growth are: access of firms to local labour markets, skilled labour, intermediary inputs and customers, including face-to-face interactions in knowledge-intensive industries, and access of households to jobs and services. As a central enabler of access to local markets, internal connectivity is thus a condition for endogenous drivers of productivity, growth and economic development.

Table 3.5. **Access to local and distant markets**

Local markets	Distant markets
Self-supporting production	Production for extra-regional demand
Endogenous, self-generated economic growth and productivity enhancements	Exogenous demand and self-generated productivity improvements stimulate economic growth
Face-to-face contact between buyers and sellers	Mediated contacts between buyers and sellers
Local competition	Global competition
Infrastructure for access to local markets	Infrastructure for access to global markets
Lower intra-regional transaction costs stimulate development	Lower extra-regional transaction costs stimulate development
Diversity and welfare depend on the size of the region	Diversity can stimulate productivity growth and exports

Source: adapted from ITF (2007).

Access to external markets can be improved locally

External connectivity improvements depend much on national policies, so the municipalities in the Agglomeration have limited means to improve access to distant markets. Nevertheless, in particular with respect to logistics transport infrastructure affecting external connectivity, local policies and measures are influential. In this respect, two projects merit heightened attention for improvements going forward:

- Emelyanovo international airport. In addition to the current improvements in customs procedures through the introduction of the IATA e-Freight system, the pricing of technical landing should be reviewed against those of major competitors. Attracting more international air cargo carriers for technical stopovers will also require developing necessary services, including the facilities and logistics for international air cargo transfer to regional markets in the Krai.

- An intermodal logistics centre. The logistics centre planned in the area of the fourth bridge could become a central element of Krasnoyarsk as an intermodal transport hub in which rail, road, air, water and container transport connect. The development of intermodal facilities and transport logistics should be well co-ordinated with developments of the overall transport system in the Agglomeration to avoid trade-offs between external and internal connectivity.

Improving access to internal markets requires an integrated and systemic approach

Internal connectivity improvements and related effects on productivity, growth and economic development need to be built on a deep integration of land-use and transport planning. Through their impact on the spatial organisation of urban development, land use and transport affect internal connectivity and access to local markets (OECD/ITF, 2008). Two types of spatial organisation and land use positively impact accessibility: compactness and mixed use. In particular, compactness contributes to increased capacity utilisation of existing infrastructures, reduces the need for new infrastructure, and shortens the need for and the distance of urban trips. Effective means to achieve compactness are infill development and redevelopment, which, if favouring mixed use, can also contribute to economic resilience. Brownfield redevelopment is particularly relevant in the context of Krasnoyarsk's plans to continue relocating industrial complexes from central urban areas to the periphery (SFU, 2012). A condition for achieving compactness and mixed use is to deeply integrate transport policies with land-use planning. Effective instruments for implementing and financing integrated land-use and transport plans are, for example, transit-oriented development (TOD) and land-value capture tools (Box 3.15).

Transport and land-use planning reaches beyond municipal boundaries and thus needs to be co-ordinated among all municipalities of the Agglomeration. In OECD metropolitan areas, transport and land-use planning are the most prominent subjects for inter-municipal co-ordination: over 80% of metropolitan governance bodies work on transport, over 70% on spatial planning and more than 55% are active in at least both fields at the same time. This is not surprising given the variety and the importance of issues to be addressed in order to territorially integrate transport and land-use planning, such as: *i)* administrative fragmentation and information gaps; *ii)* private versus public sector leadership; *iii)* individual municipal decisions versus metropolitan impact; *iv)* diverging time horizons. In many cases, these issues are addressed through multi-purpose inter-municipal joint authorities, which can represent the needs and interest of all of the involved municipalities and can plan for a larger territory. A good example is the Chicago Metropolitan Agency for Planning (CMAP), which co-ordinates transport and land-use planning, among other issues, across the three states of Illinois, Indiana and Wisconsin (OECD, 2012b).

Box 3.15. Transit-oriented development and value capture tools

Transit-oriented development (TOD) concentrates urban development around existing or new public transport station. In most cases, TOD consists of residential and commercial mixed use and dense development, often in redeveloped urban areas. The city of Toyama, Japan, for example, at the occasion of renovating its mass-transit system, incentivised people to move from suburbs into targeted areas close to mass-transit stations. This intensified the use of urban land, increased public transport demand and reduced car dependency (OECD, 2012a).

An effective instrument for financing urban redevelopment and TOD is land-value capture. A number of land-value capture tools allow generating revenues from indirect benefits of new or retrofitted (public) transport infrastructure, for example from increased real estate value in proximity to transport infrastructures. These revenues can be used to complement the capital financing of transport infrastructure projects. Land-value capture tools have proven successful in different circumstances, mostly for road, metro and rail infrastructures, and include:

- tax increment financing districts, i.e. earmarking future growth in property taxes to fund infrastructure investments and other economic development activities
- development charges, i.e. a one-time charge on the land-value gain attributable to adjacent infrastructure investment or a tax on private developers to finance capital costs of greenfield development
- transferable development rights from the rent or sale of public land or building rights. Such rights can be traded by landowners to free land for new transport infrastructure against land for built up in other areas
- joint property development, i.e. a formal arrangement in which private stakeholders either pay public authorities or agree to share the capital costs of development.

Sources: OECD (2012a), *Compact City Policies: A Comparative Assessment*, OECD Green Growth Studies, OECD Publishing, Paris, http://dx.doi.org/10.1787/9789264167865-en; Ang, G. and V. Marchal (2013), "Mobilising private investment in sustainable transport: The case of land-based passenger transport infrastructure", *OECD Environment Working Papers*, No. 56, OECD Publishing, Paris, http://dx.doi.org/10.1787/5k46hjm8jpmv-en.

While integrated land-use and transport planning brings medium- and long-term benefits, congestion also needs to be addressed in the short term, through a range of complementary measures. As long as economic activity, income levels and car ownership in the Agglomeration are growing, congestion will continue to be a challenge. In order to effectively address congestion, a balanced approach is needed, which considers demand- and supply-side policies as well as public and private transport solutions. Congestion occurs when demand for road capacity exceeds supply at certain hours of the day, notably around bottlenecks. Providing more road infrastructure temporarily relieves pressure on roads, but soon leads to more traffic, new bottlenecks and congestion again (UKDT, 1994; ITF, 2007). An exclusive focus on providing public transport infrastructure is not likely either to reduce kilometres travelled in a given territory (Duranton and Turner, 2011). Demand-side policies should therefore be taken into account to curb congestion, including traffic management and road pricing, for example via parking fees. Parking fees are effective and flexible. They can be tailored to different (price) zones and different times of the day. Introducing parking fees in Krasnoyarsk needs to be coupled with decisive efforts in enforcing traffic rules, for example through effective fines. On the other hand, public transport needs to become more attractive. Priorities should include increasing the coverage of public transport and improving the system's performance. Finally, measures to help overcome the social stigma of public transport as being reserved for the underprivileged could significantly contribute to increase demand for public transport.

Seamless intermodal transport among public modes and interoperability between public and private transport are two priorities for systemic improvements in the Agglomeration's transport system. A lack of physical proximity between stations, separate ticketing systems and uncoordinated schedules among different modes and routes of public transport make switching from one mode to another difficult, expensive and time consuming today. Important objectives therefore should be to spatially better integrate public transport stops of different modes, creating one harmonised ticketing system that covers all public modes, and providing full and easily accessible information on routes, schedules and trips. Furthermore, interoperability between public and private transport needs to be improved, in particular in relation to the planned transfer points at the periphery of Krasnoyarsk. The success of such transfer points depends much on frictionless transfer between car and public transport as well as on pricing. Trips via transfer points should be less expensive than end-to-end car trips from surrounding municipalities into the city centre. One option for adapting pricing accordingly is to implement parking fees or other road pricing measures in the city centre.

The transport system needs an integrated strategy

Finally, making the Agglomeration's transport system the backbone of economic development needs a fully integrated strategy. An overarching aim of such a strategy should be to align the objectives for external and internal connectivity improvements and to identify synergies between the two. A good understanding of the economic implications and consequences that transport infrastructure and land use have through the way in which they influence the spatial organisation of the Agglomeration must be the basis for an integrated transport (and land-use) strategy. Furthermore, public and private transport should not be thought of as substitutes, but rather as complementing means and modes of transport that have to inter-operate as one system. In this respect, an integrated strategy should:

- be informative for national transport policy makers as to the needs and strategic direction of developing the Agglomeration's transport system
- guide implementation of national transport policy consistently with land-use and transport plans and decisions in the Agglomeration
- systematically assess the potential for building an international air and intermodal transport hub based on both airports and intermodal transport and logistics facilities in the Agglomeration
- take into account potential trade-offs and synergies between measures that improve internal connectivity and measures that improve external connectivity
- deeply integrate land-use policies and transport planning to maximise the benefits from compact and mixed use for urban spatial and economic development
- co-ordinate land-use and transport planning across municipalities, for example by establishing a multi-purpose inter-municipal joint authority
- analyse challenges such as congestion through cost-benefit analyses, at the territorial scale of the Agglomeration, and identify the economically most efficient systemic improvements

- balance supply- and demand-side policies as well as public and private transport solutions for addressing congestion in the long, medium and short term
- improve intermodal connectivity among public transport modes and interoperability between private and public transport, in particular at transfer points on the urban periphery.

Co-ordination tools for effective multi-level governance

Horizontal and vertical co-ordination are fundamental to the effective governance of the Agglomeration. While competition among municipalities can improve public service delivery, municipal fragmentation in metropolitan areas often leads to inefficiencies, redundancies and inter-jurisdictional externalities from local actions with regional impacts. Externalities can be internalised through horizontal coordination, which helps overcoming jurisdictional fragmentation and thus reducing redundancies and increasing efficiency. Co-ordination should be targeted and tailored to areas with strong inter-jurisdictional externalities and should not compromise the diversity and the responsiveness of solutions driven by competition. In turn, it should enable positive inter-jurisdictional spill-overs, help aligning sectoral policies and reduce institutional fragmentation. Furthermore, policies need to be aligned across different levels of government. A lack of co-ordination at higher levels may weaken the effect of local co-ordination. Conversely, a coherent national and regional policy framework can enhance the potential of a locally integrated approach. Effective horizontal co-ordination paired with vertical co-ordination can significantly improve conditions for territorial and economic development of the Agglomeration.

Horizontal co-ordination should be at the heart of governance in the Agglomeration

As is clear from the foregoing, metropolitan governance of the Krasnoyarsk Agglomeration needs a solid basis that is flexible enough to enable tailored approaches for addressing local needs and freeing local potential. The quasi absence of experience with co-ordination and cooperation among municipalities in the Agglomeration calls for a reliable framework for co-ordination and guidance were needed. Given the different sizes and economic weights of the municipalities, a key challenge is to integrate the interests and stakes of all territories, notwithstanding the powerful position of Krasnoyarsk city. This is in fact a condition for garnering broad support and the willingness of all stakeholders to equally contribute. The common ambitions and potentially differing interest of municipalities need to be substantiated and taken account of in a general and common agreement. This should spell out the common vision, long-term strategic objectives and aligned economic, social and environmental policy goals. It should steer long-term development and enable integrated plans, strategies and programmes with immediate impact. Guided by the Krai government, the conception of such a commonly agreed approach needs to be co-ordinated also with the main bodies already identified to co-ordinate implementation of policies and programmes in different areas: *i)* the Investment Council, *ii)* the Commission on Strategic Development of Krasnoyarsk Krai, *iii)* the Council for Innovative Development.

The implementation of the Agglomeration's vision and strategic objectives is shaped by federal law, in the framework of which municipalities can notably establish contractual relations. In the absence of a legal status of the Agglomeration and a more institutionalised approach to metropolitan governance in Russia, current federal law[7] determines the possible models and instruments for implementation. It enables municipalities to cooperate on a voluntary or contractual basis, and allows to unite municipal units, e.g. in an urban district. Different forms and instruments of collaboration include:

- **Voluntary nets and association of municipalities**, taking into account their territorial and organisational foundations. Municipalities can unite around shared challenges to find common solutions. This can include pooling financial, material and other resources to address local challenges. Such inter-municipal nets are usually purpose bound and would be subsumed under one association that heads and coordinates inter-municipal cooperation in different fields, such as health services or transportation. Such an association would be open to regional and federal representatives and thus also enhance vertical coordination across levels of government, in junction with inter-municipal and inter-sectoral coordination. While such a loose association would have no legal power, it may significantly enhance horizontal and vertical coordination.
- **Independent non-profit organisation,** established by Krasnoyarsk Krai, municipalities or city districts can act as executive bodies for specific management tasks in the Agglomeration, e.g. of Agglomeration wide development programs. Together with business entities and the participation of the state, region and municipalities, they could also play a role in centralising service provision, e.g. health care, within the Agglomeration.
- **Contracts and agreements** between organs of local self-management can be used flexibly to a wide range of purposes. Given that no regulatory procedure exists for contractual agreements in the Russian legislation, they need a higher supervising (and enforcing) body, which in practice is enacted by the Krai administration.
- **Foundations** may be established at the level of municipalities to raise additional funds for the implementation of development projects.

Overarching co-ordination and supervision of inter-municipal cooperation in the Agglomeration is currently ensured by the Krai government and could be improved. On one hand, a higher governmental body in the Agglomeration that coordinates and partly steers co-ordination and cooperation arrangement among municipalities offers oversight, strategic planning and arbitration power. On the other hand, the Krai government is not elected for the Agglomeration, which risks making it more of a "top-down" project than is desirable. The first attempt to agree on an Agglomeration strategy gives a good example. It failed to find consensus in part because not all municipalities saw their interests and concerns to be well enough represented. For the Krai government to s provide overarching co-ordination in the Agglomeration, it needs to enable municipalities to play their part in shaping the strategic direction and to represent their respective constituencies.

Rather than seeking one ideal governance solution, a variety of approaches and models may be considered and suitable approaches identified for different purposes. In OECD countries, metropolitan governance bodies – broadly defined as bodies organising responsibilities among public authorities in metropolitan areas (including voluntary associations of municipalities, with few or no legal powers) – are very common. Over two thirds of 200 metropolitan areas over 500 000 inhabitants have a metropolitan governance body. However, the types of governance arrangements vary widely, usually taking one of the four most established (Table 3.2). These types of governance arrangements are not mutually exclusive, rather, several of them can co-exist. Informal/soft co-ordination arrangements are the most common among OECD metropolitan areas with a metropolitan governance body are. Over half of metropolitan areas have such arrangements, whereas around one quarter have introduced inter-municipal joint authorities, 16% established supra-municipal authorities and 3% enjoy a special status of a "metropolitan city" (OECD, 2014a). In refining the metropolitan governance approach for the Krasnoyarsk Agglomeration, this classification and experience with metropolitan governance arrangements can help establishing and operationalising targeted governance arrangements for specific areas and goals.

Any type of metropolitan governance arrangement applied in the Agglomeration needs to build on a culture of and effective incentives for co-ordination. Beyond horizontal co-ordination across municipalities, key policy sectors need to be coordinated as well as different levels of government. This triple co-ordination challenge, horizontally across actors, public and private, among municipalities and vertically across levels of governments, tends to be most successful in a culture of co-ordination that enables going beyond institutional reform and that allows co-ordination arrangements to evolve flexibly and to adjust over time to the changing needs of different actors involved. Building such a co-ordination culture is a condition for the Krasnoyarsk Agglomeration to develop the different dimensions of co-ordination as keys to successfully integrating strategic planning and to design coherent and effective policy instruments and implementation processes. As the central coordinating actor in the Agglomeration, the Krai government may need to foster co-ordination through additional incentives. Financial incentives from higher levels of government might be necessary when municipalities are reluctant to cooperate, in particular when such reluctance is rooted in history or path-dependency. In France, for example, a group of municipalities can receive additional grants from the central government, if they join a *Communauté d'agglomération*.

Several instruments and approaches to co-ordinated implementation in the Agglomeration have proven useful so far:

- **State (municipal) order.**[8] Municipalities can be incentivised to collaborate through the placement of the state (municipal) order. This can be, for example, the development of a standard for public and municipal services to which all municipal organs, public institutions and non-profit organisations would need to comply with. Such standards and regulations can also be developed by the organisation operator of the strategic development of the Krasnoyarsk Agglomeration.
- **Inter-municipal investment projects**. Inter-municipal investment projects require a business plan and project documentation developed in accordance with the federal legislation and approved by the highest body of the executive authority of Krai. Such projects should address local issues of two and more municipalities, such as through the construction or reconstruction of social and engineering municipal infrastructure, and have positive social and economic effects. They are financed at the expense of the Krai, municipal budgets and corporate funds. Agreements for inter-municipal investment projects are signed by all parties of the project and the Krai government.
- **Inter-municipal business entities.**[9] Representative bodies of municipalities can create inter-municipal business entities in the form of closed joint stock and

limited liability companies to work together on local issues. They also can create non-profit organisations in the form of autonomous non-profit organisations and foundations. Furthermore, municipalities may establish associations (unions) for co-operation and implementation of their own interests.

The above are being applied in different ways in a number of large inter-municipal projects in the Agglomeration. The parties having agreed to the draft scheme of spatial planning of the Agglomeration and corrections to general plans of development of Krasnoyarsk, Divnogorsk, Sosnovoborsk and Sukhobuzim. State enterprises of the Krasnoyarsk Krai have been set up to implement the construction of municipal infrastructure in Krai municipalities (Centre of communal services) and to construct new facilities to increase the capacity of power grids (Centre of transport logistics). Another example is inter-municipal cooperation on waste management, which is planned to be managed Agglomeration-wide; as well as transport projects that are being planned and implemented in cooperation with several municipalities, such as the new railway connecting Krasnoyarsk with Sosnovoborsk and Zheleznogorsk.

The Agglomeration may consider creating a dedicated authority for co-ordinate the planning and implementation of transport infrastructure and land use. As elaborated in more detail above, planning and implementation of transport infrastructure and land use needs to be better co-ordinated and done in cooperation among municipal other public and private actors. This need is not unique to Krasnoyarsk, rather it is the most commonly addressed challenge in OECD metropolitan areas. Of these areas, more than 80% have governance bodies working on transportation and regional development, and over 70% on spatial planning; over 55% of metropolitan governance bodies engage with all three fields at once. OECD metropolitan areas with a public transport authority represent around 60% (OECD, 2014a). It is worth noting that OECD metropolitan areas with a public transport authority are found to have lower air pollution and higher satisfaction public transport users, two indicators for the effectiveness of such authorities (OECD, 2014a).

While financing and implementation of transport infrastructure in the Agglomeration is governed at different levels, and legislation is not entirely conducive to inter-municipal cooperation, federal law[10] allows creating representative bodies of inter-municipal networks, economic entities and organisations. Such bodies are based on voluntary contractual agreements and should aim at pooling financial, material and other resources (BR). In the light of experience from OECD metropolitan areas, an inter-municipal transport authority, which might covers spatial planning and regional development as well, should be considered for the Agglomeration. Such an authority would go beyond an inter-municipal advisory body for land use and transport planning, as discussed previously. It would be composed by representatives from the Agglomeration's municipalities and different government levels, pool resources, co-ordinate planning, and guide cooperation among municipal and other public and private actors that implement transport infrastructure, land and economic development projects. In addition to improving external connectivity, including logistics infrastructure, such a body would be best placed to focus on public transportation with the aim to decrease congestion and air pollution in central urban areas in the Agglomeration.

Closer co-ordination across levels of government can improve investment conditions

The Russian legal and legislative framework gives little guidance on vertical coordination across levels of government, but allows for contractual agreements, including public-private partnerships. In the absence of legislation and general rules for joint implementation of state tasks among organs of state authority and organs of local self-management, constitutional, budgetary, municipal and administrative law still offer possibilities to conclude multi-level public agreements or public-private partnerships. Also, organs of the Federation and organs of state authority of the subjects of the Federation can agree to delegate powers[11]; and organs of local self-management and communities can agree to delegate powers at the expense of local budgets.[12]

Agreements between the Krai and municipal governments in the Agglomeration, possible in a number of sectors, are regulated at the federal level. According to the Civil Code of the Russian Federation (article 124), subjects of the Federation and municipalities are subject to civil law. This gives the Krasnoyarsk Krai and municipalities in the Agglomeration the right to enter into civil contracts or agreements.[13] Among those provided for in the Civil Code, a simple partnership contract (of joint activity, chapter 55 of the Civil Code) is the most appropriate to determine joint management mechanisms in the Agglomeration. The main fields or sectors for contractual agreements are territorial planning and urban development, transport, health, waste recycling, support for young and small firms (entrepreneurs), sports, culture and entertainment and youth (BR). Every agreement determines: *i)* a list of specific issues (the powers of the state authorities and local self-management), specifying municipal-regional (inter-municipal) cooperation; *ii)* a list of state and local authorities responsible for the cooperation on specific issues; *iii)* organisation of the coordinating body in the relevant field; *iv)* basic procedures for cooperation in the respective field (sector).

Key actors for vertical coordination are the Krai ministries of Economy and Regional Development (MERD) and of Investment and Innovations (MII) of Krasnoyarsk Krai. The MERD is responsible for socio-economic development programmes of municipalities as well as for preparing and implementing investment projects, including nationally funded ones. It also maintains a register of complex programs of socio-economic development of municipalities and the register of complex programs of socio-economic development of urban and rural municipal territories of Krasnoyarsk Krai. The MII holds executive power for cooperating with the Ministry of Economic Development of the Russian Federation and for implementing agreements between the latter and the Krai Government for state support of small and medium-sized businesses, including in agriculture. The MII also organizes the interaction between executive authorities of Krasnoyarsk Krai with the federal government, the state authorities of the Russian Federation, public organisations, major Russian and foreign companies engaged in business activities in the region, as well as with international investment and financial institutions.

Another important actor for vertical coordination of domestic and foreign investments, including public-private partnerships, is the Krasnoyarsk Krai Investment Council. Created in 2008, the Investment Council acts as an advisory board, facilitating interaction between federal executive authorities, public authorities of Krasnoyarsk Krai, local authorities, institutions, enterprises and other organisations, to implement investment projects in Krasnoyarsk Krai. It coordinates investment policy and projects, both for domestic and foreign direct investment. Its core activity is to improve investment conditions, notably through improving regulative frameworks and policies that influence financial (e.g. credit) and fiscal conditions and thus investment decisions. It helps removing administrative barriers to attract and promote investments that contribute to regional economic development. Engaging actors from different levels of government, including the public authorities of Krasnoyarsk Krai and local government bodies, the

Investment Council also prepares individual offers for investors, choosing the most effective forms of state support for the investment, and gives advice on the implementation of investment projects, based on its record of experience with investment projects in Krasnoyarsk Krai.

Growing investments in Krasnoyarsk Krai and the Agglomeration are concentrating in traditional sectors and in Krasnoyarsk city. Over the past years, investments have been growing faster in Krasnoyarsk Krai than Russia on average. In 2011, overall investments in the Krai amounted to RUB 303.9 billion. Increasingly attracting international investors, the Krai's long-term credit rating was corrected upwards by Fitch Ratings from a stable (BB) to positive (BB +) in June 2012. Over the past decade, the Krai's investment policy focused on medium- and large-scale projects, notably in the area of natural resource extraction. More recently, it started emphasising economic diversification and promoting social, transport, energy and innovation infrastructure development. In late 2010, the largest share of investments went into commercial projects (45% of total investments) and engineering infrastructure (44%), while only a small share went into social projects (7%), R&D (4%) and R&D infrastructure (0.06 %). Capital-formation concentrates in transport and communications, construction, production and distribution of electricity, gas and water. Geographically, the main investments are planned in the city of Krasnoyarsk (representing 57% of planned investments) and the Emelyanovo district (40%). Almost half of all planned investments involve more than one municipality and can thus be expected to positively affect adjacent territories.

Private investments in the Agglomeration mainly target productive capacity, notably in resource extraction, whereas federal, regional funds and local funds are primarily invested in social, innovation and transport infrastructures. This being said, 87% of investments in the Agglomeration are done in some form of public-private partnership (e.g. co-financing, partial subsidisation of expenditures or interest payments on loans, concessions), often involving several levels of government. Getting vertical coordination for public-private partnerships right is thus an important condition for successful investment in the Agglomeration.

As noted above, PPPs are an essential part of investment activities across the Agglomeration. This being said, 87% of investments in the Agglomeration are done in some form of public-private co-operation, even not a PPP (e.g. co-financing, partial subsidisation of expenditures or interest payments on loans, concessions). Often these involve several levels of government. A number of areas lend themselves particularly well to municipal-private or other public-private partnerships: infrastructure, including the expansion and modernisation road networks, heat and water systems or waste recycling. The currently largest public-private partnership in Agglomeration is the housing, utility and infrastructure project Novoland, co-financed by the Investment Fund of the Russian Federation. While Novoland is an example for a successful multi-level PPP, it also shows the difficulty of implementing such projects. For example, the absence of a clear mechanism and rules for financing investment projects through the RF Investment has also posed difficulties in the case of the Novoland project; so do frequent changes in federal legislation that have contributed to slowing down progress of the project (SFU, 2012). Given the importance of multi-level PPPs for the agglomeration, clear coordination mechanisms and rules for implementing PPPs, including across government levels, are needed.

Current investments projects are mainly aimed at specific sectors, lacking co-ordination among sectors, including at higher levels of government. Large investment projects tend to reflect territorial development policies. The current large investment projects in the Agglomeration are mostly in isolated sectors, such as transport, logistics, housing or utilities. For a more integrated territorial development approach, the fragmentation among different sectoral policies and respective investment strategies needs to be overcome. Policies in different areas need to be co-ordinated not only at the municipal level, but, in particular in the view of multi-level PPPs and investments projects that affect several municipalities, across levels of government. A municipal-private partnership for Agglomeration wide waste management, for example, should be co-ordinated not only among the participating municipalities, but also with federal investments in transport and housing that affect both the production of new waste and the ability to handle waste disposal and recycling logistics.

A stronger identity of the Agglomeration may help marketing the Agglomeration to foreign investors. A comprehensive strategy for the Agglomeration should also aim to better define the local identity that characterises it Agglomeration. A strong identity as a territory, its people, qualities and culture makes the Agglomeration easier recognisable for non-locals, including investors. Creating a regional brand that clearly communicates what the Agglomeration can offer, what makes it unique and worthwhile can, in addition to providing transparent data on the business environment, increase trust and the attractiveness of a place. Special events for investors could build on local customs and festivities that enable showing Krasnoyarsk and the Agglomeration beyond the objective information investors can get at a distance. Better identifying, strengthening and communicating the quality of the place are important conditions for building the Agglomeration's reputation as an attractive place to make business in Russia.

Looking ahead: A final word on lessons for success

Recent OECD work on metropolitan governance reforms has identified some basic success factors that appear to hold good across a large number of countries (OECD, 2014a). These are summarised in Table 3.6. A quick scan of these factors suggests three conclusions for Krasnoyarsk. The first is that many of them look like simple common sense. They may thus appear trivial. However, the reality is that important factors are missing in many cases and that even mobilising these very common-sensical factors can require political will and strategic foresight. The second is that the task is never done: many of these factors are not one-off considerations to be addressed at the birth of the reform. They require continuing attention, negotiation and engagement with public and private-sector actors, a fact which underscores the vital importance of the second factor – metropolitan leadership. Thirdly, the experience of the Krasnoyarsk Agglomeration to date looks broadly positive when viewed in these terms, particularly as regards flexibility and time frames (the evolution of the project over time must be seen as a positive response to changing circumstances. However, there are clear additional steps to be taken, particularly in respect of citizen engagement, financing and communication: in particular, a clearer, sharper definition of the vision for the Agglomeration could frame the big picture against which progress could be assessed.

Table 3.6. **Effective metropolitan governance reforms: Lessons from OECD countries**

Identify a common cause for collaboration and build on (as well as communicate) successful collaboration outcomes. Starting with small-scale and concrete projects can sometimes help rally forces and progressively lead to setting a 'big picture', as success breeds success and trust.	*In Barcelona, three sectoral inter-municipal authorities (transport, environment, and planning) were created in 1987. After participating in the elaboration of a metropolitan strategic plan with the municipality of Barcelona in 1999, a metropolitan authority of Barcelona was set up in 2011.*
Develop metropolitan leadership and/or ownership. A relevant personality and/or institution often plays a pivotal role in steering change and creating and maintaining momentum for reform. The reform needs a strong advocate as the engine of the process. Such clear demand for reform may stem from different constituencies.	*In France, impetus towards governance reforms in the three largest metropolitan areas has been largely (albeit not exclusively) driven by the central government in Paris; local governments in Lyon (municipalities and département); and the private sector as well as the central government in Marseille*
Empower and engage stakeholders at an early stage, and ensure accountability and transparency. Those who are the ultimate recipients of governance/policy (and have the continuity that political bodies do not), such as citizens, businesses, and universities, need to be brought on board at the very beginning of the process. Policymakers, citizens and relevant parties require clear information both on short-term and long-term gains/losses.	*The Montreal Metropolitan Community created a mixed committee of elected officials and citizens to jointly organise a biennial set of debates among elected officials and civil society to discuss the implementation of the strategic metropolitan plan 2031. The first series of debates took place in February and March 2013.*
Strengthen the evidence base and track progress. Solid background research and scrutiny from unbiased experts can help create and sustain credibility for the reform. Strong, reliable instruments for monitoring and evaluation contribute to fostering continuous improvement.	*In Canada, the Greater Toronto CivicAction Alliance convened all three levels of government with business, labour, academic and non-profit sectors since its diagnostic report "Enough Talk: An Action Plan for the Toronto Region" (2003). It convenes a Greater Toronto Summit every four years to drive collective action on pressing issues such as transportation, energy and socioeconomic inclusion.*
Provide (or secure) sources of financing. Metropolitan public finance is often the nexus of political resistance as governments are torn between the search for fiscal autonomy and dissuasive taxation. Securing an appropriate stream of financial resources helps to avoid unfunded mandates and often determines effective collaboration. In addition to traditional fiscal tools (e.g. own taxes, grants and transfers, fees), strategic partnerships with the business and financial community can be instrumental in gathering additional resources for public investment.	*Former mayor of London Ken Livingstone built a close relationship with the London Chamber of Commerce and Industry, the local branch of the Confederation of Business Industry, and London First – he then invited them to sit on the newly created London Business Board (2000) and convened them frequently*
Balance clear time frames and flexibility. Providing visibility on the short and long term will allow actors to anticipate next steps of the process while leaving room for trial and error as well as midway adjustments.	*In Sweden, governance reforms have first been tested in a few pilot regions (Västra Götaland around Gothenburg, and Skåne around Malmö) with a multiannual timeline and evaluation mechanisms, before extending the possibility to other interested regions.*

Source: OECD (2015), *Governing the City*, OECD Publishing, Paris, http://dx.doi.org/10.1787/9789264226500-en.

Notes

1. This reflects in part the fact that the world "metropolitan has a distinct meaning in Russian: it refers to underground urban railways.
2. See Ahrend, Gamper and Schumann (2014) for details
3. Governance structures that result in lack of transport infrastructure and congestion would also be expected to contribute to fragmented labour markets, thereby harming economic efficiency and increasing unemployment. Maybe even more importantly, longer commutes have a direct negative impact on well-being, and leave less time for parents to take care of their kids or for community tasks, which can endanger education outcomes and decrease the social cohesion and resilience of neighbourhoods.
4. The American general Dwight Eisenhower reportedly said, "In preparing for battle, I have always found that plans are useless, but planning is indispensable." Something similar may be said of regional development planning.
5. See data at http://urbanica.spb.ru/?cat=27 (accessed 10 December 2013).
6. The construction of a metro system advanced from 1995 until 2011, leaving 3.2 kilometres of metro tunnels under Krasnoyarsk. Public funds, including federal funds, stopped in 2011.
7. Federal Law from 06.10.2003 № 131-FZ (points 3, 4 Art. 8) (№131-FZ).
8. Under Federal Law № 94-FZ.
9. According to Art. 68-69, Federal Law of 06.10.2003 № 131.
10. Federal Law No 131-FZ.
11. Article 78 of the Constitution of the Russian Federation.
12. Article 15 of the federal law from 06.10.2003 №131-FZ.
13. Both provided and not provided directly by the legislation (Part 2 of Article 421 of the Civil Code of the Russian Federation).

Bibliography

ADB and the World Bank (2006), *Best Practices for Private Sector Investment in Railways*, prepared by TERA International Group, Inc., Final Report, available at: www.adb.org/Documents/Reports/Consultant/bestpractices-railways/Study-Report.pdf.

Ahrend, R. and A.C. Lembcke (2015), “Economic and demographic trends in cities”, *OECD Regional Development Working Papers*, OECD Publishing, Paris, forthcoming.

Ahrend, R. and A. Schumann (2014), “Does Regional Economic Growth Depend on Proximity to Urban Centres?”, *OECD Regional Development Working Papers*, 2014/07, OECD Publishing, Paris, http://dx.doi.org/10.1787/5jz0t7fxh7wc-en.

Ahrend, R., C. Gamper and A. Schumann (2014), “The OECD Metropolitan Governance Survey: A Quantitative Description of Governance Structures in large Urban Agglomerations”, *OECD Regional Development Working Papers*, 2014/04, OECD Publishing, Paris, http://dx.doi.org/10.1787/5jz43zldh08p-en.

Ahrend, R. et al. (2014), “What Makes Cities More Productive? Evidence on the Role of Urban Governance from Five OECD Countries,” *OECD Regional Development Working Papers*, 2014/5, OECD Publishing, Paris, http://dx.doi.org/10.1787/5jz432cf2d8p-en.

Aircargonews (2009), “Lufthansa Cargo shifts Asian hub to Krasnoyarsk”, Aircargonews website, www.aircargonews.net/news/single-view/news/lufthansa-cargo-shifts-asian-hub-to-krasnoyarsk.html (accessed 16 February 2014).

Alklychev, A. and K. Zoidov (2012), “Railroad Transportation for the Territorial Development of Siberia and the Far East”, *Problems of Economic Transition*, Vol. 55, No.7, pp. 88-98.

Amaral, M., S. Saussier and A. Yvrande-Billon (2008), “Auction procedures and competition in public services: The case of urban public transport in France and London”, paper submitted to the Working Party No. 2 on Competition and Regulation on 25 February 2013, Competition Committee, OECD, Paris.

Ang, G. and V. Marchal (2013), “Mobilising private investment in sustainable transport: The case of land-based passenger transport infrastructure”, *OECD Environment Working Papers*, No. 56, OECD Publishing, Paris, http://dx.doi.org/10.1787/5k46hjm8jpmv-en.

Argus (2011), “Argus Russian jet fuel prices”, Argusmedia, available at: https://media.argusmedia.com/~/media/Files/PDFs/White%20Paper/Argus-Russian-Jet.pdf.

ASDG (2013), “Gorodskie aglomeratsii: vzglyad rukovoditelei munitsipal’nykh obrazovanii Rossii”, Association of Siberian and Far Eastern Cities, April.

Bartholomy, M. and A. Krutik (2013), "Russian real estate", Law Business Research, http://whoswholegal.com/practiceareas/13/real-estate (accessed 30 November 2013).

Beregovskih, A. et al. (2010) "Russian Urban Planning: modern ideas (Legislative Base, Spatial Planning, Transport and Ecology, GIS Technology)", working paper at http://www.corp.at/archive/CORP2010_239.pdf.

Bertaud, A. and B. Renaud (1995), "Cities without land markets: Location and land use in the socialist city", *Policy Research Working Paper*, The World Bank, Washington, DC.

Boeing (2013), "Current market outlook, 2013-2032, Boeing, available at: www.boeing.com/assets/pdf/commercial/cmo/pdf/Boeing_Current_Market_Outlook_2013.pdf.

Crouch, M. (1979) "Problems of Soviet urban transport", *Soviet Studies*, Vol. XXXI, No. 2, pp. 231-256.

Department of Transport Krasnoyarsk (DOTK) (2011), "Concept for the development of passenger transport in the city of Krasnoyarsk from 2011-2015, looking towards 2020", Polytechnic Institute FGOU Federal Siberian University, DOTK, www.admkrsk.ru/citytoday/transport/proposal/Pages/koncepciya.aspx (accessed 9 August 2013).

Donchenko, V. (2013), "Towards the sustainable mobility in Russian cities: Problems, challenges and risks", paper presented at the International symposium OPTOSOZ, Moscow, 14 March.

Duranton, G. and M.A. Turner (2011), "The fundamental law of road congestion: Evidence from US cities", *The American Economic Review*, Vol. 101, No. 6, pp. 2 616-2 652.

Dye, R. and D. Merriman (2006), "Tax Increment Financing: A Tool for Local Development", *Land Lines*, Vol. 18, No. 1, January, available at: https://www.lincolninst.edu/pubs/dl/1076_Jan2006-Final.pdf.

Emelyanovo Airport (2014), "Emelyanovo airport summary", press release, www.yemelyanovo.ru/doc.php?id=2680 (accessed 16 February 2014).

Emelyanovo Airport (2013), "Emelyanovo airport summary", press release, www.yemelyanovo.ru/doc.php?id=1822 (accessed 16 February 2014).

Emelyanovo Airport (2012), "Emelyanovo airport has joined the pilot project on implementation of IATA e-Freight standard in Russia", press release, www.yemelyanovo.ru/en/doc.php?id=1218 (accessed 16 February 2014).

Ernst & Young (2012), *How to Make PPP Work in Russia*, Ernst & Young, available at: http://ey.com/Publication/vwLUAssets/Russian-PPP-Survey-2012-ENG/$FILE/Russian-PPP-Survey-2012-ENG.pdf.

Federal State Statistics Service (FSSS) (2013), "Main indicators – Transport and communication", FSSS website, www.gks.ru/wps/wcm/connect/rosstat_main/rosstat/en/figures/transport (accessed 15 February 2014).

FSSS (2012), "Passengers transport by public transport modes", FSSS website, http://gks.ru/wps/wcm/connect/rosstat_main (accessed 16 February 2014).

Filina (2012), "Russian market of transport services in international container transport", *Studies on Russian Economic Development*, Vol. 23, No. 2, pp. 153-161.

Finogenov, A. (2012), "Modern Russia and Urban-Planning Reality of a Post-Soviet City", *Urbanica: Spatial Planning*, at www.urbanica.spb.ru/?pageid645&lang=en (accessed 10 December 2013).

Francke, E., J. Macías and G. Schmid (2012), "The mobilisation of private investment for low-carbon, climate-resilient infrastructure: The case of Metrobus Bus Rapid Transit System in Mexico City", draft case study prepared by CTS EMBARQ Mexico for the OECD.

Fujita, M. and J.-F. Thisse (2002), *Economics of Agglomeration: Cities, Industrial Location and Regional Growth*, Cambridge University Press.

GEF (2002), Results from the GEF Climate Change Program: Evaluation Report No. 1-02, Global Environment Facility, Washington, DC

Gel'man, V. and S. Ryzhenkov (2011), "Local regimes, sub-national governance and the 'power vertical' in contemporary Russia", *Europe-Asia Studies*, Vol. 63, No. 3, pp. 449-465

Glubchikov, O. (2006), "Urban planning in Russia: Towards the market", *European Planning Studies*, Vol. 12, No. 2, pp. 229-247, http://dx.doi.org/10.1080/0965431042000183950.

Hildebrandt, A. (2013), "Canadian cities, take note of Detroit's downfall", CBC News, 21 July, http://www.cbc.ca/news/canada/canadian-cities-take-note-of-detroit-s-downfall-1.1391656 (accessed 12 December 2013).

Hirt, S. (2012), "Mixed use by default: How the Europeans (don't) zone", *Journal of Planning Literature*, Vol. 4, No. 27, pp. 375-393.

Hunter, H. (1965) "Transport in Soviet and Chinese development", *Economic Development and Cultural Change*, Vol. 14, No. 1 (Oct. 1965), pp. 71-84.

IERT (Institute of Economy and Transport Development) (2012), *The Reference and Analytical Paper on the Railway Infrastructure Development in the Regions of the Russian Sea Ports Until 2015*, IERT, Moscow.

International Union of Railways (IUR) (2012), *2012 Report on Combined Transport in Europe*, IUR, Paris.

Interros (2013), "International cargo traffic at Emelyanovo airport in 2012 has almost doubled", http://www.interros.ru/en/press/releases/ (accessed 16 February 2014).

ITF (2007), "Transport infrastructure inside and across urban regions: Models and assessment methods", in: OECD and ITF, *The Wider Economic Benefits of Transport: Macro-, Meso-, and Micro-Economic Transport Planning and Investment Tools*, OECD Publishing, Paris, http://dx.doi.org/10.1787/9789282101834-en.

Iyer, S.D. (2003), "The urban context for adjustments to the planning process in post-Soviet Russia: Responses from local planners in Siberia", *International Planning Studies*, Vol. 8, No. 3, pp. 201-223, http://dx.doi.org/10.1080/747355569.

Kinossian, N. (2013), "Urban agglomerations in Siberia: tackling peripherality by aggravating spatial disparities?", Paper for the RGS-IBG Annual International Conference, London, August.

Krai (2013), "Krasnoyarsk Kray. The territory of development", Government of the Krasnoyarsk Kray, Krasnoyarsk.

Krasnoyarsk (2013a), "Enterprises and individual entrepreneurs engaged in bus transport routes of the city of Krasnoyarsk", Krasnoyarsk city website, www.admkrsk.ru/citytoday/transport/Pages/enterprise.aspx (accessed 19 December 2013).

Krasnoyarsk (2013b), "The city today", Krasnoyarsk city website, www.admkrsk.ru/citytoday/transport/proposal/pages/default.aspx (accessed 14 September 2013).

Krasnoyarsk (2013c), "Developing a network of light rail", Krasnoyarsk city website, www.admkrsk.ru/citytoday/transport/proposal/Pages/speed.aspx (accessed 22 February 2014).

Larionova, T. (2013), "Sozdat Pravovoe Pole" (To create the legal base), *Transport of Russia*, No. 25 (780), Moscow.

LH Consulting (2012), "Air service development for Russia's Yemelyanovo International Airport in Krasnoyarsk", Lufthansa Consulting website, www.lhconsulting.com/company/news/article/air-service-development-for-russias-yemelyanovo-international-airport-in-krasnoyarsk (accessed 16 February 2014).

McKinsey Global Institute (2013), *Infrastructure Productivity: How to Save $1 Trillion a Year*, McKinsey&Company.

Ministry of Transport (2013), "Doklad o Rezultatah I Osnovnih Napravleniyah Deyatelnosti Ministerstva Transporta Rossiiskoy Federatsii v 2012 godu i na 2013-2015 gody" (Report on the results and main directions of the Ministry of Transport's activities in 2012 and up to 2012-2015), Ministry of Transport, Moscow.

Ministry of Transport (2012), "Gosudarstvennaya Programma Razvitia Transportnoy sistemy, 2013-2020" (Russian Federation State Program "Transport system development, 2013-2020"), Ministry of Transport, Moscow.

Ministry of Transport (2011), "Koncepcia Razvitia Aerodromnoy (Aeroportovoi) Seti Rossiiskoi Federacii na period do 2020 Goda" (Concept of Russia's airport network development until 2020), Ministry of Transport, Moscow.

Moses, J.C. (2010), "Russian local politics in the Putin-Medvedev era", *Europe-Asia Studies*, Vol. 62, No. 9, pp. 1 427-1 452.

Mu, R. et al. (2012), "The future of the modal split in China's greenest city: Assessing options for integrating Dalian's fragmented public transport system", *Policy and Society*, No. 31, pp. 51-71, http://dx.doi.org/10.1016/j.polsoc.2012.01.002.

New York City Global Partners (2012), "Best practice: Metrobus Bus Rapid Transit System", NYC Global Partners, www.nyc.gov/html/unccp/gprb/downloads/pdf/Mexico%20City_Metrobus.pdf.

NIIAT (State Scientific and Research Institute of Road Transport) (2011), "Nauchnoe issledovanie Tehnologichaskih Parametrov Sistemi vzimania Platy s Tyazhelich Gruzovih Avtomobiley" (The research of the technological parameters of the heavy vehicle charging system), NIIAT, Moscow.

Nord-News (2013), "Skorost Gruzovih Poezdov na Seti Zheleznih Dorog v Janvare 2012 Goda Virosla" (The speed of freight trains increased in January 2013), http://nord-news.ru/news/2013/02/04 (accessed 15 February 2014).

OECD (2015), *Governing the City*, OECD Publishing, Paris, http://dx.doi.org/10.1787/9789264226500-en.

OECD (2014a), *OECD Regional Outlook 2014: Regions and Cities: Where Policies and People Meet*, OECD Publishing, Paris, http://dx.doi.org/10.1787/9789264201415-en.

OECD (2014b), *OECD Economic Surveys: Russian Federation 2013*, OECD Publishing, Paris, http://dx.doi.org/10.1787/eco_surveys-rus-2013-en.

OECD (2013a), *OECD Regional Statistics* (database), http://dx.doi.org/10.1787/region-data-en.

OECD (2013b), *Regions at a Glance*, OECD Publishing, Paris, http://dx.doi.org/10.1787/reg_glance-2013-en.

OECD (2013c), *Green Growth in Cities*, OECD Green Growth Studies, OECD Publishing, Paris, http://dx.doi.org/10.1787/9789264195325-en.

OECD (2012a), *Compact City Policies: A Comparative Assessment*, OECD Green Growth Studies, OECD Publishing, Paris, http://dx.doi.org/10.1787/9789264167865-en.

OECD (2012b), *OECD Territorial Reviews: The Chicago Tri-State Metropolitan Area, United States*, OECD Publishing, Paris, http://dx.doi.org/10.1787/9789264170315-en.

OECD (2012c), *Recommendation of the Council on Principles for Public Governance of Public-Private Partnerships*, OECD, Paris, May, available at: www.oecd.org/gov/budgeting/PPP-Recommendation.pdf.

OECD (2011), "From lessons to principles for the use of public-private partnerships", 32nd meeting of the Network of Senior Budget Officials, Luxembourg, 6-7 June, OECD, Paris, available at: www.oecd.org/gov/budgeting/48144872.pdf.

OECD (2008), *Public-Private Partnerships: In Pursuit of Risk Sharing and Value for Money*, OECD Publishing, Paris, http://dx.doi.org/10.1787/9789264046733-en.

OECD (2007), *Infrastructure to 2030 (Vol.2): Mapping Policy for Electricity, Water and Transport*, OECD Publishing, Paris, http://dx.doi.org/10.1787/9789264031326-en.

OECD (2001), *Towards a New Role for Spatial Planning*, OECD Publishing, http://dx.doi.org/10.1787/9789264189928-en.

OECD/ECMT (2008), *Managing Urban Traffic Congestion*, OECD Publishing, Paris, http://dx.doi.org/10.1787/9789282101506-en.

OECD/ITF (2013), "Spending on transport infrastructure 1995-2011", International Transport Forum/OECD, Paris, www.internationaltransportforum.org/statistics/investment/data.html (accessed 7 August 2013).

OECD/ITF (2008), *Transport Infrastructure Investment: Options for Efficiency*, OECD Publishing, Paris, http://dx.doi.org/10.1787/9789282101568-en.

Okulov, V (2013), "Opening markets", presentation at the 4th International Forum on Freight Air Travel, available at: www.c-ca.ru/assets/files/AirCargoForum-2013%20pres/Okulov%20IV%20AirCargoForum%20Slides.pdf.

Okulov, V. (2012), "Concept of air cargo transport development in Russia until 2020", presentation at the TIACA Executive Summit and Annual General Meeting, Moscow.

Okulov, V. (2011), "The Russian Ministry of Transport initiatives in air cargo transport development on domestic and international markets", presentation at the 2nd AirCargoForum, Moscow, available at: http://c-ca.ru/assets/files/AirCargoForum_24_11_11_V_Okulov_Presentation.pdf.

Pucher, J. (1990) "Capitalism, socialism, and urban transport policies and travel behavior in the east and west", *Journal of the American Planning Association*, Vol. 56, No. 3, pp. 278-296, http://dx.doi.org/10.1080/01944369008975773.

Puzanov, A. (2009), "Development of the real estate rights system in Russia, 1989-2009", Institute of Urban Economics, Moscow, 9 October, http://www.urbaneconomics.ru/eng/publications.php?folder_id=19&mat_id=86 (accessed 30 November 2013).

RBK-Research (2011), "Market of transport-logistic services in 2010-2011 and the forecast until 2014", analytic survey, RBK, Moscow.

Romer, P.M. (1986), "Increasing returns and long-run growth", *Journal of Political Economy*, No. 94, pp. 1 002-1 037.

Ross, C. (2011), "Introduction: Russian regional politics under Putin and Medvedev", *Europe-Asia Studies*, Vol. 63, No. 3, pp. 361-366.

Ross, C. and A. Campbell (2009), *Federalism and Local Politics in Russia*, Routledge, Oxford.

Rosavtodor (2011), *Methodical Recommendations on the State Policy Implementation in the Sphere of Investments into the Road Development and Utilisation*.

Russian Survey (2013), "Krasnoyarsk. The grand city on a grand river", Russian Survey website, www.russian-survey.com/russia/177-krasnoyarsk#sthash.iktVVUKL.dpuf (accessed 16 February 2014).

RZhD (Russian Railways), (2011), "Godovoi otchet kompanii 2011" (Annual Report 2011), RTZ, Moscow.

SFU (2012), "Background report for the OECD Territorial Review of Krasnoyarsk", Siberian Federal University, Krasnoyarsk, Russian Federation, November.

Slider, D. (2009), "Putin and the election of regional governors", in: Ross, C. and A. Campbell (2009), *Federalism and Local Politics in Russia*, Routledge, Oxford.

Solodkij, A. and A. Gorev (2013), "System approach to elimination of traffic jams in large cities in Russia", *World Applied Sciences Journal*, Vol. 23, No. 8.

UCLG (2010), "Policy Paper on Urban Strategic Planning: Local Leaders Preparing for the Future of Our Cities", United Cities and Local Governments, Barcelona.

UKDT (UK Transport Department) (1994), "Trunk roads and the generation of traffic", HMSO, London, available at: http://webarchive.nationalarchives.gov.uk/+/http:/www.dft.gov.uk/pgr/economics/rdg/nataarchivedocs/trunkroadstraffic.pdf.

UNECE (2013), *Good Practices for Energy-Efficient Housing in the UNECE Region*, United Nations, Geneva.

Veneri, P. and V. Ruiz (2013), "Urban-to-Rural Population Growth Linkages: Evidence from OECD TL3 Regions", *OECD Regional Development Working Papers*, 2013/03, OECD Publishing, Paris, http://dx.doi.org/10.1787/5k49lcrq88g7-en.

Vetrov, V. and I. Zaitseva (2005), "Municipal governance in modern Russia", conference paper for the 45th Congress of the European Regional Science Association, August, Amsterdam.

Voevodin, V. (2012), "Navigatsia na volnakh polozhitelnoy dinamiki" (Navigation on the positive development waves), RZhD partner, Moscow.

Wollmann, H. and E. Gritsenko (2009), "Local self-government in Russia: Between decentralisation and recentralisation", in: Ross, C. and A. Campbell (2009), *Federalism and Local Politics in Russia*, Routledge, Oxford.

World Bank (2012), *Eurasian Cities. New Realities Along the Silk Road*, The World Bank, Washington, DC.

World Bank (2009), *Intergovernmental Reforms in the Russian Federation*, The World Bank, Washington, DC.

World Bank (2002), *Cities on the Move. A World Bank Urban Transport Strategy Review*, The International Bank for Reconstruction and Development/The World Bank, Washington, DC, available at: http://siteresources.worldbank.org/INTURBANTRANSPORT/Resources/cities_on_the_move.pdf.

World Economic Forum (WEF) (2011), *The Russia Competitiveness Report 2011*, WEF, Eurasia Competitiveness Institute.

Zadonsky, G. (2013), "Mortgage in the Russian Federation", Gaidar Insitute for Economic Policy, *Russian Economic Developments*, *Working Papers Series*, No. 11, pp. 26-29.

Zadonsky, G. (2012), "Mortgage in the Russian Federation", Gaidar Insitute for Economic Policy, *Russian Economic Developments*, *Working Papers Series*, No. 12.

Zhuravskaya, E. (2010), "Federalism in Russia", Centre for Economic and Financial Research at New Economic School, *Working Paper Series*, No. 141, April.

ORGANISATION FOR ECONOMIC CO-OPERATION AND DEVELOPMENT

The OECD is a unique forum where governments work together to address the economic, social and environmental challenges of globalisation. The OECD is also at the forefront of efforts to understand and to help governments respond to new developments and concerns, such as corporate governance, the information economy and the challenges of an ageing population. The Organisation provides a setting where governments can compare policy experiences, seek answers to common problems, identify good practice and work to co-ordinate domestic and international policies.

The OECD member countries are: Australia, Austria, Belgium, Canada, Chile, the Czech Republic, Denmark, Estonia, Finland, France, Germany, Greece, Hungary, Iceland, Ireland, Israel, Italy, Japan, Korea, Luxembourg, Mexico, the Netherlands, New Zealand, Norway, Poland, Portugal, the Slovak Republic, Slovenia, Spain, Sweden, Switzerland, Turkey, the United Kingdom and the United States. The European Commission takes part in the work of the OECD.

OECD Publishing disseminates widely the results of the Organisation's statistics gathering and research on economic, social and environmental issues, as well as the conventions, guidelines and standards agreed by its members.

OECD PUBLISHING, 2, rue André-Pascal, 75775 PARIS CEDEX 16
(04 2015 04 1 P) ISBN 978-92-64-22936-5 – 2015-17

www.ingramcontent.com/pod-product-compliance
Ingram Content Group UK Ltd.
Pitfield, Milton Keynes, MK11 3LW, UK
UKHW051501290926
15471UKWH00008B/1333

9 789264 229365